Savoring Tuscany

WILLIAMS-SONOMA

Savoring Tuscany

Recipes and Reflections on Tuscan Cooking

Recipes and Text
LORI DE MORI

General Editor
CHUCK WILLIAMS

Recipe Photography
NOEL BARNHURST

Travel Photography
JASON LOWE

Illustrations
MARLENE McLOUGHLIN

TIME
LIFE
BOOKS

ITALIA

EMILIA-ROMAGNA

MUGE

LIGURIA

MASSA-CARRARA

GARFAGNANA

ABETONE

LUCCA   PISTOIA

FIRENZE

CARRARA

BAGNO

PISTOIA

PRATO

FORTE DEI MARMI

GOLFO
DI
GENOVA

VIAREGGIO

TORRE
DEL
LAGO

LUCCA   LAMPORECCHIO

FIRENZE
FIESOLE   SETTIGNA

PISA

PISA

GREVE IN CHIAN
MONTE

PAN FOR

LIVORNO

SAN GIMIGNANO
VOLTERRA

SIEN

ARCIPELAGO

LIVORNO

TOSCANA

MASSA MARITTIMA

MONTAI

GROSSETO

PIOMBINO

GROSSETO

MAREMMA

ISOLA D'ELBA

TOSCANO

ISOLA PIANOSA

ORBE

MARE TIRRENO

Contents

POPPI

ANGHIARI

AREZZO

CORTONA

MONTEPULCIANO

PIENZA

PITIGLIANO

LAZIO

UMBRIA

KM
0   10   20   30

0   10   20
MILES

Above top: The Sanatorio dell'Immacolata Concezione quietly presides over its setting amid the rolling golden hills surrounding Volterra. **Above:** During the olive harvest in late autumn, the fruits are gently gathered in vast nets spread beneath the trees. Careful harvesting by hand minimizes any bruising of the olives—which would raise their acidity level—and thus ensures the sweet fruitiness of the crop. **Right:** A table at an elegant *caffè* provides a restorative moment for the *signore*.

INTRODUZIONE

The Tuscan Table

THE ROOM WAS LIKE A CHAPEL. Or a sanctuary. Walls the color of a deep winter sky, golden light billowing through the thick windows of the vaulted ceiling. In the center of the room, towering over the crowd of mere mortals hovering at his lustrous marble feet, was Michelangelo's *David*. How well I thought I knew that gargantuan form. I had seen his image in countless postcards, his replica both in Florence's Piazza della Signoria, where the original once stood, and at Piazzale Michelangelo, with its sweeping view of the town. Yet nothing prepared me for the breathtaking perfection of the real thing.

Tuscany can have much the same effect on the unwitting traveler. Birthplace of the Renaissance, the region gets its name from the Etruscans, the most powerful civilization of pre-Roman Italy. Its walled cities, cypress-lined roads, and patchwork hills have been written about and photographed with such unrivaled enthusiasm that the image of the place seems to have insinuated itself into the public consciousness, even in the minds of those who have yet to set foot on its fertile soil. A cynic might expect the "real" Tuscany to disappoint, for how could it live up to all the attention it has received? And yet whenever I come home to Tuscany—even after the shortest absence—its startling beauty, its richness and abundance strike me with a freshness that belies the many years I have spent here.

In all truth, it is a place whose gifts are almost too large to embrace. Stendhal was so stunned by Florence's transcendent beauty that he is said to have staggered around its streets in stuporous delight. Siena, Lucca, Arezzo, and Pisa, cities that thrived as independent republics from the 1300s until Italy's unification in 1861, each have uniquely glorious histories, traditions, and artistic treasures, from the riotously colorful Palio, the twice-yearly bareback horse race held in Il Campo, Siena's great scalloped square, to Piero della Francesca's magnificent frescoes in Arezzo.

Many passageways lead into the heart of this land, but I prefer to travel one over all others. Simply put, if art, literature, and architecture are the gold and silver filaments in the exquisitely loomed tapestry that is Tuscany, then food and culinary life in all its guises are the bright silk threads woven through the whole of the fabric, bringing it to life.

Pellegrino Artusi, the celebrated nineteenth-century food writer who divided his time between Florence and Viareggio, put it plainly: "The hypocritical world doesn't want to give any importance to food; but there isn't a holiday, religious or secular, where we don't lay out the tablecloth and try to eat as well as we possibly can." Artusi's comment, at least as it relates to Tuscany, can safely be expanded even further: the pleasures of the table are so essential to Tuscan life that almost any meal, from the most humble to the most refined, is seized as an opportunity to share the best of nature's bounty in the company of family or friends.

The Tuscan table is a picture of artful simplicity. For the most part, culinary theatrics, whether through the use of exotic imported ingredients, complicated preparation techniques, or fussy presentation, provoke more skepticism than admiration. Raw ingredients are everything—olive oil from the inland hills; heavy loaves of coarse saltless bread; woodland mushrooms, chestnuts, and wild game; exquisitely fresh fish and shellfish from the sea—and they are expected to be able to speak for themselves.

But it was not always so. During the Renaissance, if one had the good fortune of being a nobleman or wealthy merchant, eating well was a highly elaborate affair. The banquets

Left: At one of the region's ubiquitous markets, a vendor arranges a selection of vegetables and fruits, seeking to tempt shoppers with bunches of succulent grapes. At home, the fruits are set out as a finish to dinner or are tucked into children's backpacks as a school-day snack, or *merenda*. **Below:** Luscious peaches bring fragrant sweetness to the Tuscan summer table, where they might be served as a refreshing dessert steeped in chilled red wine. **Below bottom:** Since the Etruscan era, artisans working in alabaster, the translucent *pietra candida* of Volterra, have created objects both useful and fanciful.

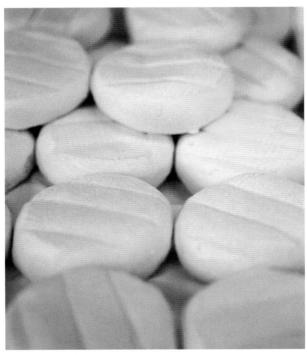

Above top: After bringing in the day's catch, fishermen turn to the task of mending their nets. **Above:** Plump rounds of fresh cheese are so tender that they bear the imprint of the draining rack. **Right:** Statues of prophets and patriarchs are among the embellishments on the lavishly ornamented facade of Siena's cathedral, a Gothic jewelcase of architectural wonders.

of Florence's ruling Medici family during the 1500s were characterized by unfathomable gastronomic excess and extravagance. Ornate sugar sculptures by Giambologna, Florence's most influential sculptor after Michelangelo's death, decorated the immense dining hall. Long tables set with intricately folded napkins and ornaments of marzipan and sugar paste were arranged around a large open stage upon which ballets, operas, and other theatrical productions were presented during the course of the meal. The banquet itself consisted of an interminable succession of hot and cold dishes: meat pies shaped like giant roses; larded turkeys (still considered an exotic bird) made to resemble fire-breathing hydras; boiled capons covered with ravioli; fried goats' heads; whole piglets; crusted veal with kidneys surrounded by grilled lemons and pomegranates. Desserts of iced cakes, citron tarts, and spiced and candied sweetmeats were followed by trays of fresh pecorino cheese, raw fennel and celery, peaches steeped in wine, candied apples, and quince jelly.

For the Medicis, food was yet another form of art—rich, complex, and highly stylized. A favorite *intingolo,* or "sauce," of Catherine de'

Medici (and one on which she once literally almost gorged herself to death) was *cibreo,* a mixture of chicken livers, combs, crests, and wattles sautéed with parsley and onion, simmered with wine and chicken broth, and then combined with egg yolks and the tiny yellow unlaid eggs from inside a freshly slaughtered hen. In my mind, it is a dish imbued with the fairy-tale aura of legend, for though Tuscan cookbooks and gastronomes have long sung praises of its delicacy and deliciousness, I've never been able to get a glimpse—or taste—of the real thing, however hard I've tried (and I have tried, though admittedly more to satisfy my curiosity than my hunger). Like the opulent life of the Renaissance court itself, the sauce has faded into history.

While the rich and titled waged their genteel battles of gastronomic showmanship, *il popolo*—"the people"—based their diet around many of the same foods that had nourished the Etruscans before them. First and foremost among these staples was the holy trinity of *pane, olio, e vino* (bread, olive oil, and wine), the three ingredients that to this day are the most basic, universal, and beloved elements of the Tuscan table. Yet despite their unmistakable importance, they are only the starting point of this delicious tale. For just as the topography changes from one province to the next, so does the culinary landscape.

Tuscany's best pecorino (sheep's milk) cheeses come from the countryside outside of Siena, where narrow roads gently wind past fortressed medieval hill towns, and timeworn farmhouses nestle among neatly tended rows of grapevines and silvery-leaved olive trees. Chickens peck and scratch in large, open henhouses or at the edge of dusty country lanes. Their firm-textured, flavorful meat is later enhanced by the fragrant culinary herbs that are a fixture in every garden in the province, among them sage, rosemary, thyme, *nepitella,* and the anise-like tarragon (rarely used outside of Siena) first brought to the area by Charlemagne's regiments in the eighth century.

Farther inland is the province of Arezzo, known for its harsh winters, poets (Petrarch and Redi among them), wealth (the city itself abounds with goldsmiths, jewelers, and antiquaries), and a cuisine based more heavily on meat than anywhere else in the region. *Scottiglia,* the province's legendary meat-and-game stew laced with wine, herbs, and spices, dates back to feudal times, but its most evocative image comes from the rural Casentino, where family and friends often converged upon a farmstead of one of their number, each household contributing a piece of meat to the cauldron: lamb or beef from the pasture;

Below: Gilt stars line the ascent to heaven inside the great dome of the Church of the Madonna di San Biagio, near Montepulciano. The graceful church, with its refined adornments, is the masterpiece of the High Renaissance architect Antonio da Sangallo il Vecchio. **Right top:** A present-day view of the Tuscan countryside looks much as the Etruscans may have seen it—softly diffused in the muted sun. **Right bottom:** Two gentlemen of Volterra enjoy the amber afternoon.

chicken, pork, or rabbit from the farm; pheasant, pigeon, or other game birds from the woods and fields.

In Lucca and the lush green hills and chestnut woods of the Garfagnana to its north, beans, grains (particularly wheatlike *farro*), and flours such as *ceci* (chickpea/garbanzo bean), *castagna* (chestnut), and polenta (cornmeal) are baked into rustic flat breads or used to thicken soups flavored with wild greens, woodland mushrooms, and vegetables from the kitchen garden or one of the area's many produce markets. At the Puccini festival in nearby Torre del Lago (where the legendary composer made his home), I made a meal of *necci*, warm chestnut crepes (mine were folded around a dollop of fresh ricotta cheese), cooked as they have been since the fourteenth century, between long-handled, thin metal plates set over a bed of smoldering embers.

The bright waters of the Mediterranean caress the Tuscan coastline, from Versilia to the north, down past the lively port town of Livorno, and then through the Pisan coast to the Maremma, whose once deadly malarial swamplands have been transformed into vast agricultural plains and into pinewoods that are home to pheasant, thrush, boar, and deer. Not far from the water's edge are *le isole,* Elba, Giglio, and a handful of smaller islands, some navigable only by foot. Although it is fair to say that the bulk of traditional Tuscan cooking comes from the inland cities and countryside, dishes such as Livorno's famed *cacciucco,* sweet-fleshed eel from the Ortobello lagoon, and *acquacotta,* the Maremma's age-old bread soup, are impressive and delicious contributions to Tuscany's culinary repertory.

In the pages that follow, you'll find a collection of the region's most beloved and delightful recipes, some steeped in tradition, others reflecting a more contemporary Tuscany. It is often said here that *l'appetito vien mangiando*—"it is the act of eating that whets the appetite." One taste of these treasures from the Tuscan table, and chances are you'll find it hard to disagree.

ANTIPASTI

The perfect antipasto teases the appetite without sating it, leaving room for the delights that follow.

Preceding pages: True to their name, these *girasoli* faithfully turn their faces to the sun and to the Chapel of San Galgano, site of the hermitage and tomb of the twelfth-century saint. **Above top:** A profusion of freshly made *panini* and *pizzette* is Italy's answer to fast food. **Above:** Central to many Tuscan antipasto plates are thick slices of wild boar sausage, *salsicce di cinghiale*. **Right:** Born of modern-day necessity, the ubiquitous motor scooter simplifies negotiation of narrow, ancient streets.

NOWHERE IS THE SIMPLICITY of the Tuscan table more evident than at the beginning of a meal. It is where the essential culinary elements—the coarse country bread, the jewel green olive oil, the famous wine—make their first appearance and where the tone of the meal is set.

I had just arrived in Tuscany when I encountered what I still consider to be the most beautiful of all antipasti. I had been invited for dinner at the home of friends who I knew loved to entertain but who were examples of that rare breed of Tuscan who hated to cook. They lived on the ground floor of a crumbling villa that had been divided up by three families. The table was set in their small walled garden under an arbor of climbing roses. Candles and bamboo torches threw a blanket of golden light over the darkness, and the night air shimmered with the scent of jasmine and the voices of crickets, cicadas, and a lone nightingale.

At the center of the table was what looked to me like the most glorious still life: wedges of crisp fennel and a few pale bulbs with their

ferny leaves still attached, tiny artichokes whose purple-tinged leaves were as smooth as plum skins, clusters of sweet tomatoes still hanging from their stems, bunches of green (spring) onions, florets of radishes, and bright yellow ribbons of sweet peppers (capsicums). At each of our plates was a small ramekin, which we were invited to fill with olive oil, then season with salt and pepper, creating our own *pinzimonio* in which to dip the vegetables. I don't remember what else we ate that evening, but it doesn't matter, for the beginning of the meal is forever imprinted in my culinary memory.

As extraordinary as it can be, *pinzimonio* is not the appetizer visitors to Tuscany are most likely to encounter. That distinction goes to the time-honored combination of flavors and ingredients known as the *antipasto toscano*. You will find these two words printed on trattoria menus everywhere, or uttered by waiters on those many occasions when no written menu exists.

When I am out at a simple trattoria with a group of friends, we frequently ask for an *antipasto toscano* for the table (at which point

Left: Olive harvesting in Tuscany is most often accomplished by hand. Both men and women climb tall wooden ladders to work among supple branches heavy with the ripening fruits. **Below:** Mesh bags of clams are ready for the local market or *pescheria*. **Below bottom:** Western Tuscany meets the sea in a ragged and precipitous coastline of dramatic beauty.

the waiter heaves a sigh of relief, since it is a snap for the kitchen to prepare and will keep us happily occupied while the rest of our meal is made). For a large gathering, the antipasto is almost always served family style, and each diner is given an empty plate, typically of thick, milk-white ceramic, to fill from platters set in the middle of the table.

There will be a platter of assorted cured meats *(affettato misto)* whose specific contents will vary slightly depending on where in Tuscany it is being served. It will always contain prosciutto, sometimes highly salted, sometimes not. Near Siena, plates of *affettato misto* usually hold a few large slices of crumbly *sbriciolona,* a soft salami flavored with fennel

seed, while other parts of Tuscany are more likely to serve *finocchiona,* a firm salami that is similar in flavor but slightly smaller in diameter. Tiny, piquant *salsicce di cinghiale* (dried wild boar sausages) are common near Grosseto, whose pinewoods abound with the bristle-haired, dusky-brown animals. One can see the boars in the wild on a hike through the Maremma's protected Parco dell'Uccellina, said to be the last stretch of virgin coastal landscape in all of Italy. One fall, I came across a pair of the mythical-looking beasts, their long snouts covered with mud, herding a string of little ones through the dappled woods.

Whatever the particular combination of cured meats, scattered alongside them will

often be an assortment of vegetables preserved in vinegar or olive oil, *sott'aceti* or *sott'olio*. My favorites are crunchy pearl onions and wispy spears of wild asparagus steeped in wine vinegar, and baby artichoke hearts and porcino mushrooms marinated in olive oil laced with peppercorns and herbs.

The final element of a traditional *antipasto toscano* is that most versatile of all Italian culinary inventions: *crostini e bruschetta*. Both have bread as their base, though *crostini* are usually made with little ovals of untoasted *frusta* (the Tuscan equivalent of the French baguette), while *bruschetta* is made with thick slices of toasted country bread. A few standards exist, but you'll find *crostini* and *bruschetta* topped

Left: Patrons at a *bar* in Arezzo relax and converse in the customary manner: standing—*in piedi*—at the long counter. **Above top:** Gold-brown rounds of scamorza cheese, typically made from cow's milk, are widely used in cooking. **Above:** Porcino mushrooms, avidly pursued by foragers in the Tuscan woodlands, are dried for adding an earthy flavor to sauces, soups, and risottos year-round.

or drizzled with any one of a vast number of items, depending on the season and the culinary whims of the chef.

The classic Tuscan *crostini,* for which every family has its own special recipe, are *crostini di fegatini,* thin slices of bread covered with a pâté of chicken livers seasoned with anchovies, capers, and red wine or sweet Tuscan *vin santo.* *Bruschetta* tends to be a more rustic creature. In the fall, after the olives have been harvested and pressed, thick slices of country bread are toasted on the grill, rubbed with garlic, and bathed in *olio nuovo,* or covered with tender *fagioli bianchi* (white beans) or boiled *cavolo nero* (Tuscan black cabbage) and the new oil.

There was a time, not so long ago, when the Tuscan world stopped for a long, multi-course *pranzo,* or "lunch," and a brief siesta, then in the early afternoon sputtered back to life. But especially in the cities, and particularly among the postwar baby boom genera-

tion, there is a trend toward simpler, quicker lunches. Many antipasti that were once preludes to a larger meal now constitute the meal itself. Such light repasts often call for the appearance of eggs in one guise or another. The frittata, popular throughout Tuscany, is an omelet of sorts, laced with any combination of vegetables, cheese, or even leftover pasta. The *tortino,* a favorite in Siena, is a rustic egg-and-vegetable pie baked in an oven. A simple salad of mixed or wild greens and a glass of wine complete the meal.

The word *insalata* doesn't necessarily refer to lettuce. Lightly dressed, lettuce-free "salads" of fresh vegetables and cheese, usually Parmesan, are a favorite Tuscan appetizer. For the everyday table, there is an *insalata di finocchio, arance, e pecorino,* a mixture of thinly sliced raw fennel, tart oranges, and pecorino cheese. For special occasions, nothing compares to an *insalata* of orange-hued *ovoli* (wild mushrooms from the Tuscan hills), black or white truffles, and Parmesan cheese.

Not surprisingly, recipes for the region's fresh seafood antipasti come from the towns and villages scattered along the Tuscan coast. I live an hour's drive from the sea, and I make the trip whenever I can, racing along the Firenze-Mare *autostrada* toward the enticing beaches of Viareggio or Livorno, or meandering through the gorgeous countryside south of Siena on my way to the Maremma or the island of Elba or Giglio. I am, like so many other travelers, merely a passing visitor on the Tuscan shores—*una turista*—and as a result, my memories of meals eaten *al mare* are tinged with that lovely carefree feeling of being *in vacanza,* of drinking a bottle of lightly chilled *vino bianco* at lunch because I knew a siesta awaited me under the welcoming shade of a wide canvas umbrella.

On the beach in Viareggio, with my feet in the warm sand, I have eaten sizzling *cozze ripiene,* mussels stuffed with bread crumbs, garlic, shallots, and herbs. Farther south, at a modest trattoria along the strip of coast between the Marina di Pisa and Livorno, I feasted on a plate of exquisitely fresh, slim anchovy fillets marinated in lemon juice and sprinkled with garlic and parsley. Waiting for the ferry to Giglio, years before I dared to cook octopus myself, I stopped for lunch at a tiny restaurant overlooking a jumble of sailboats and *pescherecce* (fishing boats) in Porto Santo Stefano and ordered a *carpaccio di polpo,* thinly sliced octopus scattered with crunchy slivers of celery and *cipolla di Tropea* (a sweet onion grown in the south of Italy).

Tuscany's crisp, clean—and, for the most part, uncomplicated—white wines are wonderfully refreshing with the region's traditional seafood antipasti. Every province has its own *vini bianchi,* but San Gimignano's Vernaccia, made from wine grapes of the same name, is undoubtedly the most famous.

The Tuscan antipasto, wherever it is eaten, is a perfect introduction to the bounty of culinary gifts this region has to offer. It teases the appetite without sating it, making its own delicious statement while leaving room for all the delights that follow.

Lucca

Frittata di Patate e Cipolle

potato and onion frittata

Eggs rarely show up at breakfast, instead making their appearance most often in a frittata, the Italian version of the French omelet. It differs from a traditional omelet in that it is not folded in the pan, but rather partially cooked on top of the stove, then placed under a broiler (griller) to set.

1 large boiling potato

8 eggs

1 tablespoon water

salt to taste

4 tablespoons (2 fl oz / 60 ml) extra-virgin olive oil

1 yellow onion, thinly sliced

2 cloves garlic, minced

leaves from 1 fresh rosemary sprig, chopped

1 tablespoon unsalted butter

freshly ground pepper to taste

✿ In a saucepan, combine the potato with water to cover. Bring to a boil and cook until tender, about 20 minutes. Drain and let cool.

✿ In a bowl, whisk the eggs until blended. Whisk in the water and salt and set aside.

✿ Preheat a broiler (griller). Peel the cooled potato and cut into bite-sized pieces. Set aside.

✿ In a large ovenproof frying pan over medium heat, warm 2 tablespoons of the olive oil. Add the onion slices and sauté until they begin to soften, about 3 minutes. Add the garlic and rosemary and sauté until softened, about 2 minutes longer.

✿ Distribute the potato pieces evenly in the pan over medium heat. Add the remaining 2 tablespoons oil and the butter and swirl the pan until the butter melts. Pour in the egg mixture, season with pepper, reduce the heat to low, and cook slowly until the sides and bottom are set but the center is still loose, about 4 minutes. Run a spatula along the sides of the pan occasionally to keep the frittata from sticking.

✿ Transfer the pan to the broiler and broil (grill) until the top sets and browns only slightly, about 2 minutes. Let cool until warm. Cut into wedges and serve at once.

serves 4

Siena

Insalata di Carciofi, Grana, e Rucola

baby artichoke, parmesan, and arugula salad

Once, lost in the heart of Chianti, I was caught for what seemed like a long time behind a farmer in his ape, "bee" in Italian, a minuscule three-wheeled truck with the motor of a scooter. The back of the vehicle was piled high with fresh-cut, long-stemmed, purple-tinged artichokes. When I finally stopped for lunch, I had this salad. It is now a staple at our house in early spring when baby artichokes are in season.

SALAD

6 baby artichokes

1 bunch arugula (rocket), tough stems removed and leaves shredded

DRESSING

¼ cup (2 fl oz / 60 ml) extra-virgin olive oil

2 tablespoons fresh lemon juice

salt to taste

2-oz (60-g) piece Parmesan cheese

freshly ground pepper to taste

✿ To make the salad, trim and slice the artichokes as directed on page 246.

✿ Once all the artichokes have been sliced, make the dressing: In a small bowl, whisk together the olive oil and lemon juice until creamy. Season with salt.

✿ Place the arugula in a salad bowl. Drain the artichoke slices and pat dry. Add to the greens and toss gently. Drizzle the dressing over the salad and, using a vegetable peeler or sharp paring knife, cut the Parmesan cheese into thin shavings, letting them fall over the top. Season generously with pepper.

serves 4

The freshest Tuscan eggs are called uova da bere, literally "eggs for drinking."

Firenze

Polenta Fritta con Acciugata

polenta crisps with anchovy sauce

The Mugello is the rugged and once desperately poor mountainous area of Tuscany bordering Emilia-Romagna. In the past, economic hardship often forced mugellani *into seasonal migration to the Maremma, the coastal area of southern Tuscany, for work. This recipe combines anchovies from the sea with polenta, a staple from the mountains. The polenta can be made the day before, refrigerated, and then sliced and fried just before serving. Tuscans often use sliced polenta just as they would use bread for* bruschetta, *topping it with anything from marinated mushrooms to a dollop of tomato sauce and a fresh basil leaf.*

POLENTA CRISPS

5 cups (40 fl oz/1.1 l) water

salt

1 cup (5 oz/155 g) coarse-grain polenta

SAUCE

⅓ cup (3 fl oz/80 ml) extra-virgin olive oil

1 clove garlic, minced

4 large olive oil–packed anchovies

2 tablespoons chopped canned tomatoes

1 tablespoon capers, rinsed and finely chopped

1 teaspoon finely chopped fresh flat-leaf (Italian) parsley

freshly ground pepper to taste

vegetable oil for deep-frying

❧ To make the polenta crisps, in a deep saucepan over high heat, bring the water to a boil and salt lightly. Pour in the polenta in a thin, steady stream, stirring constantly. Reduce the heat to low and cook, stirring continuously with a wooden spoon, for about 40 minutes. The polenta is ready when it becomes quite thick and pulls away from the sides of the pan as you stir it. Remove from the heat.

❧ Oil the bottom and sides of a 9-by-12-inch (23-by-30-cm) baking pan. Pour the polenta into the prepared pan, smoothing the surface with the back of a spoon. Let the polenta cool for a few hours or overnight in the refrigerator.

❧ Invert the polenta onto a cutting board. Cut into 2-by-1-inch (5-by-2.5-cm) rectangles.

❧ To make the sauce, in a saucepan over low heat, warm the olive oil. Add the garlic and sauté until fragrant, about 1 minute. Add the anchovy fillets and, using a wooden spoon, break them apart in the pan. Cook, stirring occasionally, until the sauce thickens slightly, about 6 minutes. Stir in the tomatoes, capers, and parsley, season with pepper, raise the heat to medium, and cook uncovered for 10 minutes. Remove from the heat, cover, and set aside.

❧ Lay a few sheets of paper towel near the stove and top with a wire rack. Select a large, deep frying pan, preferably of cast iron. Pour vegetable oil to a depth of 3 inches (7.5 cm) into the pan and heat to 350°F (180°C) on a deep-frying thermometer. Working in batches, fry the polenta, turning once, until crisp and golden on both sides, about 10 minutes total. Using a slotted utensil, transfer the slices to the wire rack to drain. Keep warm in a low oven until serving.

❧ Arrange the hot polenta crisps on a warmed serving platter and top each slice with a teaspoon of the sauce. Serve immediately.

serves 6

Lucca

Cozze Ripiene

stuffed mussels

For this dish, be sure to look for the common blue mussel, with its deep blue-black shell, rather than the much larger green-lipped mussel.

about 2 cups (16 fl oz / 500 ml) dry white wine

5 lb (2.5 kg) large mussels (see note), scrubbed and debearded

¼ cup (2 fl oz / 60 ml) extra-virgin olive oil

2 tablespoons finely chopped shallots

2 cloves garlic, minced

3 tablespoons coarse dried bread crumbs (page 248)

3 tablespoons finely chopped fresh flat-leaf (Italian) parsley

salt and freshly ground pepper to taste

lemon wedges

☙ Pour the wine to a depth of ½ inch (12 mm) into a large pot. Add the mussels, discarding any that fail to close to the touch, cover, and place over high heat. Cook, shaking the pot occasionally, until the shells open, 5–6 minutes. Transfer the mussels to a large roasting pan. Discard any mussels that failed to open. Reserve the cooking liquid.

☙ Preheat a broiler (griller).

☙ In a heavy frying pan over medium–high heat, warm the olive oil. Add the shallots and garlic and sauté for 1 minute. Add 1 tablespoon of the cooking liquid and cook for 1 minute. Remove from the heat and stir in the bread crumbs, parsley, salt, and pepper.

☙ Remove the top shell of each mussel and discard. Using a sharp knife, sever the muscle connecting each mussel to its bottom shell, leaving each mussel on its half shell. Top with about 1 teaspoon of the bread crumb mixture. Place on a baking sheet and slip under the broiler until the mussels begin to sizzle and brown, 1–2 minutes. Transfer the mussels from the sheet to a warmed platter. Garnish with lemon wedges and serve.

serves 6

Arezzo

Funghi Sott'olio

mushrooms in olive oil

Not long ago, preserving vegetables was the only way to eat them once their brief, glorious seasons had passed. Even though the circumstances that necessitated preservation have changed, the tradition itself remains. Serve the mushrooms as part of an antipasto plate, or chop them coarsely, mix with a mild, soft cheese, and use as a spread for crostini.

2 cups (16 fl oz/500 ml) water

2 cups (16 fl oz/500 ml) red wine vinegar

1 lb (500 g) fresh button mushrooms, brushed clean, with stems intact

1 tablespoon salt

3 whole cloves

1 small cinnamon stick

2 bay leaves

4 peppercorns

about 1½ cups (12 fl oz/375 ml) extra-virgin olive oil

❦ In a nonaluminum saucepan over high heat, combine the water and vinegar and bring to a boil. Add the mushrooms, the salt, 2 of the cloves, the cinnamon, and 1 of the bay leaves. Reduce the heat to medium and simmer, uncovered, for 20 minutes. Drain the mushrooms, discarding the seasonings, and spread on a kitchen towel to dry for 6 hours.

❦ Spoon the mushrooms, peppercorns, and remaining clove and bay leaf into a sterilized 1-pt (16–fl oz/ 500-ml) glass jar. Pour in enough olive oil to cover the mushrooms. Let the jar rest, uncovered, for a couple of hours while the contents settle. Add additional oil if necessary to cover the mushrooms, then cap the jar tightly. Set in a dark, dry place for at least 5 days before serving.

❦ Serve the mushrooms with toothpicks. Once the jar is opened, refrigerate it; return the mushrooms to room temperature before serving.

makes 1 pt (16 fl oz/500 ml)

Il Bar

Every Tuscan town or village, no matter how small or grand, has a *bar,* or more likely several. This is where the Tuscan day begins, and where the life of the town hovers until evening. Newspapers are read; politics and soccer are loudly debated; cigarettes are lit.

In the morning, glass counters are filled with brioches and sandwiches, which together with an espresso or a cappuccino constitute the average Tuscan breakfast. Locals tend to spend their time *in piedi* (standing up) at the long counter. Anyone who doesn't have to rush off to work or run errands lingers at a table, although there is sometimes a price for such privilege, indicated by menus that list two prices next to each item. Another flurry of activity occurs around midmorning when the working world abandons the office to gulp down an espresso.

My favorite ritual of all—the *aperitivo* hour— begins sometime between 6:00 and 7:00 in the evening. In a small *bar,* a couple of bowls filled with *salatini* (little salted crackers) and olives will be set on the counter, to nibble on while drinking a Campari soda, a glass of wine or *spumante,* or some other lightly alcoholic drink. An exception to the "lightly alcoholic" category is the Negroni, a concoction of Campari, gin, and sweet vermouth purported to have originated in Florence.

Fancier places offer more elaborate choices during the *aperitivo* hour—a platter of crisp raw vegetables such as radishes, carrots, celery, and fennel; little bowls of olives, brine-cured capers, sweet gherkins, and pickled onions; and slivers of hard cheese and various cured meats.

You could make a meal out of these offerings, but restraint is advised. The *aperitivo* is simply meant to tease the appetite, to begin the slow descent from the bustle of the day's activities to the leisure of the evening meal.

Siena

Pinzimonio

dipping vegetables and olive oil

Tuscans are always looking for ways to highlight that most precious of all local ingredients, olive oil. The word pinzimonio *doesn't actually refer to the confetti of colorful raw vegetables, which should always be the freshest, most tender available, but to the seasoned oil in which they are dipped. Although the vegetables are presented on a single large platter, everyone at the table gets his or her own ramekin to fill with oil and season with salt and pepper. To make the dipping even easier, the ramekins are often propped forward with a table knife.*

2 baby artichokes

2 fennel bulbs

4 carrots

1 head celery

4–6 radishes

4–6 green (spring) onions

1 head Belgian endive (chicory/witloof)

extra-virgin olive oil

salt and freshly ground pepper to taste

❦ Trim the artichokes as directed on page 246, cutting each into quarters lengthwise.

❦ Remove the feathery leaves and the tough outer layers from the fennel and cut the bulbs into medium-sized wedges. Peel the carrots and, if large, cut in half lengthwise and then into serving-sized pieces. Trim the celery head, separate into stalks, and slice the heart lengthwise into medium-sized pieces. Trim the tops from the radishes, leaving a small section of stem, and then slice off the root ends. Cut an X into the bottom of each radish. Trim the green tops and the root end from each green onion, then make a few lengthwise slices in the bulb. Separate the leaves of the endive.

❦ Put a small ramekin at each place setting. Drain the artichoke pieces, pat them dry, and arrange on a large serving platter along with the fennel wedges, carrot pieces, celery stalks and pieces, radishes, green onions, and endive leaves. Bring to the table along with a cruet of olive oil, salt, and a pepper grinder. Let each diner season his or her own oil.

serves 4–6

Lucca

Salvia Fritta

fried sage leaves

Italy's warm Mediterranean climate is perfect for growing sage. In Tuscany, not only is it one of the most widely used of all culinary herbs, but the leaves are also dipped in batter and fried. Choose especially large, fresh, attractive leaves, and serve plain or use as a dramatic garnish for grilled fish or steaks.

24 large fresh sage leaves

1 egg

2 tablespoons water

1 cup (5 oz/155 g) all-purpose (plain) flour

½ teaspoon salt, plus salt to taste

corn oil or soybean oil for deep-frying

♨ Rinse the sage leaves well, shake off as much water as possible, and lay them on a clean kitchen towel to dry.

♨ In a shallow bowl, beat the egg until blended. Beat in the water and set aside. Sift the flour onto a plate and mix in the ½ teaspoon salt.

♨ Line a tray with paper towels and set a wire cooling rack on top. Place next to the stove.

♨ Pour the oil to a depth of 1 inch (2.5 cm) into a deep, heavy frying pan, preferably cast iron, and heat to 350°F (180°C) on a deep-frying thermometer.

♨ While the oil is heating, gently slip the leaves into the egg mixture. Once the proper temperature has been reached, working quickly, take out 1 leaf at a time, allowing the excess egg to drain off. Coat with the flour, shaking off the excess, and carefully place in the hot oil. Repeat with additional leaves, being careful not to crowd the pan. Fry the leaves until lightly golden, about 3 minutes. Do not allow them to brown. Using a wire skimmer, transfer the leaves to the wire rack to drain.

♨ When all the leaves have been fried, sprinkle them with salt. Arrange the leaves in a single layer on a platter and serve immediately.

serves 6

Firenze

Tonno, Fagioli, e Cipolla

tuna, white beans, and sweet onion

This is Florentine comfort food, the sort of dish a local makes upon a late return from a long journey, or prepares during a torrid summer day when turning on the stove, even to boil a pot of water for pasta, is unthinkable.

In a perfect world, this dish would be made with freshly shucked cannellini beans, simmered until their skins were soft and tender in water flavored with sage, garlic, and a bit of olive oil. In reality, this truly delicious staple of Florentine cuisine requires little more than a sweet onion, some fruity Tuscan olive oil, one tin each of good-quality tuna and white beans, and a can opener.

4 cups (28 oz / 875 g) drained, canned or cooked dried cannellini beans (page 246)

1 can (7 oz / 220 g) olive oil–packed tuna

1 large sweet onion (page 249), coarsely chopped

6 tablespoons (3 fl oz / 90 ml) extra-virgin olive oil

salt and freshly ground pepper to taste

☙ Place the beans in a serving bowl.

☙ Lightly drain the tuna and use a fork to flake it over the beans. Scatter the onion over the top.

☙ Drizzle with olive oil, and season with salt and pepper. Serve at room temperature.

serves 4

Il Lardo di Colonnata

It isn't every day that a new culinary sensation hits Tuscany. Of course, *lardo di Colonnata*—the hard layer of fat just below the skin of the pig's back, preserved in a brine of salt water, garlic, herbs, and spices—isn't actually new. For centuries, it has been a staple of marble cutters in Colonnata, a quarry town in the white-marbled Apuan Alps above Carrara. Now, however, the secret is out, and restaurants and food shops all over the region are clamoring for pale white *lardo*, with its soft, buttery texture and aromatic spicing.

What makes Colonnata's version so special, and totally different from its rather unappealing counterpart, common lard, is the way it's preserved and aged. Every winter, vats or troughs built of local marble are filled with slabs of the fat, which are then covered with water, salt, and some combination (every family has its own recipe) of bay leaves, pepper, juniper berries, thyme, and *nepitella*. The vats are stored in cool, dark cellars for at least six months while the *lardo* cures, during which time it soaks up the herbs and turns as white as the marble in which it is aged. Not surprisingly, the best way to eat *lardo* is also the most traditional: in thin slices on warm toasted bread.

Firenze

Tortino di Carciofi

artichoke omelet

This dish is called a tortino *because it is baked in the oven. If it were cooked on the stove top, it would be called a frittata. Zucchini (courgettes), cardoons, and eggplant (aubergine) can all be substituted for the artichokes. Serve the* tortino *for Sunday brunch or a light supper, and accompany with coarse country bread and a simple salad.*

6 baby artichokes

½ cup (2½ oz/75 g) all-purpose (plain) flour

1 teaspoon salt, plus salt to taste

½ cup (4 fl oz/125 ml) extra-virgin olive oil

1 clove garlic, minced

6 eggs

2 tablespoons water

freshly ground pepper to taste

lemon wedges

☙ Preheat an oven to 350°F (180°C).

☙ Trim and slice the artichokes as directed on page 246. After all the artichokes have been sliced, drain the pieces well and pat dry.

☙ Combine the flour and the 1 teaspoon salt on a plate and stir to mix well. In a large ovenproof pan over medium heat, warm the olive oil. Add the garlic and sauté until golden, about 1 minute. Dust the artichoke slices with the flour mixture, shaking off the excess, and add them to the pan. Fry the slices, turning once, until browned, about 5 minutes.

☙ Meanwhile, in a bowl, lightly beat the eggs until blended. Beat in the water and season with salt and pepper. When the artichokes are well browned, pour in the egg mixture. The eggs should sizzle when they hit the pan. Swirl the pan to distribute the eggs evenly, and immediately put into the oven. Bake until the *tortino* is set on the surface, 20–25 minutes.

☙ Bring to the table at once, cut into wedges in the pan, and serve with lemon wedges, or slide onto a serving plate and bring the plate to the table.

serves 4

Grosseto

Baccalà con i Ceci

chickpeas with salt cod

Chickpeas, which hold their shape beautifully during cooking, are a wonderful match for the salty flavor and firm texture of salt cod.

6½ oz (200 g) salt cod

⅔ cup (4 oz/125 g) dried chickpeas (garbanzo beans)

1 small carrot, peeled and cut into pieces

1 small yellow onion, quartered

1 small celery stalk, cut into pieces

1 clove garlic, crushed

salt to taste

⅓ cup (3 fl oz/80 ml) extra-virgin olive oil

juice of ½ lemon

freshly ground pepper to taste

4 large cupped lettuce leaves

2 tablespoons finely chopped fresh flat-leaf (Italian) parsley

In a bowl, combine the cod with water to cover. Refrigerate for 48 hours; change the water 8 times during that time.

Pick over the chickpeas, discarding any grit or misshapen beans. Rinse well and place in a saucepan. Add water to cover by 3 inches (7.5 cm) and bring to a boil. Reduce the heat to low, cover partially, and simmer until tender, 1½–2½ hours. Drain well.

Drain the salt cod. In a saucepan, bring water to a depth of 3–4 inches (7.5–10 cm) to a boil. The water must be deep enough to submerge the fish. Add the carrot, onion, celery, and salt cod, reduce the heat to low, cover, and simmer until the cod is tender, about 10 minutes. Drain, discarding the vegetables. Peel away the skin from the fish, then flake it, removing any bones. Place in a bowl and add the chickpeas.

Place the garlic clove in a small bowl, sprinkle with salt, and mash with a spoon or pestle. Whisk in the oil and then the lemon juice to make a dressing. Pour over the fish and beans, season with pepper, and toss gently but thoroughly.

Place a lettuce leaf on each individual plate. Top with the cod and beans, and garnish with the parsley. Serve warm or at room temperature.

serves 4

Firenze

Fettunta

toasted bread with garlic and olive oil

More than anything, the food of Tuscany is defined by its ingredients. Recipes rely much more on raw materials than on complex culinary techniques. So while bread and oil might sound like the humblest of dishes, when you use heavy, unsalted Tuscan bread and jewel-green olive oil from the countryside, simplicity becomes sublime.

My kids would eat fettunta (without garlic when they were smaller) five times a day if I let them. Most adults would, too. If I have a fire in the kitchen hearth and friends over for dinner, rather than make the fettunta myself, I set out a few cloves of garlic and a bottle of olive oil and send my guests to the fireplace to toast the bread on a grill over the embers.

1 lb (500 g) coarse country bread, thickly sliced

2 cloves garlic, halved

extra-virgin olive oil

salt to taste

Prepare a fire in a grill, or preheat a broiler (griller).

Place the bread slices on the grill rack or a broiler pan and grill or broil, turning once, until golden on both sides, about 4 minutes total; do not allow the slices to scorch. Transfer the slices to a work surface and rub the cut side of the garlic over one side of each piece of toast.

Arrange the slices on a serving platter, garlic-rubbed side up. Drizzle liberally with olive oil and sprinkle with salt. Serve immediately.

serves 6

Come late fall, olives are harvested and pressed, and the precious olio nuovo is quickly bottled.

Il Pane

Tuscans are extraordinarily proud of their bread, but at first bite you may wonder why. True, the heavy golden loaves piled one atop the other at the local bakery are gorgeous to look at, their crusts appealingly thick, their pale interiors dense and textured. I remember my first mouthful, eaten over twenty years ago when I spent a summer in Florence learning Italian. I was staying at a small *pensione* in the heart of the old city. On each table in the brightly lit dining room was a basket of thickly sliced bread. My first thought was that it had no taste. It took me a moment to realize that what it lacked was not flavor but salt.

Some pundits contend that Tuscan bread is saltless (or *sciocco,* meaning "insipid," as it is called here) because historically salt carried a tax, and saltless bread was a way around it. Others say that Tuscan cooking has such strong flavors that it requires a bland, but well-textured bread.

There is no doubt, however, that the best Tuscan bread is made from stone-ground flour, uses a natural leavening agent, and is baked in wood-burning ovens, as it was in the old days when meals were made of *pane e*

companatico—bread and something to go with the bread. The absence of salt in the bread means that as the loaf goes stale, it hardens but doesn't mold, so day-old bread is never wasted. It is an ingredient in such Tuscan classics as *acquacotta* (a soup from the Maremma made of vegetables, egg, and bread), *ribollita* (bread-and-vegetable soup), *pappa al pomodoro* (tomato-and-bread soup), and *panzanella* (bread salad with tomatoes, cucumbers, onions, and basil).

Once you get used to it—toasted and drizzled with olive oil, covered with summer tomatoes and basil, or as a tool for soaking up flavorful sauces—it is difficult to imagine a bread more suited to Tuscan food.

That said, the best Tuscan *panifici* use organic flours and filtered spring water to make salted loaves of whole wheat, farro, corn, rye, or mixed grains. Some are sprinkled with sesame seeds, others laced with anything from rosemary and walnuts to black olives and fiery *peperoncini*. All these loaves are delicious, but they are no substitute for the humble *pane sciocco* when it comes time to make a *ribollita*.

Firenze

Fette col Cavolo Nero

black cabbage bruschetta

Every summer, my family sows cavolo nero, or Tuscan "black cabbage," in the garden, and although it grows leafy and tall all summer long and throughout the fall, it isn't ready to eat until after the first frost, which is usually in November. Late fall is also when the olives are pressed and harvested, and the rich taste of the black cabbage is offset beautifully by the sharp, fruity flavor of the new oil.

1 bunch black cabbage (page 76) or kale

2 cloves garlic

6 slices coarse country bread, ½ inch (12 mm) thick

extra-virgin olive oil

salt and freshly ground pepper to taste

💮 Remove the center rib from the black cabbage. If using kale, cut off the heavy bottom stalks. Cut the cabbage or kale leaves into coarse strips. Crush 1 of the garlic cloves.

💮 Bring a large saucepan three-fourths full of salted water to a boil over high heat. Add the cabbage or kale and the crushed garlic clove, cover, adjust the heat as necessary, and boil until the greens are wilted and tender, about 20 minutes. Drain and let cool. When the greens are cool enough to handle, squeeze out the excess liquid, then roughly chop the leaves. (This step can be done up to 1 day in advance and the greens refrigerated.)

💮 Toast the bread. Cut the remaining garlic clove in half and rub 1 side of each piece of toast with a cut side of the garlic.

💮 Arrange the hot slices, garlic side up, on a platter or individual plates and divide the greens evenly among them. Drizzle generously with olive oil. Season with salt and pepper and serve at once.

serves 6

Grosseto

Insalata di Polpo

octopus salad

I came to Italy with an unfounded aversion to octopus. Finally I succumbed and tried it. The texture is wonderfully meaty, and when chilled and thinly sliced, it almost takes on the flavor of lobster.

2 lb (1 kg) octopus

2 tablespoons coarse salt, plus salt to taste

1 clove garlic, crushed

½ cup (4 fl oz / 125 ml) extra-virgin olive oil

juice of 1 lemon

2 green (spring) onions, including tender green tops, sliced crosswise

1 red bell pepper (capsicum), seeded and cut into small dice

2 inner celery stalks, thinly sliced

freshly ground pepper to taste

✧ A day in advance, clean each octopus: Invert the head sac and trim away the beaks visible in the mouth region, discarding these along with the eyes and all viscera. Remove and discard the ink sac. Rinse the octopus well under running cold water. Place in a large lock-top freezer bag and freeze overnight to tenderize the flesh. Thaw before proceeding.

✧ In a saucepan, combine the octopus with water to cover and bring to a boil over high heat. Add the 2 tablespoons salt and the garlic, cover, reduce the heat to low, and simmer, without lifting the lid, for about 45 minutes. The octopus should turn white.

✧ Drain the octopus and set aside until cool enough to handle. Cut the cooked octopus into bite-sized pieces and place in a serving bowl. Add the olive oil and lemon juice, cover, and let marinate for at least 1 hour at room temperature or for up to 4 hours in the refrigerator.

✧ Just before serving, add the green onions, bell pepper, and celery and toss well. Season with salt and pepper and toss again, then serve slightly chilled.

serves 4

Firenze

Schiacciata

tuscan flat bread

While the basic Tuscan unsalted loaf of bread is as plain as plain can be, Tuscany's other favorite bread, schiacciata, is anything but. It is the midmorning snack of choice for every school-age child I know, my own included. On the way to school, we often stop at the neighborhood bar to buy freshly cut squares of the flat, salty bread, still warm from the oven and dripping with olive oil, for slipping into their backpacks. The bread is delicious for sandwiches, albeit a bit tricky to slice in half horizontally.

1 cake (1 oz/30 g) fresh yeast or 2½ teaspoons (1 envelope) active dry yeast

½ cup (4 fl oz/125 ml) lukewarm water (110°F/43°C)

½ teaspoon sugar

2½ cups (12½ oz/400 g) all-purpose (plain) flour

½ teaspoon salt

5 tablespoons (2½ fl oz/75 ml) extra-virgin olive oil, plus oil for drizzling (optional)

½ cup (4 fl oz/125 ml) cold water

coarse salt

☙ In a small bowl, sprinkle the yeast over the luke-warm water and stir gently. Stir in the sugar and let the mixture stand until creamy, about 5 minutes.

☙ In a large bowl, mound the flour and make a well in the center. Pour the yeast mixture into the well. Add the salt and 2 tablespoons of the olive oil to the well. Stir in a circular motion, slowly incorporating the dry ingredients. When roughly half of the flour has been incorporated, add the cold water. Continue working the ingredients until the mixture forms a cohesive ball.

☙ Turn the dough out onto a lightly floured work surface and knead until it becomes smooth and elas-tic, 10–15 minutes.

☙ Shape the dough into a ball and place in a lightly oiled bowl. Turn to coat with oil, cover with a damp kitchen towel, and set in a warm place to rise until the dough has doubled in volume, 1½–2½ hours.

☙ Lightly oil a 10½-by-15-inch (26.5-by-37.5-cm) baking pan. Punch down the risen dough, then return to the floured work surface and knead again for a couple of minutes. It will be very elastic, spring-ing back when you press down on it with a finger. Roll out the dough on the floured work surface, shaping it to the size of the baking pan. Transfer the rolled-out dough to the prepared pan, cover with a damp kitchen towel, and set in a warm place to rise for 30 minutes.

☙ Preheat an oven to 400°F (200°C).

☙ Dimple the surface of the dough with your finger-tips, spacing the dimples about 1½ inches (4 cm) apart. Pour the remaining 3 tablespoons oil over the surface and sprinkle with coarse salt.

☙ Bake until golden on top, 25–30 minutes. Remove from the oven and drizzle with additional olive oil, if you wish. Remove the bread from the pan and cut into squares to serve. The bread can be stored, well wrapped, for up to 2 days and reheated or served at room temperature.

serves 6–8

Firenze

Involtini di Bresaola, Ricotta, e Rucola

sliced cured beef stuffed with ricotta and arugula

I first ate a version of this recipe one summer night on the outdoor patio of trattoria Quattro Leoni in Florence. So simple, the combination seemed obvious, but I would probably never have thought of it myself. I let my children assemble this appetizer when we have friends coming out to our farmhouse for a visit. Bresaola, mild cured lean beef popular in northern Italy but appreciated in Tuscany as well, is ruby red and close in texture to prosciutto. It is available in fine delicatessens outside Italy.

¾ cup (6½ oz/200 g) fresh ricotta cheese

¼ cup (2 oz/60 g) mascarpone cheese

3 tablespoons chopped arugula (rocket), plus whole leaves for garnish

½ teaspoon minced garlic

1 teaspoon grated lemon zest

24 paper-thin slices bresaola (see note)

☙ In a bowl, combine the ricotta and mascarpone cheeses, chopped arugula, garlic, and lemon zest. Mix well. Scatter the arugula leaves on a serving platter.

☙ Lay a *bresaola* slice on a work surface. Dip a spoon into cold water, then scoop out 1½ teaspoons of the cheese mixture and place in the center of the *bresaola* slice. Starting at one end, roll up the slice and place it seam side down on the platter. Repeat with the remaining *bresaola* and filling.

☙ Garnish the platter with whole arugula leaves. Cover and refrigerate for 30 minutes before serving.

serves 6

In warm weather, prosciutto slices arrive draped over sweet summer melon.

L'Affettato

One of the standards of Tuscan cuisine—even though it involves no cooking—is the ubiquitous *affettato misto*. It appears on nearly every buffet table and on trattoria menus in cities and in the countryside. Indeed, it is found just about everywhere but at a formal dinner. And although the two words simply mean "sliced mixed," every Tuscan knows that what is sliced is some combination of cured meats.

First and foremost of all *affettati* is prosciutto. In Tuscany, you will find it *dolce*, referring to the mildly salted varieties from northern Italy, and *toscano*, the highly salted local product, considered a perfect accompaniment to saltless Tuscan bread. Usually it is very thinly cut on a slicing machine, but sometimes (and I love this) it is hand-cut into somewhat thicker pieces.

A Tuscan platter of cured meats will most often include a few slices of *salame toscano*, a full-bodied local salami flavored with peppercorns, garlic, and white wine, and *finocchiona* or *sbriciolona*, delicious soft salamis (the latter so soft that it literally crumbles) flavored with fennel seed.

Less common, though no less delectable, is the meat of wild boar. It is often used to make prosciutto, salami, and *coppa*, cured boneless pork—in this case boar—shoulder. *Prosciutto di cinghiale* has a beautiful deep red cast and an appealing subtle earthiness.

Grosseto

Insalata di Ovoli e Tartufi

ovoli and truffle salad

Several years ago, I walked into a small produce shop in the center of Grosseto and eyed a wicker basket lined with laurel leaves and filled with the most extraordinary-looking—and extraordinarily expensive—mushrooms I had ever seen. They had brilliant orange caps and pale cream stems. "Why do ovoli cost so much?" I asked the shopkeeper. "Because they are so rare and so wonderful" was his answer. Ovoli are always cut into thin slivers and eaten raw. The only thing better than a salad of ovoli is a salad of ovoli and truffles. If your budget won't permit such extravagance, substitute small white mushrooms for the ovoli and omit the truffle.

1 lb (500 g) ovoli or white mushrooms, brushed clean

1 celery heart, finely julienned

1 white or black truffle, about 1 oz (30 g)

2-oz (60-g) piece Parmesan cheese

6 tablespoons (3 fl oz/90 ml) extra-virgin olive oil

juice of ½ lemon

pinch of salt

freshly ground pepper to taste

❀ If using *ovoli*, trim only the very base of the stems. If using white mushrooms, remove the stems. Slice the mushrooms very thinly (a mandoline works nicely) and put into a salad bowl. Scatter the celery on top of the mushrooms.

❀ Brush away the dirt from the truffle with a mushroom brush or kitchen towel, slice as thinly as possible, and add to the celery and mushrooms. Using a vegetable peeler or sharp paring knife, cut the Parmesan cheese into thin shavings, letting them fall over the top of the salad.

❀ In a small bowl, whisk together the olive oil and lemon juice until creamy. Add the salt and season with pepper. Pour over the salad and serve at once.

serves 6

Livorno

Crostini di Pesce Spada

smoked swordfish toasts

Tuscan kitchens are notoriously gadget free. Vegetables are chopped by hand, using one of the few indispensable tools of the kitchen, the mezzaluna, or "half-moon," a curved knife with a handle at each end. Tuscan cooks will almost always use this kitchen implement for a recipe such as this one, rolling the blade back and forth over the vegetables and fish, never lifting the knife from the cutting surface, until everything is chopped to the perfect consistency. If you cannot find smoked swordfish, smoked trout can be used with equally delicious results.

1 green (spring) onion, white part only, finely chopped

1 carrot, peeled and finely chopped

1 tender inner celery stalk, finely chopped

2 tablespoons finely chopped fresh flat-leaf (Italian) parsley

¼ lb (125 g) smoked swordfish fillet, thinly sliced

¼ cup (2 fl oz/60 ml) extra-virgin olive oil

juice from ½ lemon

freshly ground pepper to taste

1 loaf ciabatta (page 246) or 1 baguette

snipped fresh chives

♛ Combine the green onion, carrot, celery, and parsley on a cutting board. Add the smoked fish and finely chop the ingredients.

♛ Transfer the fish mixture to a glass bowl. Pour in the olive oil and lemon juice, combine to mix well, and season with pepper. Cover and refrigerate for at least 4 hours or for up to 24 hours.

♛ Just before serving, cut the bread into slices ¼ inch (6 mm) thick and toast lightly.

♛ Spread the fish mixture on the slices of toast, dividing evenly. Garnish with the chives and serve the toasts at once.

serves 6

Grosseto

Code Affogate al Sughetto Rosso di Magro

poached shrimp in garlic tomato sauce

The Maremma, an area within Grosseto, is home to some of Italy's most stunning shoreline. This recipe comes from Grosseto, the Maremma's largest town.

SHRIMP

1 lb (500 g) large shrimp (prawns) in the shell

1½ teaspoons salt

1 tablespoon finely chopped fresh flat-leaf (Italian) parsley

SAUCE

2 cloves garlic, halved

heart of 1 small sweet onion (page 249), chopped, plus ½ small onion, finely chopped

4 fresh basil leaves, torn into pieces

1 tablespoon white wine vinegar

pinch of ground red chile

4 plum (Roma) tomatoes, peeled, seeded, and chopped

juice of ½ lemon

1 tablespoon finely chopped fresh flat-leaf (Italian) parsley

salt and freshly ground pepper to taste

½ cup (4 fl oz/125 ml) extra-virgin olive oil

1 head butter (Boston) or romaine (cos) lettuce, leaves separated and cut into ribbons

❦ To prepare the shrimp, bring a saucepan three-fourths full of salted water to a boil. Add the shrimp and cook for about 2 minutes. Drain and then peel and devein. Place in a bowl and stir in the salt and parsley. Cover and refrigerate for 1–3 hours.

❦ To make the sauce, place the garlic in a mortar. Add the onion heart and basil and, using a pestle, mash to a fine paste. Stir in the vinegar and ground chile. Transfer to a bowl. Mix in the tomatoes, chopped onion, lemon juice, and parsley. Season with salt and pepper. Cover and refrigerate for 1 hour.

❦ Add the shrimp to the tomato mixture and cover with the olive oil. Stir to incorporate. Make a bed of the lettuce on individual plates, arrange the shrimp in its sauce on top, and serve.

serves 6

Lucca

Uova Ripiene

stuffed eggs

Is there a cuisine in the world that does not serve stuffed eggs? Or anyone who can resist them? Eggs prepared this way usually appear as part of a buffet table or are passed with wine as a handheld appetizer. The saltiness of the anchovies and the tartness of the capers are mellowed by the egg and mayonnaise. The filled eggs can be stored, covered, in the refrigerator for up to 12 hours; remove 30 minutes before serving.

6 eggs, hard boiled and peeled

¼ cup (2 fl oz/60 ml) mayonnaise

6 olive oil–packed anchovy fillets or 1 teaspoon anchovy paste

2 tablespoons finely chopped fresh flat-leaf (Italian) parsley

1 teaspoon capers, rinsed and finely chopped

1 tablespoon snipped fresh chives

❦ Cut the eggs in half lengthwise. Carefully scoop out the yolks into a bowl and mash with a fork. Arrange the whites, hollow side up, on a serving tray.

❦ Add the mayonnaise, anchovy fillets or paste, parsley, and capers to the mashed yolks and blend with the fork until smooth.

❦ Spoon the mixture into the egg halves, mounding attractively and dividing evenly. Or spoon the mixture into a pastry (piping) bag fitted with a large star tip and pipe into the egg halves. Garnish with a sprinkling of chives and serve.

serves 6

In the Maremma, farmhouses dot fields of sunflowers, and the woods shelter boar and hare.

Pisa

Alici Marinate al Limone

marinated anchovies

For years I thought I didn't like anchovies. Then I realized that what I didn't like was the overpowering flavor of tinned salted anchovies (and even this is a taste I am slowly acquiring). A fresh anchovy, with its iridescent blue-green back, silvery underbelly, and subtle, delicate flavor, is another creature entirely. There's no denying that it takes work to clean a batch, but the results are well worth the effort.

This dish is almost always eaten along the Tuscan coast where freshly caught anchovies are readily available. For a variation, substitute a few cloves of minced garlic and a scattering of finely chopped fresh flat-leaf (Italian) parsley for the onion.

1 lb (500 g) fresh anchovies

1 tablespoon salt

1 small white onion, thinly sliced

juice of 6 lemons

extra-virgin olive oil

freshly ground pepper to taste

☙ Using the tip of a sharp knife, carefully make a slit on the underside of each anchovy from head to tail. Slip your thumb up the inside of the slit to push out the viscera. Cut off and discard the head and tail. Open the fish like a book. Grasp the tail end of the spine between your thumb and forefinger, then pull it out and discard.

☙ Lay the splayed fish in a single layer on a large concave dish. Sprinkle the salt over the fillets.

☙ Cover the anchovies with the onion slices and pour the lemon juice over to cover. Let marinate for 1½ hours, but no longer.

☙ Drain the marinade off the fish and onions. Drizzle lightly with olive oil and season with pepper. Serve immediately. The anchovies will keep, covered, for up to 1 week in the refrigerator.

serves 4

Siena

Crostini di Fegatini

crostini with chicken liver pâté

Here is the quintessential Tuscan appetizer. Rare is the trattoria that doesn't serve crostini. *Rarer still is the* casalinga *(housewife) who doesn't have her own special recipe for them. Whole dinner-party conversations have centered around the debate as to what constitutes the perfect pâté. Among the controversies: spleen* (milza) *or no spleen. A friend's mother tells me it gives* quella punta d'amaro, *a touch of bitterness (without which the pâté is* troppo dolce, *or "too sweet").*

Another line of division is the way the ingredients are processed. Home cooks of the old school would always use a mezzaluna *and work the ingredients manually. The result is a coarse paste, somewhat more difficult to spread than the smooth (and, they would say, suspiciously artificial looking) mixture that results from using a food processor or blender. Some add a splash of wine, others a bit of pickled vegetables. Still others have their own secrets with which they will not part. The following is a very fine basic recipe. The bread slices may be toasted before being spread with the pâté.*

5 tablespoons (2½ fl oz / 75 ml) extra-virgin olive oil

½ small yellow onion, chopped

1 small clove garlic, crushed

4 large chicken livers, trimmed of membranes and connective tissue

salt to taste

¼ cup (2 fl oz / 60 ml) vin santo (page 222)

2 salt-packed anchovy fillets, rinsed, or 2 olive oil–packed anchovies

1 tablespoon capers, rinsed and minced

½ cup (4 fl oz / 125 ml) chicken broth (page 247), if needed

¼ cup (2 oz / 60 g) unsalted butter, cut into small pieces

freshly ground pepper to taste

1 baguette, thinly sliced

☙ In a large frying pan over medium heat, warm the olive oil. Add the onion and sauté until soft and translucent, about 5 minutes. Add the garlic and cook until lightly fragrant, about 2 minutes longer. Add the livers, sprinkle with salt, and stir to coat with the oil. Then add the *vin santo* and let the alcohol bubble away for about 3 minutes. Reduce the heat to low and cook gently, turning occasionally, until the livers are a deep, rich brown on the outside and tender pink on the inside, 8–10 minutes.

☙ Transfer the livers to a cutting board and slice them open down the middle. Return them to the pan, cut side down. Add the anchovy fillets and capers, raise the heat to medium-high, and continue cooking, stirring often, until the livers are no longer pink, about 5 minutes longer.

☙ Using a food processor or hand blender, reduce the mixture to a thick paste, adding a little chicken broth if it is too stiff and dry. Blend in the butter, stirring until it has melted into the pâté. Season with salt and pepper.

☙ Spread the sliced bread generously with the pâté, arrange on individual plates, and serve immediately.

serves 10

Il Pecorino

Walk into any cheese shop in Tuscany and you will find among the lovely straw-colored wedges of Parmesan from the north and the soft, milky mozzarella balls from the south round upon round of the local sheep's milk cheese known as pecorino. This specialty seems to come in as many varieties as there are producers.

As with most things Tuscan, nothing is wasted in the cheese-making process. From the whey is made a delicate, light ricotta that can be eaten fresh with olive oil, salt, and pepper, or incorporated into a variety of pasta dishes. The pecorinos themselves range from the soft, almost sweet fresh pecorino to piquant flavorful ones aged for varying lengths of time and more or less dense, salty, and rich in taste and smell.

Some producers lace their pecorino with various herbs, garlic, chile, parsley, spicy arugula (rocket), or, my favorite, slivers of wild truffles. Others are returning to the medieval technique of aging their cheeses in earthen pits to re-create the famous *pecorino di fossa,* a hard, yet moist cheese with the texture of a fine Parmesan and a ripe, spicy flavor. Still others are combining traditional pecorino-making techniques with those of other cheeses—Gorgonzola, for example—with spectacular results.

Massa-Carrara

Torta di Erbe Pontremolese

green vegetable tart

The Lunigiana is a small, little-visited area in the northwestern part of Tuscany, just below Liguria. At its heart are the towns of Massa and Carrara, which for centuries have provided Italy's sculptors, Michelangelo among them, with exquisite soft, white marble carved from the local mountains.

This savory torta *comes from the small village of Pontremoli, and it uses a mixture of greens, including cucumber-scented borage, which grows wild in the area. Since it is as delicious at room temperature as it is warm, the* torta *is often served as part of a buffet at large gatherings. Make one to bring to a friend's house to start off a simple dinner— you'll find that it will be as well received as the most luscious homemade sweet.*

PASTRY

2 cups (10 oz/315 g) all-purpose (plain) flour

½ teaspoon salt

½ cup (4 oz/125 g) chilled unsalted butter, cut into ½-inch (12-mm) pieces

about 6 tablespoons (3 fl oz/90 ml) water

FILLING

1 lb (500 g) Swiss chard

2 tablespoons extra-virgin olive oil

1 clove garlic, crushed

2 oz (60 g) borage or 1 head Belgian endive (chicory/witloof), chopped

1 leek, including pale green portion, chopped

2 eggs, beaten

⅔ cup (5 oz/155 g) ricotta cheese

2 tablespoons grated Parmesan cheese

½ teaspoon salt

freshly ground pepper to taste

1 egg lightly beaten with 1 tablespoon water

To make the pastry, in a large bowl, combine the flour and salt. Add half of the butter and, using your fingers, work the butter into the flour. Add the remaining butter and continue to work into the flour until the mixture resembles coarse crumbs. Slowly incorporate the water into the flour-butter mixture,

stirring lightly with a fork and adding only enough to make a dough that holds together. Shape into a ball, wrap in plastic wrap, and refrigerate while you make the filling.

♛ To make the filling, trim away the ribs and any battered or tough leaves from the chard. Bring a large saucepan three-fourths full of salted water to a boil. Add the chard and boil until the chard is wilted, about 3 minutes. Drain well and let cool. Squeeze out the excess water, then chop coarsely.

♛ In a large, heavy frying pan over medium heat, warm the olive oil. Add the garlic to the pan and sauté until fragrant, about 2 minutes. Remove and discard the garlic.

♛ Add the chard, the borage or endive, and the leek to the pan and sauté until the borage or endive is wilted, about 5 minutes. Remove from the heat.

♛ In a large bowl, combine the eggs, ricotta and Parmesan cheeses, and salt. Season with pepper, add the sautéed vegetables, and mix well.

♛ Position a rack in the lower third of an oven and preheat to 375°F (190°C).

♛ To assemble the *torta,* divide the dough in half. On a lightly floured work surface, roll out half of the dough into an 11-inch (28-cm) round ⅛ inch (3 mm) thick. Drape the round over the rolling pin and carefully ease it into a 9-inch (23-cm) tart pan with a removable bottom, pressing it into the bottom and sides. (Alternatively, roll out the dough between 2 sheets of plastic wrap, peel off the top sheet, and use the other sheet for transferring the pastry round to the pan.)

♛ Spoon the filling into the pastry-lined pan. Roll out the remaining dough half into a 10-inch (25-cm) round. Lay the dough round over the filling and trim the edges. Crimp lightly to form an attractive rim. Brush the top crust with the egg mixture.

♛ Bake the *torta* until the crust is golden brown, about 45 minutes. Transfer to a rack and let cool for 10 minutes. Cut the *torta* into slices and serve warm or at room temperature.

serves 6

PRIMI

Soup, pasta, rice,
gnocchi, polenta,
crespelle ~ Tuscans
prepare a primo for
every palate, every season.

Preceding pages: Corn, when ground to a coarse meal, cooks into polenta, the foundation for diverse regional dishes.
Above top: In the marble-rich town of Pietrasanta, an exhibition of sculptures by Botero fills the Piazza del Duomo.
Above: An order of *porchetta*—whole roasted pig—is carved in a busy *salumeria*. **Right:** In the northwest, sprawling chestnut trees stand in counterpoint to neatly rolled bales of hay.

WALK INTO A TUSCAN HOUSE around mealtime and follow the subtly enticing perfume that beckons you into the kitchen like a crooked finger. Chances are your nose will lead you to a pot of gently simmering soup. The majority of Tuscan soups originated as peasants' dishes and embody that most elemental and enviable aspect of Tuscan cooking: the ability to make something both nourishing and delicious from whatever is available, whether a handful of herbs and fresh vegetables, half a loaf of day-old bread, or a few ladlefuls of beans. Soups speak of an era when life moved at a slower pace, and time (soups won't be rushed) was more abundant than money.

Traditionally, *minestre* or *zuppe* of one sort or another appeared on Tuscan tables at least once a day. The former generally refers to broth-based soups but is also a generic term for first courses as a whole. The latter is used for thick soups made or served with bread, like Florence's famous *pappa al pomodoro* made with tomatoes, basil, and day-old saltless bread, and *ribollita,* a deliciously thick, cool-weather soup made with carrots, greens, white beans, and country bread. As I write these words, a soup is bubbling

on my own stove. It contains a handful each of *farro,* brown and red lentils, split peas, and white beans, and some onions, carrots, celery, and tiny nuggets of spicy pancetta. The recipe comes from a busy trattoria located just outside the ancient walls of Lucca, a brightly lit place with tiled floors, battered wooden tables, a few spartan rooms upstairs to rent to travelers, and a kitchen run by two grandmotherly women who were as delighted to tell me their culinary secrets as I was to hear them.

All this talk of soup never fails to surprise the vast majority of non-Tuscans who assume—as I did when I first came to Tuscany—that *il primo,* or the first course, is largely synonymous with pasta. Until about fifty years ago, pasta had an aura of luxury to it and was eaten on Sundays or other occasions that called for a touch of extravagance. Today, most of the pasta eaten in Tuscany is factory made. But during the Middle Ages and the Renaissance, lasagne, ravioli, and *maccheroni* (handmade, of course)

were considered *piatti ghiotti* (gastronomic delicacies), and paradise, as described by Boccaccio in the *Decameron* (set in the plague-ridden Florence of 1348), was a place where "grapevines were tied down with sausages... and there was a mountain of grated parmesan, atop which were people who did nothing but make *maccheroni* and ravioli, cook them in capon broth, then toss them down the mountain, and the more people took, the more that appeared."

Pasta fatta in casa, or "homemade pasta," is still the stuff of dreams throughout much, but not all, of Tuscany. Every housewife *di una certa età* (of a certain age) in Borgo San Lorenzo, off the old road from Florence to Bologna, is as skilled at making *tortelli di patate,* pasta stuffed with puréed herb-and-spice seasoned potatoes, as her neighbor is in Emilia-Romagna, the epicenter of Italian homemade pasta that lies to the north. In the province of Siena—but rarely outside it—you can peek into a restaurant kitchen and catch a glimpse of *pici* (or

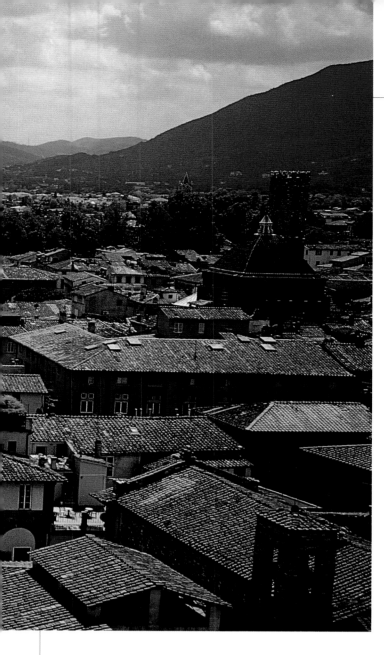

Left: The lovely town of Lucca is a peaceful and well-ordered world, rich in Romanesque churches and medieval towers. **Below:** Packaged pastas ensure that the busy cook need never do without. **Below bottom:** Eminent among the Tuscans' taste for winter squashes is the formidable pumpkinlike *zucca*.

Above top: It is a pleasing paradox that goats thrive in the rockiest areas of Tuscany, scrambling for sparse vegetation, and then yield milk for the making of some of Italy's most delicate cheeses. **Above:** Beans of every stripe come together in the soup pot to cook up a hearty *zuppa toscana*. **Right:** Cultivated for millennia, the fertile hills and valleys of the region ceaselessly give forth the grape harvest, *la vendemmia,* for Tuscany's wealth of celebrated wines.

pinci, as they are also known) being rolled between open palms into long, plump strands of pasta. Take a seat in the dining room and order them covered with a rich, savory *ragù* made with fresh pork sausages, dried porcini, tomatoes, and onions.

Ever resourceful in the kitchen, Tuscan cooks will make use of just about anything for a pasta sauce—from the savory juices of roasted meats to bright garden vegetables cooked with olive oil, garlic, onion, and herbs. My favorite version of the latter (and surely the most interestingly named) is *sugo finto,* literally "fake sauce." What at first glance looks much like a meat ragù is really a thick rustic sauce made from aromatic vegetables and herbs. There is nothing fake about its delicious flavor.

Although most Tuscans seem to derive as much pleasure from the act of cooking as from the results themselves, there isn't always time to knead flour and eggs into a silky dough, wait while a pot of vegetables and water slowly transforms into a soup, or even chop, sauté, and simmer a bit of this or that into a proper sauce for dried pasta. The Tuscan solution for such gastronomic emergencies is the same as it is throughout most of Italy: *una bella spaghettata,* "a nice plate of spaghetti." The underlying principle for this *primo* is that the sauce can be assembled or cooked in the time it takes for the pasta to boil. In Elba or Giglio, the largest islands of the Tuscan archipelago (where your excuse for not having time to cook might be that you had better things to do, such as swim in the warm waters of the Mediterranean), spaghetti is tossed with garlic-infused olive oil and parsley, or shards of *bottarga* (the dried roe of gray mullet or tuna) and chopped raw tomatoes.

Of course, wherever there is water there is fish, and wherever there is fish there will be markets whose tables are heaped with treasures from the sea: mesh bags of tiny gray-shelled clams; cuttlefish, their opaque bodies still filled with velvety black ink; mussels with tightly closed blue-black shells. Versilia's beaches are lined with brightly painted cabanas, bars, and restaurants vying to cater to beachgoers' every need. But it was once a much simpler place, where weather-beaten fishing boats set out to sea before dawn and delivered their catch to the *"ristoranti,"* usually little more than ram-shackle fishing huts perched on the sand and run by the fishermen's wives.

Another humble, yet indispensable, staple in every Tuscan kitchen is *il riso,* or "rice." Despite the fact that risotto in Tuscany has nowhere near the culinary importance that it has in the Veneto and Piedmont, every Tuscan home cook I know is skilled in the art of coaxing pearly grains of rice to a creamy, flavorful finish. The variations are limitless, but the technique for making this archetypal rice dish remains more or less the same: a bit of sautéed onion, the rice tossed in the pan and lightly toasted, a splash of wine, and then the slow addition of broth until the grains become tender and creamy.

But risotto isn't all Tuscans make with rice. A handful of grains sprinkled into a broth or vegetable soup and boiled until they've plumped up to three times their size and turned soft enough to feed to a baby was all a traditional *casalinga* needed to create a real *sfamafamiglia*— a humble dish capable of feeding the whole family. Northern Italians can't seem to help but poke fun at the Tuscan way with rice, as did eighteenth-century Venetian dramatist Carlo

Goldoni in *Sior Todero Brontolon:* "I've been to Florence, that's where I learned how to cook rice. They boil it for three hours; and half a lira of rice is enough for eight or nine people."

Last among the Tuscan first courses, but of no less importance, are gnocchi, polenta, and crepes. The elegant spinach-filled *crespelle* of Florence hark back to the Renaissance and the Medici court. Gnocchi and polenta take us into the countryside, to the gentle hills of the Casentino where soft, fresh ricotta cheese and finely chopped spinach are fashioned into hearty gnocchi, and to the coastal marsh and pinewoods of the Maremma where golden cornmeal is simmered into a thick, warming polenta and covered with *sugo di cinghiale* made from wild boar.

The sheer range and diversity of Tuscan first courses is astonishing. Whether a bowl of hearty soup drizzled with olive oil, a delicate lasagne flavored with woodland mushrooms, or a plate of pasta tossed with colorful spring vegetables, there is something for every season and every palate.

Left: In Lucca, the church of San Michele in Foro displays the ambition and invention that characterized the Pisan Romanesque style. Although construction of the church began in the eleventh century, the completion of the ornate arcading was the pride of fourteenth-century *lucchesi.* **Above top:** *Pecora* is the Italian word for "sheep," and pecorino is Tuscany's renowned sheep's milk cheese, the best of which is protected by a *denominazione di origine controllata,* indicating that it was made within a circumscribed area and by a specific process. **Above:** Among the world's earliest cultivated grains, *Triticum dicoccum* is grown in the rugged Garfagnana of northern Tuscany, where it is known as *farro.*

Arezzo

Gnocchi di Ricotta e Spinaci con Brodo

spinach and ricotta gnocchi in broth

The forests of the Casentino in the province of Arezzo are a world unto themselves. Green and cool, they are dotted with rural villages and are home to the lovely eleventh-century monastery of Camaldoli, where many of the monks have taken vows of silence. The wonderful ricotta cheese from the area finds its way into many traditional recipes, such as these light and savory gnocchi.

The gnocchi are often served in broth, as they are in this recipe. Otherwise they are cooked lightly in salted water (in which case you should make the gnocchi smaller, using about 1 tablespoon of filling for each dumpling), then drained and dressed with melted butter and Parmesan, ragù, the juices of roasted meat seasoned with pepper and nutmeg, or a creamy besciamella (white sauce).

Gnocchi, which go by the name topini in parts of Tuscany, are also made with potatoes, eggs, and flour, although this version is nowhere near as prevalent in Tuscany as it is in the north. But when made with floury baking potatoes, seasoned with nutmeg, and bathed in a light fresh tomato sauce, potato gnocchi are as welcome on the table as the most traditional Tuscan soup.

1 lb (500 g) spinach, stems removed

1½ cups (12 oz/375 g) ricotta cheese

4 egg yolks, lightly beaten

1 cup (4 oz/125 g) grated Parmesan cheese, plus Parmesan cheese for serving

pinch of freshly grated nutmeg

salt and freshly ground pepper to taste

2 cups (10 oz/315 g) all-purpose (plain) flour

2½ qt (2.5 l) meat broth (page 247)

☙ Place the spinach in a saucepan with only the rinsing water clinging to the leaves, cover, and cook until tender, 4–8 minutes. Check the pan from time to time and add a bit of water if needed to prevent scorching. Drain and rinse under running cold water to cool completely. Form the spinach into a ball and squeeze forcefully to remove as much water as possible. Finely chop the spinach, then squeeze again to force out any additional water and transfer to a bowl.

☙ To the bowl holding the spinach, add the ricotta cheese, egg yolks, 1 cup (4 oz/125 g) Parmesan cheese, and nutmeg. Using a wooden spoon, combine the ingredients into a homogeneous paste. (Do not use a food processor, as the processor tends to force out liquid.) Season with salt and pepper.

☙ Pour the flour onto a work surface. Dust your hands with some of the flour and scoop out a golf ball–sized portion of the spinach mixture. Roll it into a ball between your palms. Place the ball on a baking sheet.

☙ Repeat the rolling process, dusting your hands regularly with flour, until all of the spinach mixture has been used.

☙ To finish the dish, set a warmed tureen near the stove. Pour the broth into a saucepan and bring to a gentle boil over medium heat.

☙ Ladle 2 scoops of the broth into the tureen. Then carefully place the gnocchi, one by one, into the simmering broth in the saucepan, adding no more than 5 or 6 gnocchi at a time to prevent sticking. The gnocchi are ready when they have risen to the surface, about 3 minutes.

☙ Using a skimmer, transfer the gnocchi to the tureen. When all the gnocchi are cooked, carefully pour the broth from the pot into the tureen.

☙ Ladle into warmed individual bowls and serve immediately. Pass the remaining Parmesan cheese at the table.

serves 6

Farmers in Arezzo tend orchards and vegetable fields and raise the province's celebrated Chianina steers.

Firenze

Pappa al Pomodoro

bread and tomato soup

Pappa is a dish so strictly associated with easy-to-digest, healthful baby food that the word is an indispensable entry in the lexicon of Italian baby talk. Children refer to any meal as pappa, and mothers run after their bambini asking, "Mangiamo la pappa?" "Era buona la pappa?" ("Shall we eat our pappa? Was the pappa good?") As my friend Riccardo Bruscagli explained, "A whole generation of Florentine baby boomers grew up on pappa al pomodoro. What was a toddler back then supposed to eat before cereals and homogenized baby foods were available?"

Pappa al pomodoro is also a favorite with adults, as it combines a handful of the ingredients that Florentines love most: tomatoes, bread, basil, and fruity olive oil. Each bowl is usually drizzled with more oil.

¼ cup (2 fl oz/60 ml) extra-virgin olive oil

4 cloves garlic, minced

2 lb (1 kg) tomatoes, peeled, seeded, and chopped

8 fresh basil leaves

4 cups (32 fl oz/1 l) light vegetable broth (page 247) or salted water

salt to taste

½ lb (250 g) day-old unsalted coarse country bread, cut into 1-inch (2.5-cm) slices and torn into medium-sized pieces

freshly ground pepper to taste

☙ In a large saucepan over medium heat, warm the olive oil. Add the garlic and sauté, stirring frequently, until the garlic begins to color, about 1 minute. Stir in the tomatoes and bring to a gentle boil. Tear 5 of the basil leaves into pieces and stir into the tomatoes. Pour in the broth or salted water, raise the heat to medium-high, and bring to a boil. Season the soup with salt, reduce the heat to low, and stir in the bread. Simmer uncovered, stirring often, until the bread softens, about 5 minutes.

☙ Remove the soup from the heat, cover, and let stand for 1 hour.

☙ Before serving the soup, adjust the seasoning with salt and pepper, stir well, and add the remaining 3 basil leaves. Reheat, if desired, or serve warm or at room temperature.

serves 4

Siena

Farfalle con Zucchini, Fiori di Zucca, e Pomodori

farfalle with zucchini, zucchini flowers, and tomatoes

The bounty of the Tuscan summer vegetable garden is almost beyond imagination. Mine is filled with pomodori of every persuasion, but the only verdura that rivals the tomatoes for sheer abundance is the zucchini.

¼ cup (2 fl oz/60 ml) extra-virgin olive oil

1 small yellow onion, chopped

2 cloves garlic, minced

4 small zucchini (courgettes), trimmed, halved lengthwise, and sliced

2 lb (1 kg) plum (Roma) tomatoes, peeled, seeded, and chopped

salt to taste

pinch of red pepper flakes

7 very fresh zucchini (courgette) flowers, pistils removed and cut lengthwise into thin strips

handful of fresh basil leaves

2 tablespoons heavy (double) cream

1 lb (500 g) farfalle

2 tablespoons coarse salt

grated Parmesan cheese

☙ In a large frying pan over medium heat, warm the olive oil. Add the onion and sauté until fragrant, about 5 minutes. Add the garlic and zucchini and sauté until the zucchini begin to soften, about 3 minutes. Stir in the tomatoes, season with salt and red pepper flakes, cover, and simmer until the zucchini are tender, about 10 minutes. Add the zucchini flowers and basil leaves and cook uncovered, stirring often, until the flowers are wilted, about 5 minutes. Remove from the heat and stir in the cream.

☙ Meanwhile, bring a large pot three-fourths full of water to a boil. Add the pasta and the coarse salt, stir well, and cook until al dente, about 9 minutes. Drain the pasta.

☙ Spoon half of the sauce into a warmed serving bowl, add the drained pasta, top with the remaining sauce, and toss well. Serve immediately. Pass the Parmesan cheese at the table.

serves 4–6

Lucca

Spaghetti al Cacio e Pizzico

spaghetti with sheep's milk cheese
and pepper

Cacio is another word for pecorino cheese. Pizzico refers to both the piquant bite of aged cheese and the spiciness of the pepper. This recipe comes from the town of Altopascio in Lucca Province, which, like much of Tuscany, has its share of fine pecorino cheeses. Although I've seen it on many restaurant menus, I think cacio e pizzico *is less a restaurant dish than a wonderfully easy pasta to make at home for a late-night meal. Most of the aged sheep's milk cheese exported from Italy is* pecorino romano *from Rome, which is quite hard and must be grated. When I make* cacio e pizzico *in Tuscany from an aged semihard pecorino, I crumble the cheese rather than grate it.*

½ lb (250 g) spaghetti

1 tablespoon coarse salt

¼ cup (2 oz/60 g) unsalted butter

3-oz (90-g) piece aged pecorino cheese

1 tablespoon extra-virgin olive oil

salt and freshly ground pepper to taste

❦ Bring a large pot three-fourths full of water to a boil. Add the pasta and the coarse salt, stir well, and cook until al dente, about 10 minutes.

❦ While the pasta is cooking, in a small saucepan over low heat, melt the butter and set aside. Grate or crumble the cheese.

❦ When the pasta is ready, drain it, reserving a ladleful of the cooking water. Transfer the pasta to a warmed serving bowl, and pour the melted butter, olive oil, and 2 tablespoons of the cooking water over the top. Toss briefly, then sprinkle with the cheese, season with salt and a generous grinding of pepper, and toss well. If the pasta seems dry, add more of the reserved cooking water as needed. Serve immediately.

serves 2

Grosseto

Polenta al Sugo di Cinghiale

polenta with wild boar sauce

The dense woods of the Maremman countryside abound with wild boar. Make this thick, flavorful boar sauce the day before serving. Like most good stews, its flavors are better on the second day. On the other hand, make the polenta right before serving, so that it will be soft and thick. Pair this dish with a bottle of Sassicaia, a prized Super Tuscan from the same area.

2 lb (1 kg) boneless wild boar

salt to taste

1 cup (8 fl oz/250 ml) extra-virgin olive oil

2 yellow onions, chopped

2 cloves garlic, minced

1 carrot, peeled and chopped

1 celery stalk, chopped

4 fresh sage leaves, chopped

leaves from 1 large fresh rosemary sprig, chopped

1 cup (8 fl oz/250 ml) dry red wine

1 lb (500 g) tomatoes, peeled, seeded, and chopped, or 1 can (14 oz/440 g) plum (Roma) tomatoes, chopped, with juice

¼ teaspoon red pepper flakes (optional)

freshly ground black pepper to taste

POLENTA

6 cups (48 fl oz/1.5 l) water

2 teaspoons salt

1¼ cups (6½ oz/200 g) coarse-ground polenta

grated Parmesan cheese

☙ To make the sauce, rinse the meat in several changes of water, pat dry, and cut into large pieces.

☙ Sprinkle the meat with salt and place in a large frying pan over medium-low heat. Cook for 10 minutes, stirring occasionally and draining the pan every few minutes of the water released by the meat. Transfer the meat to a plate.

☙ Rinse and dry the frying pan and return it to the stove. Add the olive oil and warm over medium heat. Add the onions, garlic, carrot, celery, sage, and rosemary and sauté until soft, about 5 minutes. Add the meat and brown well on all sides, about 10 minutes.

☙ Raise the heat to high, pour in the wine, and deglaze the pan, stirring to scrape up any browned bits from the pan bottom. Cook until the wine has reduced by half, about 5 minutes. Add the tomatoes and the red pepper flakes, if using. Stir well, cover, and cook, stirring occasionally, until the sauce is thick and the meat begins to fall apart, about 1½ hours.

☙ Using tongs, transfer the meat to a cutting board. Cut the meat into smaller pieces, then mince using a heavy, sharp knife. Return the minced meat to the pan and stir well to combine with the other ingredients. Adjust the seasoning with salt and black pepper.

☙ To make the polenta, in a heavy saucepan, bring the water to a gentle boil. Add the salt. Pour in the polenta in a thin, steady stream, stirring continuously with a wire whisk so that no lumps form. Reduce the heat to medium. After a few minutes, when the polenta begins to thicken, reduce the heat to low and cook, stirring continuously with a wooden spoon. The polenta will bubble and spew as the mixture thickens. Cook, stirring nearly continuously, until the polenta comes away easily from the sides of the pan, 30–40 minutes.

☙ To serve, begin reheating the sauce gently about 30 minutes before the polenta is ready. Spoon the polenta directly onto individual plates. Cover each portion with 1 cup (8 fl oz/250 ml) of the sauce. Pass the Parmesan cheese at the table.

serves 4–6

Il Cavolo Nero

Literally translated, *cavolo nero* means "black cabbage," and although this handsome brassica is not black, it is as deep a green as any vegetable you'll ever see. It is an essential ingredient in the classic Tuscan soup, *ribollita,* and in the days following the olive harvest, it is boiled and heaped on toasted country bread rubbed with garlic and slathered with newly pressed oil. My friend and neighbor Beatrice Contini chops the cooked cabbage finely, mixes it with a bit of fresh ricotta cheese, and uses it as a sauce for pasta.

Although botanically a cabbage, *cavolo nero* has a pleasantly green bitterness not usually associated with cabbage. The plume-shaped crinkled leaves are harvested and eaten after the first frost, which considerably softens their rather heavy texture. Unfortunately, *cavolo nero* is nearly impossible to find outside of Italy. The good news is that it can be grown from seed in nearly any backyard garden. There's no reason not to pick up a few packets on your next trip to Tuscany. Sow the seeds during the summer and enjoy *cavolo nero* all winter long.

Firenze

Ribollita

twice-boiled soup with black cabbage
and white beans

I have eaten ribollita *a thousand times in restaurants, which probably explains why it took me so long to make it myself. Why cook something that you can find so well prepared all over town? I have called it a soup, but it is much thicker and denser than a soup, so much so that Fabio Picchi, owner of the well-known Cibrèo Restaurant, serves his with a fork. The dish begins as a typical Tuscan bread and vegetable soup, which you can eat on the first day as such. It becomes* ribollita *on the second day, when, as its name implies, it is reboiled.*

BEANS

1 cup (7 oz/220 g) dried cannellini beans

5 cups (40 fl oz/1.25 l) water

1 clove garlic

1 fresh sage sprig

SOUP

8 tablespoons (4 fl oz/125 ml) extra-virgin olive oil

1 large yellow onion, chopped

1 clove garlic, finely chopped

2 leeks, white part and 1 inch (2.5 cm) of the green, chopped

2 carrots, peeled and thickly sliced

2 zucchini (courgettes), trimmed and thickly sliced

2 tomatoes, peeled, seeded, and chopped

1 celery stalk, thickly sliced

1 potato, peeled and cut into chunks

salt to taste

4 cups (32 fl oz/1 l) hot water

½ head savoy cabbage, core removed and coarsely sliced

1 bunch Swiss chard, ribs removed, leaves coarsely chopped

1 bunch black cabbage or kale, ribs removed and leaves coarsely chopped

1 fresh rosemary sprig

1 fresh thyme sprig

6 slices day-old coarse country bread, toasted

freshly ground pepper to taste

❦ Pick over the beans, discarding misshapen beans or stones. Rinse well, place in a bowl, and add water to cover generously. Let soak overnight.

❦ Drain the beans and place in a large saucepan along with the water, garlic, and sage sprig. Bring to a boil over high heat, reduce the heat to low, cover partially, and simmer gently until tender, 1½–2 hours, depending on the age of the beans.

❦ Meanwhile, begin making the soup: In a soup pot over medium heat, warm 3 tablespoons of the olive oil. Add the onion and sauté until fragrant, about 3 minutes. Add the garlic and sauté until it begins to color, about 2 minutes. Add the leeks, carrots, zucchini, tomatoes, celery, and potato, season with salt, and sauté, stirring frequently, until the vegetables are soft, about 10 minutes.

❦ Pour in the hot water and add the savoy cabbage, Swiss chard, black cabbage or kale, rosemary, and thyme. Cover and simmer over medium heat, stirring occasionally, until the soup is thick, about 1 hour.

❦ Using a slotted spoon, transfer half of the beans to a food mill fitted with the medium disk held over

the soup pot, and purée directly into the soup. Scoop out the remaining beans with the slotted spoon and add to the pot along with 2 cups (16 fl oz/500 ml) of the cooking liquid and the toasted bread. Season with salt and pepper, and gently stir the contents of the pot.

❦ Place the soup over medium heat, cover, and simmer for 10 minutes to blend the flavors. Remove from the heat, uncover, and let cool, then re-cover and refrigerate overnight.

❦ The following day, preheat an oven to 375°F (190°C). Transfer the soup to an earthenware or other ovenproof baking dish.

❦ Bake the soup, stirring occasionally for the first 20 minutes only to allow a thin crust to form, until heated through, about 30 minutes. Remove from the oven.

❦ Bring the soup to the table, drizzle with the remaining 5 tablespoons (2½ fl oz/75 ml) olive oil. Season abundantly with pepper and serve.

serves 6–8

Lucca

Lasagne con Funghi

lasagne with mushrooms

Lasagne with mushrooms is a favorite first course in the hills of the Garfagnana, where woodland mushrooms flourish. You can make this elegant dish with store-bought dried lasagne sheets, but it will never match the lightness and delicacy that you will achieve with homemade noodles. In Tuscany, the mushrooms would almost always be sautéed with a pinch of nepitella, *a mint-scented wild herb known as calamint in English. It has a milder, more delicate flavor than mint, however. Serve with a Pomino Bianco from the Marchesi Frescobaldi.*

WHITE SAUCE

4 cups (32 fl oz/1 l) milk

1 cup (8 fl oz/250 ml) chicken or meat broth (page 247)

5 tablespoons (2½ oz/75 g) unsalted butter

5 tablespoons (2 oz/60 g) all-purpose (plain) flour

salt and freshly ground pepper to taste

½ cup (2 oz/60 g) grated Parmesan cheese

pinch of freshly grated nutmeg

PASTA DOUGH

about 3 cups (15 oz/470 g) all-purpose (plain) flour

pinch of salt

5 eggs

MUSHROOMS

2 tablespoons unsalted butter

1 tablespoon extra-virgin olive oil

2 cloves garlic, minced

1½ lb (750 g) fresh porcino or cremini mushrooms, brushed clean and cut into slices ½ inch (12 mm) thick

½ teaspoon fresh nepitella *(page 249) or thyme leaves*

salt and freshly ground pepper to taste

2 tablespoons coarse salt

grated Parmesan cheese

❦ To make the white sauce, pour the milk and broth into a saucepan and place over medium heat until small bubbles appear along the edges of the pan. In another saucepan over low heat, melt the butter.

Slowly add the flour and, using a whisk, stir continuously until the mixture thickens and smells faintly of biscuits but does not brown, 2–3 minutes. Slowly add the hot milk and broth, whisking constantly. Season with salt and pepper. Cook over low heat, stirring occasionally, until a creamy sauce forms, about 10 minutes. Reduce the heat to very low and cook the sauce, whisking occasionally, for 2 minutes longer. Remove the sauce from the heat and stir in the Parmesan cheese and nutmeg. You should have about 4½ cups (36 fl oz/1.1 l). Set the sauce aside, stirring occasionally to prevent a skin from forming.

❦ To make the pasta dough, follow the directions on page 250. Roll out the dough as directed by hand or on a machine. Cut into 12 pieces each 3 inches (7.5 cm) wide and 12 inches (30 cm) long. Bring a large pot three-fourths full of water to a boil. Stir in the coarse salt. One at a time, add the lasagne sheets to the boiling water and cook, stirring gently to keep the pasta from sticking together, until pliable, about 1 minute. Remove from the heat and drain off about two-thirds of the water, leaving the pasta in the pot. Refill the pot with cold water and set aside.

❦ Preheat an oven to 350°F (180°C).

❦ Butter a 9-by-12-inch (23-by-30-cm) baking dish with 3-inch (7.5-cm) sides. Remove 3 lasagne sheets from the water, spread flat on a clean kitchen towel, and pat dry. Lay the sheets in a single layer on the bottom of the pan. Remove ½ cup (4 fl oz/125 ml) of the white sauce and set aside to use later. Spread 1 cup (8 fl oz/250 ml) of the remaining sauce evenly over the pasta. Repeat to make 3 more layers in the same manner, finishing with a layer of sauce. Bake until golden, about 35 minutes.

❦ Meanwhile, prepare the mushrooms: In a frying pan over medium heat, melt the butter with the olive oil. Add the garlic and sauté until fragrant, about 1 minute. Add the mushrooms and *nepitella* or thyme, season with salt and pepper, cover, and cook until the mushrooms release their liquid, about 5 minutes. Uncover and sauté, stirring frequently, until all of the liquid has cooked away, 3–5 minutes. Remove from the heat.

❦ Remove the lasagne from the oven, cover with the reserved white sauce, and scatter the mushrooms over the top. Sprinkle with Parmesan cheese. Return the pan to the oven until bubbling, about 5 minutes.

❦ Remove from the oven and let stand for 15 minutes, then cut into portions to serve.

serves 6–8

Firenze

Carabaccia

onion soup

Carabaccia *(also known as* cipollata *and* zuppa di cipolle) *is a mysterious name of disputed origin for what is essentially a humble—and extraordinarily tasty—onion soup. The dish has evolved over the centuries. During the Renaissance, when the recipes of the court were highly spiced and elaborate,* carabaccia *included ground almonds, vinegar, sugar, and cinnamon. The modern version is much simplified and arguably as good as any soupe à l'oignon you'll eat in a bistro in Paris.*

6 tablespoons (3 fl oz /90 ml) extra-virgin
olive oil

2 lb (1 kg) yellow onions, quartered, then sliced

2 celery stalks, minced

2 carrots, peeled and minced

6 cups (48 fl oz /1.5 l) chicken broth (page 247)

salt and freshly ground pepper to taste

6 slices day-old coarse country bread, toasted

1 clove garlic, halved lengthwise

½ cup (2 oz /60 g) grated Parmesan cheese

In a soup pot over medium heat, warm the olive oil. Stir in the onions, celery, and carrots and sauté, stirring often, until the onions break apart easily with a wooden spoon, about 30 minutes.

Pour in the broth, season with salt and pepper, and simmer for 30 minutes.

Rub the toast with the cut sides of the garlic clove and distribute among warmed individual soup bowls.

Taste the soup and adjust the seasoning with salt and pepper. Ladle the hot soup over the toast and sprinkle with the Parmesan, dividing evenly. Serve immediately.

serves 6

Firenze

Penne Strascicate

penne with meat sauce, florentine style

Penne strascicate, *literally penne "dragged through" their sauce, is not so much a recipe as an age-old Florentine method for combining pasta and sauce. The noodles (always penne, which for some undefined reason are far and away Tuscany's preferred pasta shape) are boiled until still quite firm to the bite, then added to a frying pan with a traditional meat sauce and a bit of butter (to bind the sauce to the pasta) to finish cooking.*

No doubt the dish originated as a way to use up leftover pasta. You'll find it in Florence's simplest trattorias and self-service restaurants, although frankly it is usually not worth ordering. But home-made, with freshly cooked pasta and a rich meat sauce, penne strascicate *is delicious.*

MEAT SAUCE

6 tablespoons (3 fl oz/90 ml) extra-virgin olive oil

1 yellow onion, chopped

1 small carrot, peeled and chopped

1 small celery stalk, chopped

1 tablespoon chopped fresh flat-leaf (Italian) parsley

½ lb (250 g) lean ground (minced) beef

½ cup (4 fl oz/125 ml) dry red wine

1 lb (500 g) plum (Roma) tomatoes, peeled, seeded, and chopped

salt and freshly ground pepper to taste

about ½ cup (4 fl oz/125 ml) meat broth (page 247)

1 lb (500 g) penne

2 tablespoons coarse salt

2 tablespoons unsalted butter

grated Parmesan cheese

♨ To make the meat sauce, in a heavy saucepan over medium heat, warm the olive oil. Add the onion, carrot, and celery and sauté, stirring often, until the vegetables are soft, about 10 minutes. Stir in the parsley and, after 1 minute, add the meat, breaking it up in the pan with a wooden spoon. When the meat loses its pinkness, after 5–7 minutes, raise the heat to high, add the wine to the pan, and stir until the alcohol has evaporated and the liquid has reduced, about 3 minutes. Reduce the heat to medium, add the tomatoes, season with salt and pepper, and cook, stirring frequently, until the liquid has reduced slightly, about 10 minutes.

♨ Add ¼ cup (2 fl oz/60 ml) of the broth, reduce the heat to medium-low, cover partially, and simmer, stirring from time to time and adding additional broth if the sauce is dry, until the sauce is thick and the flavors are blended, about 40 minutes.

♨ Bring a large pot three-fourths full of water to a boil. Add the pasta and the coarse salt, stir well, and cook until tender but still quite firm to the bite, about 8 minutes. Drain the pasta.

♨ Transfer the sauce to a large frying pan placed over medium-high heat. Add the cooked pasta and the butter and stir until the sauce is almost completely absorbed, about 7 minutes.

♨ Transfer to a warmed serving bowl and serve immediately. Pass the Parmesan cheese at the table.

serves 4–6

Rigatoni all'Ortolano

rigatoni with spring vegetables

Rigatoni, a thick tube pasta with a lightly ridged surface, is the perfect vehicle to soak up the colorful confetti of vegetables in this sauce from Grosseto.

1 large artichoke

½ cup (2½ oz/75 g) young, tender shelled fava (broad) beans or lima beans

¼ cup (2 fl oz/60 ml) extra-virgin olive oil

1 small yellow onion, finely chopped

1 carrot, peeled and finely chopped

3 asparagus spears, tough ends removed, cut into 1-inch (2.5-cm) pieces

1 cup (2 oz/60 g) stemmed spinach leaves, coarsely chopped

½ cup (2½ oz/75 g) shelled English peas

¼ cup (2 fl oz/60 ml) water

salt and freshly ground pepper to taste

1⅓ cups (8 oz/250 g) drained canned plum (Roma) tomatoes

1 lb (500 g) rigatoni

2 tablespoons coarse salt

grated Parmesan cheese

❧ Trim and slice the artichoke as directed on page 246. If using fava beans, peel as directed on page 246. Bring a saucepan three-fourths full of water to a boil, add the beans, and boil for 3 minutes, then drain.

❧ In a frying pan over medium heat, warm the olive oil. Add the onion and carrot and sauté until the onion is translucent, 5–7 minutes. Add the artichoke slices, beans, asparagus, spinach, peas, water, salt, and pepper. Reduce the heat to medium-low and simmer uncovered, stirring frequently, until the artichoke slices are tender, about 5 minutes. Stir in the tomatoes and simmer, breaking them up with a wooden spoon, until thickened, about 15 minutes.

❧ Bring a large pot three-fourths full of water to a boil. Add the pasta and the coarse salt, stir well, and cook until al dente, about 10 minutes. Drain the pasta.

❧ Spoon one-third of the sauce into a warmed serving bowl, add the pasta, top with the remaining sauce, and toss well. Pass the Parmesan at the table.

serves 4–6

Il Mercato

When I was still new to Tuscany, to the Italian language, and to the habits and customs of this place that had so enchanted me, I found marketing to be both exhilarating and intimidating. I was used to the anonymity of fluorescent-lit supermarkets where I could wander unnoticed and pile things into my giant metal cart. Of course, supermarkets do exist in Tuscany, but in many senses even they are a collection of tiny markets within a market, and require a level of interaction between shopkeeper and shopper that I initially found novel and somewhat challenging.

Wherever you shop—whether at the weekly open-air markets where itinerant merchants gather to sell fruits, vegetables, meats, breads, cheeses, and housewares; at the family-run butchers, bakers, greengrocers, and delicatessens scattered throughout every town and city; or at the modern supermarket—a reverence for raw ingredients exists that you cannot fail to notice. An elderly man bearing his wife's shopping list asks the greengrocer for *un grappolo d'uva, che più dolce non si può* (the very sweetest bunch of grapes). Something as simple as buying a loaf of bread is infused with a certain lighthearted seriousness. At the bakery, one person asks for a kilo of bread *cotto bene,* or "well cooked"; another wants it *non troppo alto,* or "not too thick." Even in the days when I could barely speak Italian, I remember the baker poking through the piles of bread, as if searching for that particular loaf he had baked just for me.

Similar scenes take place wherever one buys food. Every shopper seems to know just how ripe she (and it generally is still a *she* who does the marketing) wants her tomatoes and how thick she wants her prosciutto sliced. And if by chance she doesn't specify any attributes, you can be sure that the shopkeeper will be able and willing to tell her.

Lucca

Infarinata

cornmeal, cabbage, and herb soup

Variations of this cornmeal and cabbage soup, each with its own colorful name and culinary twists, are common throughout the Garfagnana, Versilia, Livorno, and the Lunigiana.

½ cup (4 fl oz/125 ml) extra-virgin olive oil

1 yellow onion, finely chopped

2 carrots, peeled and finely chopped

1 celery stalk, finely chopped

leaves from 1 fresh sage sprig, chopped

2 cups (12 oz/375 g) crushed canned plum (Roma) tomatoes with juice

salt and freshly ground pepper to taste

8 cups (64 fl oz/2 l) hot water

2 potatoes, peeled and cut into large cubes

1 lb (500 g) savoy cabbage, cored, halved, and sliced

1 cup (5 oz/155 g) polenta

2 cups (14 oz/440 g) drained, cooked cannellini beans (page 246)

❦ In a large saucepan over medium heat, warm the oil. Add the onion, carrots, celery, and sage and sauté, stirring frequently, until the vegetables begin to soften, about 8 minutes. Stir in the tomatoes and their juice, season lightly with salt, and simmer until thick, about 15 minutes.

❦ Pour in the hot water, raise the heat to medium-high, bring the mixture to a boil, and add the potatoes and cabbage. Reduce the heat to medium-low, cover, and simmer until the potatoes are tender, about 20 minutes. Uncover and pour in the polenta in a thin, steady stream, stirring continuously with a wooden spoon. Stir continuously for 40 minutes while the polenta bubbles and thickens.

❦ Stir in the beans and adjust the seasoning with salt and pepper. The *infarinata* should be fluid and soft. Add a bit of hot water if it appears too dense. Ladle into warmed individual bowls and serve.

serves 6

Lucca

Zuppa di Arselle

clams poached in white wine, garlic,
and tomato

*Arsella is another word for vongola, or "clam."
When used in Versilia, it generally refers to the
smallest, most tender clam with the sweetest, most
delicate meat of any clam you'll ever eat.*

*2 lb (1 kg) small hard-shelled clams such as
manila or littleneck*

*6 tablespoons (3 fl oz/90 ml) extra-virgin
olive oil*

*2 cloves garlic, thinly sliced, plus 1 clove,
halved lengthwise*

*1 tablespoon finely chopped fresh flat-leaf
(Italian) parsley, plus 2 teaspoons for garnish*

½ cup (4 fl oz/125 ml) dry white wine

*1 lb (500 g) tomatoes, peeled, seeded,
and chopped*

¼ teaspoon red pepper flakes

salt to taste

4 slices coarse country bread, toasted

❦ Scrub the clams. Place in a bowl with lightly
salted water and let soak for 2 hours. Drain and rinse
well, discarding any that fail to close to the touch.

❦ In a large, wide pot over medium heat, warm the
olive oil. Add the sliced garlic and 1 tablespoon parsley and sauté for about 2 minutes. Pour in the wine
and let the alcohol evaporate, about 2 minutes. Stir in
the tomatoes and the red pepper flakes, season with
salt, cover, and cook, stirring occasionally, until the
liquid has reduced, about 10 minutes. Add the clams,
cover, and cook until the shells open, about 5 minutes. Discard any that have not opened.

❦ Rub the toasted bread with the cut sides of the
garlic clove and set a slice in each warmed bowl.
Ladle the clams and their juices into the bowls,
dividing evenly. Sprinkle the *zuppa* with the 2 teaspoons parsley and serve.

serves 4

Arezzo

Risotto con la Zucca

pumpkin risotto

Oddly enough, winter squashes are one of the joys of my summer garden. Everything else—tomatoes, lettuces, peppers (capsicums), and eggplants (aubergines)—gets picked, but the squashes just sit heavily in the garden and grow. As the summer garden slows to a halt and the days grow shorter and cooler, I harvest the crop. I use the long, camel-colored butternut squash, which is commonly cut into thick wedges and sold by the piece in Tuscan markets, to make this risotto.

5 cups (40 fl oz/1.25 l) chicken broth
(page 247) or bouillon

1¼-lb (725-g) piece orange-fleshed winter
squash, peeled and seeded

4 tablespoons (2 oz/60 g) unsalted butter

4 tablespoons (2 fl oz/60 ml) extra-virgin
olive oil

1 yellow onion, finely chopped

2 oz (60 g) pancetta or bacon, finely cubed

pinch of salt, plus salt to taste

2 cups (14 oz/440 g) Arborio rice

¼ cup (2 fl oz/60 ml) dry white wine

⅓ cup (1½ oz/45 g) grated Parmesan cheese

white pepper to taste

In a saucepan over medium heat, bring the broth or bouillon to a gentle simmer. Adjust the heat to maintain a bare simmer.

Cut the squash into finger-sized strips. In a saucepan over low heat, melt 2 tablespoons of the butter with 2 tablespoons of the olive oil. Add half of the onion and all of the pancetta or bacon and sauté until it begins to sweat its fat and the onion begins to soften, about 5 minutes. Add the squash, stir to coat with the onion, and sauté gently for a couple of minutes. Add ½ cup (4 fl oz/125 ml) broth or bouillon and a generous pinch of salt and cook over low heat for 20 minutes, stirring occasionally. The squash will take on the consistency of a chunky purée. Remove from the heat and set aside.

In a large, heavy saucepan over medium heat, warm the remaining 2 tablespoons olive oil. Add the remaining onion and sauté until soft, about 5 minutes. Add the rice, mixing well with the other ingredients to coat the grains with the oil. Cook and stir for 1–2 minutes to toast the grains lightly. Pour in the wine and cook, stirring, until the rice absorbs most of the liquid, about 3 minutes.

Add a ladleful (about ½ cup/4 fl oz/125 ml) of the broth or bouillon, reduce the heat to low, and stir continuously as the rice absorbs the liquid. Continue adding the liquid in ½-cup (4–fl oz/125-ml) increments, stirring after each addition, until the rice has absorbed most of the liquid.

When the rice has cooked for 12 minutes, stir in the squash and continue adding the liquid in small increments and stirring continuously. When the grains are tender yet firm to the bite and the risotto has a creamy consistency (after 16–18 minutes total), remove from the heat and stir in the remaining 2 tablespoons butter and the Parmesan. Season with salt and white pepper.

Remove the risotto from the heat and let rest for a couple of minutes before serving. Spoon onto warmed individual plates or bowls and serve.

serves 4

Firenze

Tortelli di Patate al Sugo di Anatra

potato tortelli with duck sauce

This is the Mugello's most famous dish. The sauce can be made up to 2 days in advance and stored, covered, in the refrigerator.

SAUCE

¼ cup (2 fl oz/60 ml) extra-virgin olive oil

1½ oz (45 g) pancetta, finely cubed

1 small red (Spanish) onion, chopped

1 small carrot, peeled and chopped

1 small celery stalk, chopped

1 tablespoon finely chopped fresh flat-leaf (Italian) parsley

½ duck with liver and heart, skin and fat removed, duck cut into quarters, and liver and heart sliced

salt and freshly ground pepper to taste

1 cup (8 fl oz/250 ml) dry red wine

4 cups (1½ lb/750 g) chopped canned plum (Roma) tomatoes with juice

PASTA DOUGH

3 cups (15 oz/470 g) all-purpose (plain) flour

pinch of salt

5 eggs

FILLING

1 lb (500 g) baking potatoes, unpeeled

1 small tomato, peeled, seeded, and diced

1 egg, lightly beaten

¾ cup (3 oz/90 g) grated Parmesan cheese

1 clove garlic, minced

2 teaspoons finely chopped fresh flat-leaf (Italian) parsley

pinch of freshly grated nutmeg

salt and freshly ground pepper to taste

2 tablespoons coarse salt

grated Parmesan cheese

To make the sauce, in a frying pan over medium heat, warm the olive oil. Add the pancetta and onion and sauté until the pancetta begins to sweat its fat, about 5 minutes. Add the carrot, celery, and parsley and sauté, stirring frequently, for 4 minutes. Add the duck pieces evenly in the pan and brown well on all

sides, about 10 minutes. Season with salt and pepper. Raise the heat to high, pour in the wine, and deglaze the pan, stirring to scrape up any browned bits on the pan bottom. When the wine has cooked away almost completely, stir in the tomatoes, reduce the heat to low, cover partially, and cook, stirring occasionally, until the sauce is very thick, about 1 hour.

Transfer the duck to a cutting board. Remove and discard the bones. Chop the meat, return to the pan, stir well, remove from the heat, and set aside.

To make the pasta dough, follow the directions on page 250, mixing together the flour and salt and adding the eggs to the well. Shape the dough into a ball, cover with a damp kitchen towel, and set aside.

To make the filling, in a saucepan, combine the potatoes with salted water to cover generously. Bring to a boil, reduce the heat to medium-high, cover partially, and cook until a sharp knife easily glides into the center of a potato, about 20 minutes. Drain the potatoes, and when they are just cool enough to handle, peel away the skins. Pass the potatoes through a food mill fitted with the medium disk onto a clean work surface. Handling them as little as possible, spread into a layer 1 inch (2.5 cm) thick. Let stand until completely cool, about 30 minutes.

Transfer the cooled potatoes to a bowl. Add the tomato, egg, Parmesan cheese, garlic, parsley, nutmeg, salt, and pepper and mix well.

Following the directions on page 250, roll out the dough by hand or with a machine. Using a pastry wheel, cut into strips 3 inches (7.5 cm) wide, making them all the same length. Dot the center of the length of 1 strip with 1½-teaspoon dollops of the filling, spacing the dollops 1½ inches (4 cm) apart and stopping within 1 inch (2.5 cm) of the ends of the strip. Brush a little water around each dollop of filling. Cover with another strip of pasta and, using your hands, gently press the pasta sheets together around the mounds of filling, forcing out any air. Using a 2-inch (5-cm) round fluted cookie cutter, cut out the *tortelli*. Transfer the *tortelli* to a lightly floured tray, then repeat with the remaining pasta strips and filling. Bring a large pot three-fourths full of water to a boil. Add the coarse salt and the *tortelli* and cook until the *tortelli* are al dente and float to the surface, about 3 minutes. Drain the pasta

Meanwhile, reheat the sauce. Pour one-third of the sauce into a warmed serving bowl, add the *tortelli*, top with the remaining sauce, and toss gently. Serve immediately. Pass the Parmesan cheese at the table.

serves 4–6

Lucca

Minestra di Farro

farro soup

*W*hen I first came to Italy, the charming town of Lucca was not yet on the tourist circuit, and it took me several years to discover the place for myself. The high walls surrounding the city are remarkably intact, and the center itself is simply stunning. I have spent many Saturday and Sunday mornings poking around Lucca's antique fair, which comes to the city the third weekend of every month. My favorite find sits on the marble work counter in my cucina below the open wooden shelf piled with glazed terra-cotta platters and bowls (many of which I've picked up at open markets and local craft fairs)—an ancient, though perfectly functional, cast-iron kitchen scale coated in brilliant Ferrari red enamel.

Once I've ambled through the fair, I take my treasures (or my unfulfilled longings, as the case may be) over to the bustling Da Giulio restaurant for a bowl of minestra di farro.

FARRO

2 cups (10 oz/315 g) farro, soaked in water to cover for 20 minutes and drained

6 cups (48 fl oz/1.5 l) water

SOUP

¼ cup (2 fl oz/60 ml) extra-virgin olive oil, plus oil for serving

1 small yellow onion, finely chopped

2 cloves garlic, minced

1 leek, white part and 1 inch (2.5 cm) of the green, thinly sliced

1 celery stalk, finely chopped

1 carrot, peeled and diced

2 tomatoes, peeled, seeded, and chopped

8 cups (64 fl oz/2 l) water

1 fresh rosemary sprig

salt to taste

2 cups (14 oz/440 g) drained, cooked dried borlotti or cranberry beans (page 246), plus cooking liquid as needed

freshly ground pepper to taste

✤ To cook the *farro,* in a large saucepan, combine the *farro* and water and bring to a boil over high heat. Reduce the heat to medium-low, cover, and simmer the *farro* until the grains swell and are lighter in color, about 35 minutes.

✤ Meanwhile, begin making the soup: In a soup pot over medium heat, warm the ¼ cup (2 fl oz/60 ml) olive oil. Add the onion, garlic, leek, celery, and carrot and sauté until the vegetables are soft, about 8 minutes.

✤ Stir the tomatoes into the vegetables, cook for 1 minute, and then add the water and rosemary sprig and season with salt. Cover partially and simmer gently until the flavors are blended, about 30 minutes.

✤ Drain the *farro* and add it to the soup pot. Re-cover partially and simmer, stirring often, until the *farro* absorbs the flavors, about 20 minutes.

✤ Uncover the pot and, using a food mill fitted with the medium disk, pass half of the beans through the mill directly into the soup, adding some cooking liquid if needed to facilitate the puréeing. Stir in the remaining whole beans.

✤ Re-cover partially and simmer until the *farro* is tender but not mushy, about 20 minutes longer. Remove and discard the rosemary sprig. Adjust the seasonings with salt and pepper.

✤ Transfer the soup to a warmed tureen, or ladle into warmed individual bowls. Top each serving with a swirl of olive oil.

serves 6

Tuscan soups, born of humble origins, speak of an era when life moved at a slower pace.

Il Farro

You wouldn't know it from all the fanfare it has been receiving the past few years, but *farro* has been around a very long time. One of the oldest grains in the world, it was known in ancient Palestine and Egypt, and it was the first grain to be introduced to Italy. When wheat began to be widely grown in the country around the first century B.C., *farro* was almost abandoned, except in those places where it grew best, such as the low mountains of the Garfagnana, an area in which it has been cultivated for millennia.

Until fairly recently, it was unusual to find *farro* on a restaurant menu far from the Garfagnana or nearby Lucchesia, and even then the grain was used primarily in soups and porridges. All that has changed, however. *Farro* has been rediscovered, not only in Tuscany but outside Italy as well. The oval grain has a faintly sweet and nutty flavor and a firm, toothy texture when cooked. These days, you'll find it in Florence replacing the bread in *panzanella,* and in the Maremma cooked like risotto and served alongside fresh fish. The grain is also ground into flour, which is used in desserts.

Livorno

Penne alla Maremmana

penne with mushrooms, eggplant,
peas, and sausage

*I like to serve this rich, flavorful pasta from the
Maremma with a Morellino di Scansano from any
of the vineyards around the hill town of Scansano in
the southern part of this coastal region. The wine is
made almost entirely from Tuscany's famed Sangiovese
grapes, has a beautiful ruby color, and is
appealingly spicy on the palate.*

1 large eggplant (aubergine), cut into ½-inch
(12-mm) cubes

salt

2 oz (60 g) dried porcini mushrooms

½ cup (4 fl oz/125 ml) extra-virgin olive oil

3 oz (90 g) fresh Italian sausage, casing removed

2 cloves garlic, minced

6 plum (Roma) tomatoes, peeled, seeded, and
chopped, or 2 cups (12 oz/375 g) chopped
canned plum tomatoes with juice

1 cup (5 oz/155 g) fresh or thawed frozen
English peas

4 fresh sage leaves, chopped

pinch of red pepper flakes

freshly ground black pepper to taste

1 lb (500 g) penne

2 tablespoons coarse salt

grated Parmesan cheese

❦ Place the cubed eggplant in a colander, sprinkle
with salt, and let stand for 30 minutes to drain off any
bitter juices. At the same time, in a small bowl, combine the mushrooms with warm water to cover and
let soak for 30 minutes.

❦ Rinse the eggplant, drain well, pat dry, and set
aside. In a large frying pan over medium heat, warm
the olive oil. Add the sausage and sauté, stirring
often, until crumbly and slightly browned, about
5 minutes. Using a slotted spoon, transfer the sausage
to a plate lined with paper towels to drain.

❦ Return the frying pan with the olive oil and
juices from the sausage to medium heat. Add the
eggplant and the garlic to the pan and sauté over
medium heat until the eggplant is golden on all sides,
about 15 minutes. The eggplant will absorb most of
the oil.

❦ Meanwhile, drain the soaked mushrooms, rinsing
them under running cold water if they appear gritty.
Chop them. When the eggplant is golden, add the
mushrooms to the pan along with the tomatoes and
peas. Sprinkle with the sage and the red pepper
flakes, cover, reduce the temperature to low, and
cook, stirring occasionally, until the flavors are
blended and the sauce is reduced, about 15 minutes.
Uncover, stir in the sausage, and cook for another
5 minutes to thicken the sauce slightly. Adjust the
seasoning with salt and black pepper.

❦ While the sauce is simmering, bring a large pot
three-fourths full of water to a boil. Add the pasta
and the coarse salt, stir well, and cook until al dente,
about 12 minutes. Drain the pasta.

❦ Pour one-third of the sauce into a warmed serving bowl, add the pasta, top with the remaining
sauce, and toss gently. Serve immediately. Pass the
Parmesan cheese at the table.

serves 4–6

Grosseto

Acquacotta

"cooked water"

For centuries, acquacotta *provided the sole sustenance for the shepherds, coal miners, woodsmen, and* butteri *(the Maremma's famous cowboys) who lived in relative isolation in what was truly Tuscany's last frontier. Although the dish is incontestably Maremman, there is no single classic recipe. It was always made with a few eggs from the henhouse, a bit of coarse bread, and whatever the garden or woods had to offer.*

½ cup (4 fl oz/125 ml) extra-virgin olive oil

2 red (Spanish) onions, chopped

¾ lb (375 g) mixed red and yellow bell peppers (capsicums), seeded and chopped

3 celery stalks, chopped

1 lb (500 g) tomatoes, peeled, seeded, and chopped

salt and freshly ground pepper to taste

8 cups (64 fl oz/2 l) water

3 eggs

½ cup (2 oz/60 g) grated Parmesan cheese

8 slices day-old coarse country bread, toasted

1 clove garlic, halved lengthwise

❀ In a soup pot over medium heat, warm the olive oil. Add the onions and sauté until fragrant, about 4 minutes. Add the bell peppers and celery and sauté until the vegetables are soft, about 10 minutes. Stir in the tomatoes. Season with salt and pepper. Reduce the heat to low, cover, and simmer gently, stirring occasionally, until the mixture is thick, about 1 hour.

❀ Pour in the water, return the soup to a steady simmer, and cook for 10 minutes longer. In a small bowl, beat together the eggs and cheese and pour into the soup. Stir briskly for a minute, then remove from the heat. Season with salt and pepper.

❀ Rub the toast with the cut sides of the garlic clove and distribute among individual soup bowls. Ladle the hot soup over the toast and serve immediately.

serves 8

Livorno

Linguine allo Scoglio

linguine with seafood

All along the Tuscan coast, this recipe appears as the jewel in the crown of restaurants specializing in seafood. Restaurants will use any combination of available shellfish, from the common clam and mussel to more unusual sea creatures like datteri di mare, *or "sea dates," named for the datelike shape of their shells;* cannolicchi, *razor clams with long, straight-edged shells; and* tartufo di mare, *a small clam reputed to have aphrodisiac properties. Many chefs add tomato to the sauce, but I like the flavor best when the shellfish is cooked in abundant white wine. If cuttlefish is unavailable, use 1½ pounds (750 g) squid.*

about 1½ cups (12 fl oz/375 ml) dry white wine

2 cloves garlic, crushed, plus 4 cloves, minced

1½ lb (750 g) mussels, scrubbed and debearded

1½ lb (750 g) clams, scrubbed, then soaked for 2 hours in lightly salted water to cover

¾ lb (375 g) small squid

¾ lb (375 g) cuttlefish

5 tablespoons (2½ fl oz/75 ml) extra-virgin olive oil

2 small dried chiles, crushed, or ½ teaspoon red pepper flakes

2½ tablespoons finely chopped fresh flat-leaf (Italian) parsley, plus 1 teaspoon for garnish

salt and freshly ground black pepper to taste

¾ lb (375 g) shrimp (prawns), heads and legs removed but shells intact

1¾ lb (875 g) dried linguine

2 tablespoons coarse salt

☙ Select a large, deep frying pan. Place over medium heat and add ½ cup (4 fl oz/125 ml) of the wine, the crushed garlic cloves, and the mussels, discarding any that fail to close to the touch. Cover and cook, shaking the pan occasionally, until the shells open, 8–10 minutes. Using a slotted spoon, transfer the mussels to a bowl, discarding any that failed to open.

☙ Pour another ½ cup (4 fl oz/125 ml) of the wine into the same pan in which the mussels were cooked, add the clams, discarding any that fail to close to the touch, cover, and cook over medium heat, shaking the pan occasionally, until the shells open, 8–10 minutes. Using the slotted spoon, transfer the clams to the bowl of mussels, discarding any that failed to open. When the clams and mussels are cool enough to handle, remove the shells from half of them and set the meats in a separate bowl. Line a sieve with cheesecloth and place over a measuring pitcher. Pour the cooking liquid remaining in the pan through the sieve. Add enough wine to make 1 cup (8 fl oz/ 250 ml) and set aside. Clean the squid and cuttlefish according to the directions on pages 251 and 248. Cut the bodies into strips ¼ inch (6 mm) wide and the tentacles into 1-inch (2.5-cm) lengths.

☙ In a large frying pan over medium heat, warm the olive oil. Add the minced garlic, chiles or red pepper flakes, and 2½ tablespoons parsley. Pour in the reserved 1 cup (8 fl oz/250 ml) wine and pan juices, add the squid and cuttlefish pieces, and season with salt and black pepper. Cover partially and cook until tender, 10–12 minutes.

☙ Meanwhile, bring a large pot three-fourths full of water to a boil.

☙ When the squid and cuttlefish are tender, add the shrimp to the frying pan and cook, stirring occasionally, until they just begin to curl, about 3 minutes. Add the unshelled mussels and clams together with any juices that have accumulated at the bottom of the bowl and stir well. Remove from the heat.

☙ Add the pasta and the coarse salt to the boiling water, stir well, and cook until al dente, about 9 minutes. Drain the pasta.

☙ Add the pasta to the pan holding the shellfish and place over low heat. Toss together to mix well and heat through. Transfer to a large warmed serving bowl. Scatter with the shelled clams and mussels, sprinkle with the 1 teaspoon parsley, and serve immediately.

serves 6–8

Few pleasures match a swim in the azure sea followed by a meal in a beachside trattoria.

Arezzo

Zuppa Frantoiana

sage-scented olive press soup

This soup gets its name from the word frantoio, *or "olive press." With just any oil, the soup would be unpleasantly heavy, but with the biting flavor of just-pressed Tuscan olive oil, it is exquisite.*

1½ oz (45 g) dried porcino mushrooms, soaked in warm water to cover for 30 minutes

8 tablespoons (4 fl oz/125 ml) just-pressed extra-virgin olive oil

1 clove garlic, minced

small handful of fresh sage leaves, finely chopped, plus whole leaves for garnish

1 large tomato, peeled, seeded, and chopped

8 cups (64 fl oz/2 l) light chicken broth (page 247)

1 cup (3 oz/90 g) broken pappardelle *or* tagliatelle *noodles (in large bits)*

2 cups (14 oz/440 g) drained, cooked dried borlotti or cranberry beans (page 246), plus cooking liquid as needed

salt and freshly ground pepper to taste

☙ Drain the mushrooms. Rinse under cold water if they are gritty. Squeeze out the excess moisture. In a soup pot over medium heat, warm 3 tablespoons of the olive oil. Add the garlic, chopped sage, and mushrooms and sauté, stirring frequently, for 3 minutes. Add the tomato and cook, stirring occasionally, until the vegetables are well blended, about 5 minutes.

☙ Pour in the broth and bring to a boil. Add the pasta and boil, uncovered, for 5 minutes. Reduce the heat to medium and pass half of the beans through a food mill fitted with the medium disk directly into the soup, adding some cooking liquid if needed to facilitate the puréeing. Stir in the remaining beans. Simmer for 5 minutes. Season with salt and pepper. Ladle the soup into warmed individual bowls, garnish with the whole sage leaves, and drizzle with the remaining 5 tablespoons (2½ fl oz/75 ml) olive oil.

serves 8

L'Olio d'Oliva

There is no ingredient more essential to Tuscan cuisine than olive oil—Tuscan olive oil. Of all the glorious patchwork of elements that make up the Tuscan landscape—neatly tended rows of grapevines, timeworn stone houses atop sloping hills, roads lined with cypress trees—it is the gnarled bark and silvery green leaves of the olive tree that speak most beautifully of this place. Locals say there is something about the soil, the slope of the land, the interplay of sun and wind and rain that conspire to produce an olive oil so unlike—so superior to—all others.

Tuscan olive oil is characterized by its ripe fruitiness and low acidity. The olives are harvested and pressed in the fall, usually sometime in November. Picking the olives is tedious and exacting work. Large tarps are spread beneath the trees, handmade ladders are propped precariously against the battered trunks, and the olives are shaken from the branches or raked off using special combs.

The *olio nuovo*—new, just-pressed oil—is jewel green and richly fruity, with a "bite" that mellows after about a month. A favorite way to enjoy new oil is by rubbing toasted bread with garlic, dipping it in the water in which cannellini beans have cooked, and smothering it with beans and oil. Another is rubbing the bread with garlic and drizzling it with oil.

The finest-quality *olio d'oliva* is labeled "extra virgin," which means that the olives were crushed in stone mortars or under granite millstones (which extract the oil without heat, so as not to compromise its flavor), and the oil has an acidity level of less than 1 percent. It is the only oil ever used in Tuscany, for cooking, for drizzling over soups, dressing salads, and dipping vegetables, and for any of the other infinite number of delicious uses.

Every fall I buy my olive oil for the whole year—about fifty liters—from friends who have olive trees. It is not inexpensive (really good olive oil never is), but there is no greater contribution I can make to the culinary well-being of my household than to keep it abundantly supplied with an olive oil so fine that it elevates the flavors of everything it touches.

Garmugia

spring vegetable soup

Few recipes celebrate early spring's bounty as deliciously as Lucca's traditional garmugia, *a beautiful soup that easily makes a complete meal on its own.*

3 tablespoons extra-virgin olive oil

1 fresh Italian sausage, casing removed and meat crumbled

3 small white onions, thinly sliced

3 oz (90 g) ground (minced) lean veal or beef

2 baby artichokes, trimmed and sliced (page 246)

½ cup (2½ oz/75 g) shelled fava (broad) beans, peeled (page 246)

½ cup (2½ oz/75 g) shelled English peas

½ cup (2 oz/60 g) asparagus tips

6 cups (48 fl oz/1.5 l) chicken broth (page 247)

salt and freshly ground pepper to taste

CROUTONS

¼ cup (2 fl oz/60 ml) extra-virgin olive oil

2 cloves garlic, crushed

4 slices coarse country bread, each ½ inch (12 mm) thick, cut into ½-inch (12-mm) cubes

1 tablespoon chopped fresh flat-leaf (Italian) parsley

❦ In a large saucepan over medium heat, warm the olive oil. Add the sausage meat and sauté until it begins to release its juices, about 3 minutes. Add the onions and the ground meat and sauté for 4 minutes. Add the artichokes, fava beans, peas, and asparagus and stir well. Pour in the broth, cover, and bring to a boil. Reduce the heat to low and cook until the flavors are blended, about 30 minutes, skimming off any froth from the surface. Halfway through the cooking time, season with salt and pepper.

❦ To prepare the croutons, in a frying pan over medium heat, warm the olive oil. Add the garlic and sauté until it begins to turn golden, about 2 minutes. Discard the garlic. Add the bread cubes and stir until golden brown on all sides, about 4 minutes. Using a slotted utensil, transfer the croutons to paper towels to drain. Sprinkle with the parsley.

❦ Ladle the soup into warmed individual bowls, garnish with the croutons, and serve immediately.

serves 6

Grosseto

Spaghetti all'Isolana

spaghetti with garlic, olive oil, and parsley

Elba may be the best-known island in the Tuscan archipelago, but it is the island of Giglio that has my heart. Half of the island is wild and roadless, accessible only by boat or the web of wildflower-strewn footpaths that traverse it. This pasta, typical of Giglio, is a variation on the much-loved mainstay of Italian cuisine, aglio, olio, e peperoncino *(garlic, olive oil, and chile). This is the pasta dish to make when you have better things to do than stay in the kitchen, but still want to eat well. In the time it takes to boil the pasta, you can make the sauce, slice tomatoes for a salad, and open a bottle of wine.*

1 lb (500 g) spaghetti

2 tablespoons coarse salt

½ cup (4 fl oz/125 ml) extra-virgin olive oil

4 cloves garlic, minced

1 bunch fresh flat-leaf (Italian) parsley, finely chopped

salt and freshly ground pepper to taste

grated aged pecorino cheese

❦ Bring a large pot three-fourths full of water to a boil. Add the pasta and the coarse salt, stir well, and cook until al dente, about 10 minutes.

❦ Meanwhile, in a saucepan over medium heat, warm together the olive oil and garlic. When the garlic turns a rich gold, after about 1 minute, sprinkle in the parsley. Stir well to coat the parsley with the garlic and oil, then remove the pan from the heat.

❦ Drain the pasta and transfer to a warmed serving bowl. Pour the herbed oil over the top and season with salt and abundantly with pepper. Toss as you would a salad, mixing well.

❦ Serve immediately. Pass the pecorino cheese at the table.

serves 4

Arezzo

Pappardelle alla Lepre

pappardelle with hare sauce

In a land of hunters, it is not surprising that one of the oldest traditional recipes is for game. Although I have eaten this delicious dish all over Tuscany, Arezzo is where it is prepared at its best. The original sixteenth-century recipe calls for the hare to be boiled with pork in the blood of both animals, a practice that, for the most part, has long since been abandoned. Purists and the nonsqueamish, however, would use the blood of a freshly caught hare instead of the broth and tomato. In a pinch, you can use store-bought pasta in lieu of homemade noodles, but the dish won't be as good. Rabbit may be substituted for the hare.

PASTA DOUGH

2½ cups (12½ oz/390 g) all-purpose (plain) flour

pinch of salt

3 eggs

1 tablespoon extra-virgin olive oil

SAUCE

½ small hare, 1½ lb (750 g), with lungs and heart

¼ cup (2 fl oz/60 ml) extra-virgin olive oil

2 oz (60 g) pancetta or bacon, finely cubed

1 yellow onion, finely chopped

1 carrot, finely chopped

1 celery stalk, finely chopped

salt and freshly ground pepper to taste

1 cup (8 fl oz/250 ml) dry red wine

about 1 cup (8 fl oz/250 ml) chicken or meat broth (page 247)

½ cup (4 fl oz/125 ml) tomato purée

2 tablespoons coarse salt

grated Parmesan cheese

✤ To make the pasta dough, follow the directions on page 250. Roll out the dough as directed by hand or with a machine. Using a straight-edged or fluted pastry wheel, cut into strips 1 inch (2.5 cm) wide and 5 inches (13 cm) long.

✤ To make the sauce, cut the hare into medium-sized pieces, and mince the lungs and heart. Set aside.

✤ In a heavy saucepan over medium heat, warm the olive oil. Add the pancetta or bacon, onion, carrot, and celery and sauté until the pancetta or bacon begins to sweat its fat and the vegetables begin to soften, about 6 minutes. Add the hare pieces and brown well on both sides, about 10 minutes.

✤ Stir in the lungs and heart, and season with salt and pepper. Raise the heat to high, pour in the wine, and deglaze the pan, scraping up any browned bits from the pan bottom. After about 3 minutes, add ½ cup (4 fl oz/125 ml) of the broth, reduce the heat to low, cover, and simmer until the hare is tender and cooked through, about 1½ hours, adding more broth if the pan gets dry.

✤ Transfer the hare pieces to a cutting board, pull out the bones, and return the meat to the pan. Add the tomato purée and simmer, stirring frequently, until the sauce is quite thick, about 15 minutes.

✤ Meanwhile, bring a large pot three-fourths full of water to a boil. Add the pasta and the coarse salt, stir well, and cook until the pasta is al dente, 2–3 minutes. Drain the pasta.

✤ Pour one-third of the sauce into a warmed serving bowl, add the pasta, top with the remaining sauce, and toss gently. Serve immediately. Pass the Parmesan cheese at the table.

serves 4–6

Grosseto

Risotto al Nero di Seppia

risotto with squid ink

Inexplicably, this recipe is always translated into English as risotto with "squid" ink, even though it is made with cuttlefish. The trick to this dish is extracting the seppia ink, which is explained below.

BROTH

2 lb (1 kg) mildly flavored saltwater fish such as cod or bass, cleaned

1 yellow onion, peel intact, quartered

1 carrot, peeled and cut into chunks

1 celery stalk, cut into chunks

1 tomato

2 cloves garlic, crushed

1 small bunch fresh flat-leaf (Italian) parsley

1 tablespoon salt

6 cups (48 fl oz/1.5 l) water

3 cuttlefish, about 1 lb (500 g) total weight, or 3 cleaned cuttlefish, plus 1 tablespoon thawed frozen ink (page 248)

6 tablespoons (3 fl oz/90 ml) extra-virgin olive oil

1 small yellow onion, finely chopped

1 clove garlic, minced

2 tablespoons finely chopped fresh flat-leaf (Italian) parsley

2 cups (14 oz/440 g) Arborio or Carnaroli rice

½ cup (4 fl oz/125 ml) dry white wine

1 tablespoon tomato paste

salt and freshly ground pepper to taste

☙ To make the broth, in a saucepan, combine the fish, onion, carrot, celery, tomato, garlic, parsley, salt, and water. Place over medium heat and bring to a boil. Reduce the heat to low, cover, and simmer for 1 hour. Using a slotted spoon, scoop out the solids and discard. Strain the broth through a colander lined with cheesecloth (muslin), discarding any remaining solids. Return the broth to the saucepan and bring to a simmer. Adjust the heat to maintain a bare simmer.

☙ If using uncleaned cuttlefish, follow the directions for cleaning on page 248. When you pull the head and tentacles from the body, the ink sac should be attached. Squeeze the sac gently, reserving the ink in a small bowl. Chop the body and tentacles of the cuttlefish into small pieces.

☙ In a large, heavy saucepan over medium heat, warm the olive oil. Add the onion and sauté gently until it begins to soften, about 4 minutes. Add the garlic and parsley and sauté until the garlic is lightly golden, about 3 minutes. Add the cuttlefish and sauté until opaque, about 5 minutes. Stir in the rice, mixing well with the other ingredients to coat the grains with the oil. Cook and stir for 1–2 minutes to toast the grains lightly. Pour in the wine and stir in the tomato paste. Cook, stirring, until the rice absorbs all of the liquid, about 3 minutes.

☙ Add a small ladleful (about ½ cup/4 fl oz/125 ml) of the broth, reduce the heat to low, and stir continuously as the rice absorbs the liquid. Continue adding the broth in ½-cup (4-fl oz/125-ml) increments, stirring after each addition, until the rice has absorbed most of the liquid. When the grains are tender yet firm to the bite, after 16–18 minutes, add the ink, stirring well to incorporate it thoroughly into the rice. The rice will turn a startling black. Add another ½–1 cup (4–8 fl oz/125–250 ml) broth to the pan so that the risotto is somewhat fluid rather than stiff. If all the broth is used before the rice is cooked, add hot water.

☙ Remove the risotto from the heat, season with salt, and grind pepper generously over the top. Cover and let rest for a couple of minutes before spooning onto warmed individual plates or bowls.

serves 6

Firenze

Fusilli alle Zucchine Crude con Mascarpone e Ricotta

fusilli with raw zucchini, mascarpone, and ricotta

This is the consummate pasta dish for a kitchen-wary cook who nonetheless wants to show off a modicum of culinary savvy. It's also a wonderful solution for anyone who wants to get off easy on a hot summer day. Nothing but the pasta is cooked—the rest of the ingredients are blended until they reach a lovely pale green paste. The mild, almost sweet taste of the mascarpone complements the other flavors, both savory and sweet.

2 small very fresh zucchini (courgettes), trimmed and cut into large chunks

¼ cup (2 oz/60 g) mascarpone cheese

¼ cup (2 oz/60 g) ricotta cheese

1 cup (4 oz/125 g) grated Parmesan cheese

½ teaspoon grated lemon zest

4 fresh basil leaves, chopped

salt and white pepper to taste

1 lb (500 g) fusilli

2 tablespoons coarse salt

☙ In a blender or food processor, combine the zucchini, cheeses, lemon zest, and basil. Process until a light green paste forms. Season with salt and white pepper. Set aside.

☙ Bring a large pot three-fourths full of water to a boil. Add the pasta and the coarse salt, stir well, and cook until the pasta is al dente, about 9 minutes. Drain the pasta, reserving ¼ cup (2 fl oz/60 ml) of the cooking water.

☙ Place all of the sauce in a warmed serving bowl and stir in the cooking water. Add the pasta and toss well to coat with the sauce. Serve immediately.

serves 4–6

Siena

Pasta e Ceci

pasta and chickpeas

This recipe is traditionally called pasta e ceci, *but it is actually a chickpea and pasta soup—just as* pasta e fagioli *is a bean and pasta soup.*

1 cup (7 oz/220 g) dried chickpeas
(garbanzo beans)

3 cloves garlic, 1 crushed, 2 minced

leaves from 1 fresh rosemary sprig

2 fresh sage leaves

1 small dried chile

2 tablespoons extra-virgin olive oil, plus oil
for drizzling

2 cups (12 oz/375 g) crushed canned plum
(Roma) tomatoes with juice

4 cups (32 fl oz/1 l) meat broth (page 247)

1½ cups (4½ oz/140 g) ditali or other
short tube pasta

salt and freshly ground pepper to taste

grated Parmesan cheese

✤ Pick over the chickpeas, discarding any grit or misshapen beans. Rinse well, place in a bowl, and add water to cover generously. Let soak overnight. Drain the beans and place in a large saucepan with the crushed garlic and water to cover generously. Bring to a boil, reduce the heat to low, cover, and cook until the beans are tender, 1½–2½ hours.

✤ On a work surface, combine the minced garlic, rosemary, sage, and chile and finely mince. In a large saucepan over medium heat, warm together the olive oil and garlic–herb mixture and sauté, stirring often, until fragrant, about 2 minutes. Add the tomatoes and broth, reduce the heat to low, cover, and cook until thickened, about 15 minutes. Raise the heat to medium, add the pasta, stir well, and cook until al dente, about 9 minutes. Using a slotted spoon, transfer half of the beans to a food mill fitted with the medium disk and purée directly into the pot, adding cooking liquid as needed to facilitate the puréeing. Add 1 cup (8 fl oz/250 ml) of the cooking liquid and the remaining whole beans. Stir well and season with salt and pepper.

✤ Ladle into warmed individual bowls and drizzle with olive oil. Pass the Parmesan cheese at the table.

serves 6–8

Firenze

Panzanella

bread salad

In Tuscany, every season has its uses for old bread, and panzanella *is summer's answer to the dilemma of a bread basket filled with* pane *that is past its prime. To think of the salad simply as a vehicle for frugality would be mistaken, however, as it is so refreshing, and does such good work with summer's best flavors, that I purposely buy more bread than my family will ever eat just to have enough to make it.*

This recipe, which relies for its success on garden-fresh tomatoes, is the basic Florentine version and the one I like best. Some cooks add any combination of celery, radishes, hard-boiled eggs, tuna, and anchovies.

1 lb (500 g) 2- or 3-day-old coarse country
bread, cut into slices 1 inch (2.5 cm) thick

6 tomatoes, peeled, seeded, and coarsely chopped

2 red (Spanish) or other sweet onions
(page 249), finely diced

2 cucumbers, peeled, halved lengthwise, seeded,
and sliced

generous handful of fresh basil leaves, torn
into pieces

about ⅓ cup (3 fl oz/80 ml) extra-virgin
olive oil

about 3 tablespoons red wine vinegar

salt and freshly ground pepper to taste

✤ In a large bowl, combine the bread with water to cover. Let stand for 15 minutes. Drain the bread and firmly squeeze out as much water as possible.

✤ Place the bread in a serving bowl. Scatter the tomatoes, onions, cucumbers, and basil leaves over the top.

✤ Dress the salad with the olive oil and vinegar. Season with salt and pepper. Toss well.

✤ Taste and adjust the seasoning with more oil, vinegar, salt, and pepper. Serve at room temperature.

serves 6

Siena

Pici alla Cipolla, Pancetta, e Pomodoro

homemade noodles with onion, pancetta, and tomato

Pinci, *as they are known in Montalcino, or* pici, *as they are called in Siena, Chiusi, Pienza, and elsewhere, are the poor man's spaghetti, made only from flour, water, and salt, without the eggs common to most fresh pasta. Each plump string of pasta dough is rolled by hand, and the irregular shape and lack of uniformity of the noodles give them a decidedly handcrafted, rustic look perfectly suited for this simple sauce or the heartier meat-based sauces that often accompany the noodles. Pici must be eaten the day they are made. The corn flour prevents the strings from sticking to one another. It also helps the strings dry without compromising their freshness. If you do go to all the effort of making* pici, *reward yourself by accompanying this dish with a bottle of one of Tuscany's finest red wines, Brunello di Montalcino.*

PASTA DOUGH

2 cups (10 oz/315 g) all-purpose (plain) flour

pinch of salt

¾ cup (6 fl oz/180 ml) water

¼ cup (1 oz/30 g) corn flour

SAUCE

1 yellow onion, quartered

3 tablespoons extra-virgin olive oil

3 oz (90 g) pancetta, cubed

1 clove garlic, minced

1 lb (500 g) tomatoes, peeled, seeded, and chopped

salt and freshly ground pepper to taste

2 tablespoons coarse salt

grated aged pecorino cheese

To make the pasta dough, in a large bowl, stir together the all-purpose flour and pinch of salt. Make a well in the center and pour the water into it. Using a wooden spoon, slowly stir to incorporate the flour, gradually pulling it in from the sides of the well to mix with the liquid. When the mixture becomes too stiff to stir, work it with your hands until it comes together to form a tough, heavy ball.

☙ Transfer the ball to a floured surface and flatten into a disk. Roll out and stretch the dough into a sheet ½ inch (12 mm) thick. Cut the sheet into ribbons of pasta no more than ½ inch (12 mm) wide.

☙ One at a time, roll each ribbon of dough between your palms until it is about ⅛ inch (3 mm) thick, then cut into 8-inch (20-cm) lengths. Lay the noodles on a clean kitchen towel sprinkled with the corn flour until ready to use.

☙ To make the sauce, in a small saucepan, combine the onion quarters with water to cover, bring to a boil, and boil until fragrant, about 15 minutes. Drain and chop coarsely, then set aside.

☙ In a frying pan over medium-high heat, warm the olive oil. Add the pancetta and sauté until it begins to sweat its fat, about 5 minutes. Add the reserved onion and the garlic to the pan and continue to sauté until fragrant, about 3 minutes.

☙ Stir in the tomatoes, reduce the heat to medium-low, and simmer uncovered, stirring occasionally, until thickened, about 15 minutes. Season with salt and pepper. Keep warm.

☙ Bring a large pot three-fourths full of water to a boil. Add the pasta and the coarse salt, stir well, and cook until al dente, 2–3 minutes. Drain the pasta.

☙ Spoon one-third of the sauce into a warmed serving bowl, add the drained pasta, top with the remaining sauce, and mix gently. Serve immediately on warmed individual plates. Pass the pecorino cheese at the table.

serves 4–6

In Tuscan kitchens, homemade pasta is still turned out by housewives of "a certain age".

I Testaroli

The Lunigiana, also known as the "Land of the Hundred Castles," is one of the most insular areas in Tuscany. Its rocky, mountainous landscape and wooded valleys form the northernmost tip of the region. It is worth a trip to the Lunigiana not only to see this evocative area but also to try a plate of *testaroli,* a delicious homemade pasta unique to the isolated villages of Pontremoli, Villafranca in the Lunigiana, Malgrate, and Bagnone. *Testaroli* are a diamond-shaped pancakelike pasta cooked first in cast-iron or terra-cotta molds, then cooled, cut, and briefly boiled in salted water.

Preparing *testaroli* the time-honored way is a labor of love, requiring a daunting mixture of patience and skill. First a thin batter is made from flour, salt, and water, and the *testaroli* mold—a flat, shallow pan with a curved lid—is set to heat over a bed of embers. A thin layer of batter is poured into the pan and cooked, covered, for about ten minutes. When it is done, the crepelike pasta is laid on a clean cloth to cool and then cut into diamonds, strips, or triangles, each about two inches (5 cm) long. The traditional sauce for this unusual pasta is a Lunigianan pesto similar to that of neighboring Liguria, except that it excludes the pine nuts from the mixture of basil, garlic, olive oil, and Parmesan and pecorino cheeses.

Firenze

Crespelle alla Fiorentina

crepes with spinach and ricotta

Throughout Italy, crespelle alla fiorentina *refers to crepes stuffed with spinach and ricotta and baked with a light* besciamella, *or white sauce. The tradition of eating crepes dates back to the time of the Medici family and may be yet another gastronomic delight influenced by the marriage of Catherine de' Medici to the Duke of Orleans, later Henry II of France.*

CREPE BATTER

1½ cups (6 oz/185 g) all-purpose (plain) flour

salt

6 eggs

½ cup (4 oz/125 g) unsalted butter, melted and cooled

2 cups (16 fl oz/500 ml) milk

FILLING

1 lb (500 g) spinach, stems removed

1 cup (8 oz/250 g) ricotta cheese

¼ cup (1 oz/30 g) grated Parmesan cheese

1 egg, lightly beaten

⅛ teaspoon freshly grated nutmeg

salt and freshly ground pepper to taste

WHITE SAUCE

2¼ cups (18 fl oz/560 ml) milk

¼ cup (2 oz/60 g) unsalted butter

6 tablespoons (2 oz/60 g) all-purpose (plain) flour

pinch of freshly grated nutmeg

salt and white pepper to taste

3 tablespoons grated Parmesan cheese

melted unsalted butter for coating pan

2 tablespoons grated Parmesan cheese

To make the crepe batter, in a bowl, stir together the flour and salt. Make a well in the center of the dry ingredients and break the eggs into the well. Add the melted butter and, using a fork, lightly beat together the eggs and butter. Using a whisk, swirl the egg mixture in a circular motion so that the flour is slowly incorporated from the sides of the well. When about half of the flour has been incorporated, slowly pour in the milk and continue to mix the batter gently until it is smooth. Allow the batter to rest at room temperature for 30 minutes before using.

To make the filling, place the spinach in a saucepan with only the rinsing water clinging to the leaves, cover, and cook until tender, 4–8 minutes. Check the pan from time to time and add a bit of water if needed to prevent scorching. Drain and rinse under running cold water to cool completely. Form the spinach into a ball and squeeze forcefully to remove as much water as possible. Finely chop the spinach, then squeeze again to force out any additional water. Place in a bowl, add the cheeses, egg, and nutmeg, and combine with a wooden spoon to form a smooth paste. Season with salt and pepper.

To make the white sauce, pour the milk into a saucepan and warm over medium heat until small bubbles appear along the edges of the pan. In another saucepan over low heat, melt the butter. Slowly add the flour, stirring continuously until the mixture thickens and smells faintly of biscuits but does not brown, 2–3 minutes. Slowly add the hot milk, whisking constantly. Add the nutmeg and season with salt and white pepper. Cook over low heat, stirring occasionally, until a creamy sauce forms, 3–4 minutes. Stir in the Parmesan cheese and set aside to cool, stirring occasionally to prevent a skin from forming.

Place a nonstick 9-inch (23-cm) frying pan over medium-high heat and coat with melted butter. When the pan is hot, pour ¼ cup (2 fl oz/60 ml) of the batter into the pan and swirl the pan until the bottom is evenly coated with the batter. Cook until the edges are firm, about 1 minute. Using a spatula, turn the crepe and cook briefly on the second side, about 30 seconds. Transfer to a plate and repeat until all the batter has been used, stacking the crepes on the plate. You should have about 18 crepes.

Preheat an oven to 350°F (180°C). Butter a 12-by-16-inch (30-by-40-cm) baking dish with 2-inch (5-cm) sides.

Spoon a few tablespoons of the filling down the center of a crepe. Loosely roll up to enclose the filling and place seam side down in the prepared baking dish. Repeat, placing the filled crepes in a single layer in the dish. Pour the sauce evenly over the crepes and sprinkle with the 2 tablespoons Parmesan cheese.

Bake until the sauce is lightly golden and bubbling, about 20 minutes. Serve the crepes directly from the baking dish.

serves 6

Siena

Risotto con Carciofi

risotto with artichokes

*Risotto is not the culinary mainstay in Tuscany
that it is in the Veneto, Piedmont, and Lombardy,
but it is served throughout the region in homes
and restaurants. Nothing compares to a risotto made
with homemade chicken broth, but many Tuscan
cooks often replace it with that beloved staple, the
dado, or bouillon cube. That the use of a tiny
foil-wrapped cube of compressed flavorings is not
considered "cheating" is a testament to the high
quality of European bouillon cubes, which are capable
of producing a broth that tastes remarkably close
to the real thing. Unfortunately, the same cannot be
said for much of the bouillon found outside of
Europe, which seems to get most of its strength from
a combination of salt and monosodium glutamate.
Look for European-manufactured bouillon cubes in
specialty stores, or for high-quality vegetable bouillon
cubes in natural-foods markets.*

3 large artichokes

6 tablespoons (3 fl oz/90 ml) extra-virgin olive oil

salt and freshly ground pepper to taste

5 cups (40 fl oz/1.25 l) chicken broth (page 247) or bouillon (see note)

1 small yellow onion, finely chopped

1 clove garlic, minced

2 cups (14 oz/440 g) Arborio rice

½ cup (4 fl oz/125 ml) dry white wine

¾ cup (3 oz/90 g) grated Parmesan cheese

salt and freshly ground pepper to taste

☙ Trim and slice the artichokes as directed on page 246. When all of the artichokes are sliced, drain well and pat dry.

☙ In a saucepan over low heat, warm 3 tablespoons of the olive oil. Add the sliced artichokes, stirring to coat them with the oil. Sauté gently until soft but not browned, 15–20 minutes, adding a bit of cold water to the pan if necessary to keep the artichokes from burning. Season generously with salt and pepper, then remove from the heat, cover, and set aside.

☙ In a saucepan over medium heat, bring the broth or bouillon to a gentle simmer. Adjust the heat to maintain a bare simmer.

☙ In a large, heavy saucepan over medium heat, warm the remaining 3 tablespoons olive oil. Add the onion and sauté until it begins to soften, a few minutes. Add the garlic and sauté until golden, about 2 minutes. Stir in the rice, mixing well with the other ingredients to coat the grains with the oil. Cook and stir for 1–2 minutes to toast the grains lightly. Pour in the wine and cook, stirring, until the rice absorbs most of the liquid, about 3 minutes.

☙ Add a small ladleful (about ½ cup/4 fl oz/125 ml) of the broth or bouillon, reduce the heat to low, and stir continuously as the rice absorbs the liquid. Continue adding the liquid in ½-cup (4–fl oz/125-ml) increments, stirring after each addition, until the rice has absorbed most of the liquid. When the grains are tender yet firm to the bite and the risotto has a creamy consistency (after 16–18 minutes), remove from the heat and stir in the artichokes and the Parmesan cheese. Taste and adjust the seasoning with salt and a generous grinding of pepper.

☙ Spoon onto warmed individual plates or bowls and serve immediately.

serves 4

Siena

Minestra di Castagne

chestnut soup

Wherever there are mountains in Tuscany, there are usually large chestnut woods. Mount Amiata, southern Tuscany's highest mountain, is covered with chestnut trees, as are the mountains near Pistoia and Arezzo and in the Mugello. Historically, dried chestnuts, which have the virtue of an extraordinarily long shelf life, were an important winter staple.

2 tablespoons extra-virgin olive oil

2 oz (60 g) pancetta, cubed

½ red (Spanish) onion, chopped

3 cloves garlic, minced

1 celery stalk, chopped

1 cup (4 oz/125 g) dried chestnuts, soaked overnight in lightly salted water and drained

¼ teaspoon fennel seed, lightly crushed

leaves from 1 fresh rosemary sprig

8 cups (64 fl oz/2 l) light chicken broth (page 247) or water

salt and freshly ground pepper to taste

1 cup (7 oz/220 g) short-grain white rice

2 oz (60 g) aged pecorino cheese, grated

In a large saucepan over medium heat, warm the olive oil. Add the pancetta cubes and sauté until they begin to soften, about 2 minutes. Add the onion, garlic, and celery and sauté, stirring frequently, until the vegetables begin to soften, about 5 minutes. Sprinkle in the chestnuts, fennel seed, and rosemary and stir well for a couple of minutes to combine.

Pour in the broth or water and bring to a boil. Reduce the heat to low, cover, and simmer until the chestnuts almost begin to fall apart, 1½–2 hours, seasoning with salt and pepper after the first hour.

Stir in the rice and continue to simmer until the rice is cooked, about 20 minutes. Taste and adjust the seasoning. Ladle into warmed individual bowls and serve. Pass the pecorino cheese at the table.

serves 6–8

Arezzo

Ravioli all'Ortica con Burro e Salvia

nettle ravioli with butter and sage

Pasta can be stuffed with almost any combination of vegetables, cheeses, meats and seasonings, but the most common filling in Tuscany is a mixture of soft ricotta cheese and finely chopped cooked greens. In the lush hills of the Casentino, north of Arezzo, ravioli are filled with the leaves of stinging nettles, a weed that grows wild throughout Tuscany, or more commonly with spinach or Swiss chard. Nettles are an extremely nutritious green with a faint tangy flavor. The best time to collect nettles is during spring and summer. Choose the smaller, tender upper leaves of the plant, being careful to wear gloves when handling them.

FILLING

1 lb (500 g) nettles, spinach, or Swiss chard, stems or ribs removed

3 tablespoons extra-virgin olive oil

1 clove garlic, minced

¾ cup (6 oz/185 g) ricotta cheese

½ cup (2 oz/60 g) grated Parmesan cheese

1 egg yolk

salt and freshly ground pepper to taste

PASTA DOUGH

2½ cups (12½ oz/390 g) all-purpose (plain) flour

pinch of salt

3 eggs

1 tablespoon extra-virgin olive oil

SAUCE

6 tablespoons (3 oz/90 g) unsalted butter

24 fresh sage leaves

2 tablespoons coarse salt

½ cup (2 oz/60 g) grated Parmesan cheese

To make the filling, place the greens in a saucepan with the rinsing water clinging to the leaves, cover, and cook until tender, 4–8 minutes. Check from time to time and add a bit of water if needed to prevent scorching. Drain and rinse under running cold water to cool completely. Form the greens into a ball and squeeze forcefully to remove as much water as possible. Finely chop the greens, then squeeze again to force out any additional water.

In a frying pan over medium heat, warm the olive oil. Add the garlic and sauté until lightly golden, about 1 minute. Add the cooked greens and sauté for about 3 minutes. Remove from the heat, let cool, and place in a bowl.

Add the cheeses, egg yolk, salt, and pepper and stir with a wooden spoon to form a smooth paste. If possible, transfer the filling to a pastry (piping) bag fitted with a large plain tip.

Following the directions on page 250, roll out the dough by hand or with a machine. Using a straight-edged pastry wheel, cut the dough into long strips 3 inches (7.5 cm) wide. Using the pastry bag or a spoon, dot the center of the length of 1 strip with 1½-teaspoon dollops of the filling, spacing the dollops 1½ inches (4 cm) apart and stopping within 1 inch (2.5 cm) of the ends of the strip. Brush a little water around each dollop of filling, then gently fold the strip over to enclose the mounds of filling. Using your hands, press the pasta sheets together around the mounds of filling, forcing out any air. Using a fluted pastry wheel, cut into 1½-inch (4-cm) squares, leaving the folded edge uncut. Transfer the prepared ravioli to a lightly floured tray, then repeat with the remaining pasta strips and filling.

Bring a large pot three-fourths full of water to a boil. Stir in the coarse salt. Add the ravioli and cook until al dente, about 3 minutes.

Meanwhile, make the sauce: In a small saucepan over medium heat, melt the butter. Sprinkle in the sage leaves, reduce the heat to low, and continue heating the butter.

When the ravioli are ready, pour the butter and sage leaves into a warmed serving bowl. Drain the ravioli, add to the bowl along with the Parmesan cheese, and toss gently. Serve immediately.

serves 6

The Tuscans are inveterate foragers, for herbs and greens, mushrooms and truffles.

Livorno

Spaghetti alla Bottarga

spaghetti with dried fish roe

Bottarga is the treated roe of gray mullet or tuna. After the fish is caught, the roe is removed and then compacted, salted, and dried. Its intense flavors are widely appreciated in the south of Italy, where it is used in antipasti and to season many secondi. *In Tuscany it appears only infrequently, however, primarily in a sauce for pasta such as this one from Elba.*

1 lb (500 g) spaghetti

2 tablespoons coarse salt

½ cup (4 fl oz/125 ml) extra-virgin olive oil

2 cloves garlic, minced

2 tablespoons finely chopped fresh flat-leaf (Italian) parsley

1 large tomato, peeled, seeded, and chopped

1½ oz (45 g) bottarga

freshly ground pepper to taste

♕ Bring a large pot three-fourths full of water to a boil. Add the pasta and the coarse salt, stir well, and cook until al dente, about 10 minutes.

♕ While the pasta is cooking, in a small saucepan, warm the olive oil over low heat. Add the garlic and parsley and sauté until the garlic begins to color, about 1 minute. Do not allow it to brown. Remove from the heat.

♕ Drain the pasta and return it to the pot. Drizzle with the seasoned olive oil and add the tomato. Toss well and distribute among warmed individual plates.

♕ Using a truffle slicer, mandoline, or vegetable peeler, cut thin shavings of *bottarga* (roughly 1 teaspoon per serving). Crumble over the pasta.

♕ Season each serving abundantly with pepper. As *bottarga* is extremely salty, no additional salt is necessary. Serve at once.

serves 4–6

Siena

Passato di Fagioli

puréed white bean soup

Among the few implements that could qualify as "gadgets" in the Tuscan kitchen is the passaverdure, *or food mill. Over the years, my food processor has begun to gather dust as I become ever more enamored of the qualities of this most simple and inexpensive kitchen helper. For example, passing the beans through a food mill removes their skins and makes for a smooth and velvety soup, while blending them with a hand blender or a food processor simply chops them into tiny pieces that then lurk in the soup.*

BEANS

1 cup (7 oz/220 g) dried cannellini beans

5 cups (40 fl oz/1.25 l) water

1 fresh sage sprig

1 fresh rosemary sprig

2 cloves garlic

SOUP

2 tablespoons extra-virgin olive oil

1 yellow onion, chopped

4 fresh sage leaves, chopped

2-oz (60-g) piece pancetta

1 clove garlic, minced

2 large tomatoes, peeled, seeded, and chopped

5 cups (40 fl oz/1.25 l) chicken broth (page 247) or water

1 fresh rosemary sprig

salt and freshly ground pepper to taste

1½ teaspoons chopped fresh flat-leaf (Italian) parsley

❦ To prepare the beans, pick over them, discarding any misshapen beans or stones. Rinse well, place in a bowl, and add water to cover generously. Let soak overnight. Drain, place in a large saucepan, and add the water. Bring to a boil over high heat and add the sage, rosemary, and garlic. Reduce the heat to low, cover partially, and simmer very gently until the beans are very soft, 1½–2 hours, depending on the age of the beans.

❦ To make the soup, in a frying pan over medium heat, warm the olive oil. Add the onion and sauté until fragrant, about 3 minutes. Add the sage and pancetta and sauté until the pancetta is golden, about

7 minutes. Add the garlic and sauté until it begins to color, about 2 minutes. Remove the cooked pancetta and discard. Reduce the heat to low, stir in the tomatoes, and simmer gently, stirring occasionally, until the tomatoes are soft, about 10 minutes.

❦ Remove the herb sprigs and garlic from the beans and discard. Using a slotted spoon, transfer the beans, in batches, to a food mill fitted with the medium disk held over a soup pot, and purée directly into the pot, adding cooking liquid as needed to facilitate the puréeing. Add 2 cups (16 fl oz/500 ml) of the cooking liquid to the broth or water and set aside. Using the food mill, purée the tomato mixture, letting it pass directly into the soup pot. Stir in the broth or water and place the pot over medium-low heat. Add the rosemary sprig, season with salt and pepper, and cook uncovered, stirring occasionally, until the soup has thickened and the flavors are blended, about 20 minutes. Discard the rosemary sprig.

❦ Transfer the soup to a warmed tureen. Sprinkle with the parsley and serve at once.

serves 4–6

SECONDI

The region's secondi are as varied and vast as the legendary landscape from which they come.

A LONG STRETCH OF COASTLINE and the Mediterranean Sea border Tuscany to the west, yet when someone mentions the region's main courses, or *secondi,* it is meat, game, and fowl that I think of first. The actual image that springs to mind is of an old farmhouse trattoria nestled among olive groves and vineyards on a hilltop in Chianti. Inside, a simply laid table stands near a cavernous hearth, the fire's crimson embers spread before the flames like jewels. Over the embers rests a grill laden with heavy, sizzling *bistecche,* the air above them thick with the smell of roasting meat.

Of all the meat dishes, *bistecca alla fiorentina* (said to have originated in the Maremma but appropriated by the Florentines) is the one for which Tuscany is most famous. The fame is deserved, for a well-prepared *bistecca* is a wondrous thing, crusty brown on the outside, red and juicy on the inside, and abundant enough to satisfy even the heartiest appetite. In a perfect world, the steaks would be from

Tuscany's prized Chianina cattle, a rare breed dating back to Roman times whose meat is reputed to be leaner, yet more flavorful than that of most other breeds. Photographs of the Tuscan countryside from the turn of the nineteenth century show the dark-eyed, pale-colored animals pulling plows through the fields. Concerns about the quality of beef worldwide have sparked increased demand for Chianina cattle, which are raised without hormones, fed only grain and hay, and butchered according to strict European Union guidelines.

On the battered grill of my own fireplace, a visitor is just as likely to find half a dozen fresh, sweet sausages dripping their juices onto the coals and sending their spicy fragrance through the house. They would undoubtedly be the result of a trip to Panzano in Chianti to see my friend and butcher, Dario Cecchini. Dario is my favorite sort of Tuscan, equal parts artist and artisan, someone who has taken the most humble of trades and infused it with

Preceding pages: When sheep graze in fields fragrant with wild herbs, the cheeses made from their milk are infused with subtle herbal scent and flavor. **Left:** Tuscany abounds in *belle viste*—"beautiful views"—unrolling in every direction. **Below:** Soft, sweet, and delectably fat, these fresh pork sausages might be simmered with cannellini beans for a savory dish of *salsicce con fagioli.* **Below bottom:** For generations, Falorni's butcher shop on the central piazza of Greve in Chianti, a lively market town south of Florence, has specialized in salt-cured *salumi* and other high-quality meats, particularly *cinghiale,* the wild boar that roams the local forests.

Above top: Corn-fed free-range chicken *(pollo ruspante)* is favored for its superior succulence. **Above:** An array of *prosciutti* makes an effective display for a local *macelleria,* or "butcher shop." **Right:** Elegantly austere, the campanile of the Abbey of Sant'Antimo, near Montalcino, encloses a bell dating to 1219.

enormous passion and creativity. I was enticed into his tiny shop by the sound of an aria drifting through the open door. Inside, he was holding court with his customers, describing the origins of a Renaissance recipe for fruit mustard while hand-cranking *salsicce* with a century-old machine handed down to him by his grandfather.

Until the 1800s, beef or veal was a nearly unattainable luxury for anyone but the bourgeoisie and those above them. Farmers raised pigs to be butchered in the fall, and although some of the meat was eaten fresh, much of it was salted, ground, flavored, or smoked and thus transformed into the region's beloved *prosciutti,* salamis, and *salsicce.* Today's Tuscan *macelleria,* or "butcher shop," is a visual feast, but it is not for the squeamish or uninformed. Unlike some places in the world where a butcher's work takes place behind closed doors and antiseptic cuts of meat are displayed in plastic containers, the Tuscan butcher shop is a place where, among the slabs of beef, veal, and pork, whole skinned rabbits, plucked chickens and ducks (heads demurely tucked under their breasts), and bowls of milky white tripe vie for the sophisticated shopper's attention.

By sophisticated I do not mean snobbish or worldly, but rather someone with a razor-sharp understanding of the trade of the *macellaio*. I am still fascinated every time I hear an eighty-year-old grandmother order a particular cut or preparation of meat with all the authority and expertise of a neurosurgeon. Exactly what she requests will depend to some extent on where she lives. In Florence, she'll have a preference for *fegatini di pollo* (chicken livers), red meat, and veal; in Siena, she'll likely ask for a free-range chicken; and in Arezzo, she'll often buy pork. Wherever in Tuscany she lives, however, she will almost certainly buy lamb to prepare for her family for Easter.

In a category all its own are Tuscan recipes for *cacciagione,* or "game." At first blush they seem a surprising departure for a cuisine whose outstanding characteristic is the simplicity and straightforwardness of its flavors. The explanation is actually a simple one: these are the recipes of the Tuscan rich and titled, throwbacks to a time, centuries ago, when hunting parties canvassed vast private landholdings on the hunt for deer, wild boar, partridge, pheasant, hare, cranes, and even peacocks (which for Renaissance banquets were usually plucked, roasted, and then "reassembled" with their feathers to look as if still alive). The intense flavor and scent of wild game were tempered by cooking it in a heady mixture of strong red wine seasoned with some combination of cinnamon sticks, cloves, nutmeg, juniper berries, orange peel, raisins, pine nuts, and even chocolate.

Although the structure of Tuscan society has changed dramatically since Renaissance times, the love of hunting and the techniques for cooking game have changed little to this day. The sumptuous flavors of these age-old delicacies beg to be paired with the region's most celebrated red wines, whether Ghiaie della Furba from the hills of Carmignano not far from Prato, Vino Nobile di Montepulciano made near the village of the same name, or one of the splendid new "Super Tuscans," such as Ornellaia or Sassicaia from Bolgheri just north of the Maremma.

I have not forgotten the Tuscan coast—
the bustling port of Livorno, the manicured
beaches of Versilia, the wild stretches of sand
and sea of the Maremma. Here more than
anywhere the emphasis is on freshness and
simplicity. Certainly few pleasures can match
that of a great seaside meal: your table steps
away from the soft carpet of sand leading to
the water, a glass of chilled wine in your hand,
and on your plate some treasure from the sea.
A bowl of *cacciucco* is itself worth the trip to
Livorno. Part soup, part stew, it is thick, spicy,
and never the same twice: its contents are less
a reflection of a rigid recipe than of whatever
fish and shellfish the *pescivendolo* has on hand.

Several years ago, I traveled farther south,
to the lagoon of Orbetello, which separates
the rocky promontory of Mount Argentario
from the mainland. I was drawn to the place
by its nature reserve (home to extraordinary
numbers of migratory birds) and the promise
of some of Tuscany's most beautiful sunsets

(true). I didn't know that the lagoon was
equally famous for the abundance and quality
of its eels, whose sweet, firm meat is roasted,
stewed, braised, and even smoked.

Except for a scattering of inland restaurants
specializing in seafood, as a general rule meat
is eaten away from the coast, and fish and
shellfish are enjoyed at the seaside. That said,
Florence has a pair of delicious seafood
recipes it can legitimately claim as its own:
baccalà coi porri and *calamari in zimino*. The
first is salt cod fried in olive oil and smothered
with garlic-scented sautéed leeks, while the
second is squid cooked in a spicy mixture
of spinach or chard laced with wine and aromatic vegetables.

The assembly of dishes that falls under
the umbrella of *secondi* is as vast and varied as
the landscape from which they come. As for
me, I'll pull up a chair at that table by the fire,
pour myself a glass of deep red Chianti, and
wait for my *bistecca*.

Left: Elba, the famous isle of exile, is the largest landmass in the archipelago just off Tuscany's central coast. **Below:** Agreeable fish vendors, or *pescivendoli,* will gladly clean their customers' purchases. **Below bottom:** Small, colorful fishing boats ply the coastal waters.

Siena

Topini in Umido

veal rolls in tomato and wine sauce

The word topini, *literally "little mice," is used in many parts of Tuscany to refer to gnocchi. In Siena, topini most often means little bundles of veal, stuffed with prosciutto and herbs and covered in tomato sauce. Make sure to use boned top round, cut against the grain. Otherwise, the meat will be stringy.*

8 veal scallops, about 1 lb (500 g) total, each about ¼ inch (6 mm) thick

freshly ground pepper to taste

8 slices prosciutto, each about ⅛ inch (3 mm) thick

8 fresh sage leaves

3 tablespoons extra-virgin olive oil

1 small carrot, peeled and finely chopped

½ small yellow onion, finely chopped

1 small celery stalk, finely chopped

½ cup (4 fl oz/125 ml) dry white wine

½ cup (4 fl oz/125 ml) tomato purée

½ cup (4 fl oz/125 ml) water or meat broth (page 247)

salt to taste

꽃 Lay each veal scallop between 2 sheets of plastic wrap and place on a work surface. Pound lightly with a meat pounder until no thinner than ¼ inch (6 mm) thick. Remove the top sheet of plastic wrap and grind some pepper over the meat. Lay a slice of prosciutto and then a sage leaf on top of each piece. Roll up each veal scallop, then fold in the sides to make a tight bundle. Secure closed with a toothpick.

꽃 In a frying pan large enough to hold the rolls, warm the olive oil over medium heat. Add the carrot, onion, and celery and sauté, stirring often, until soft, about 8 minutes. Raise the heat to medium-high and add the rolls. Brown well on all sides. Add the wine and cook until the alcohol evaporates, about 5 minutes. Add the tomato purée, water or broth, and salt, reduce the heat to medium, and cook, uncovered, until the sauce thickens, about 15 minutes.

꽃 Transfer the rolls to a plate. Pool the sauce on the bottom of a warmed serving platter. Remove the toothpicks from the rolls and arrange on top of the sauce. Serve immediately.

serves 4

Firenze

Rosticciana con le Olive

pork ribs with black olives

This is real food—hearty, flavorful, messy, and delicious. It is accompanied in trattorias with white beans or a salad of wilted greens. I like to pour soft, golden yellow polenta on a large serving plate and spoon the ribs and sauce over the top.

4 lb (2 kg) baby back pork ribs, in slabs

salt and freshly ground pepper to taste

¼ cup (2 fl oz/60 ml) extra-virgin olive oil

2 cloves garlic, crushed

1 fresh rosemary sprig

1 bay leaf

½ cup (4 fl oz/125 ml) dry white wine

1 can (1 lb/500 g) plum (Roma) tomatoes, crushed, with juice

pinch of ground red chile

½ cup (2½ oz/75 g) pitted black olives

꽃 Pull away the thin opaque membrane that covers the underside of the rib slabs. Sprinkle both sides with salt and generously with pepper. Divide the slabs into smaller pieces, cutting them into 3-rib sections.

꽃 In a frying pan large enough to hold all the ribs, warm the olive oil over medium heat. Add the garlic, rosemary, and bay leaf and sauté gently until fragrant, about 3 minutes. Raise the heat to high, add the ribs, and brown well on both sides, turning often. This should take about 15 minutes. Drain off most of the fat from the pan.

꽃 Pour the wine over the ribs, reduce the heat to medium-high, and cook, stirring occasionally and turning the ribs in the pan to coat them in the pan juices, until the alcohol evaporates and the wine reduces slightly, about 5 minutes. Stir in the tomatoes and ground chile, cover, and cook over low heat for 2–2½ hours. The sauce should maintain the consistency of a dense tomato sauce. If it becomes too dry, add water, ½ cup (4 fl oz/125 ml) at a time. The ribs are ready when the meat is moist and tender and falls away from the bone.

꽃 Just before removing the ribs from the heat, discard the bay leaf and rosemary. Add the olives, cooking them just long enough to flavor the sauce, about 3 minutes. Serve the ribs topped with the sauce.

serves 4

Livorno

Cacciucco

seafood stew

It has been said that the residents of Livorno are like their well-known seafood stew: a harmonious mixture, a melting pot. Livorno is historically the most heterogeneous city in Tuscany. In the fifteenth century, when Italy was still a collection of city states rather than a unified country, this coastal town was sold to the Florentines by Genoa. Florence's Medici family built a new port, fortified the town, and opened it for trade, attracting Greeks and Armenians from the south, English and Dutch from the north, and a large population of Jews escaping Spanish persecution.

Cacciucco is Livorno's most famous dish, and like many of the best Tuscan recipes, it began with the most humble ingredients, which were coaxed with the help of wine, herbs, chiles, and tomato into a flavorful stew that is gorgeous to look at as well. Since then, fish has become pricey but the stew remains delicious.

4 lb (2 kg) assorted fish and shellfish such as clams, mussels, mullet, smelt, snapper, cod, haddock, striped bass, squid, shrimp (prawns) in the shell, and crabs, in any combination

3 cloves garlic

¼ cup (2 fl oz/60 ml) extra-virgin olive oil

1 large yellow onion, chopped

3 tablespoons chopped fresh flat-leaf (Italian) parsley

1 teaspoon red pepper flakes

1 cup (8 fl oz/250 ml) dry white wine

3 cups (24 fl oz/750 ml) tomato purée

salt and freshly ground black pepper to taste

6 thick slices coarse country bread

☙ If using clams, soak them in lightly salted water to cover for 2 hours, then drain and scrub well, discarding any that fail to close to the touch. If using mussels, scrub well, debeard, and discard any that fail to close to the touch. Clean any whole fish, remove and discard their heads and tails, remove their skin, and cut crosswise into thick slices on the bone. If using squid, clean as directed on page 251; cut the body into rings and the tentacles into medium-sized pieces. Place all the seafood in a bowl of salted cold water and set aside.

☙ Mince 2 of the garlic cloves and cut the third clove in half lengthwise. Set aside.

☙ In a large saucepan over medium heat, warm the olive oil. Add the onion and sauté until soft and fragrant, about 3 minutes. Add the minced garlic and 2 tablespoons of the parsley and cook, stirring frequently, until the garlic is fragrant, about 2 minutes.

☙ Raise the heat to high, add the red pepper flakes, and pour in the wine. Let the alcohol bubble away for a couple of minutes, then reduce the heat to medium, pour in the tomato purée, and simmer uncovered, stirring occasionally, until the flavors are blended, about 5 minutes.

☙ Begin adding the seafood to the soup, starting with the squid, adding the full-fleshed fish pieces after 10 minutes, and ending with the shellfish. After all the seafood is added, reduce the heat to low and cook, uncovered, at a slow simmer for 15 minutes. Season to taste with salt and black pepper.

☙ Meanwhile, toast the bread and rub the surface with the cut sides of the halved garlic. Place 1 bread slice in each individual soup bowl.

☙ Transfer the stew to a warmed tureen. Sprinkle with the remaining 1 tablespoon parsley.

☙ Bring the tureen to the table and serve immediately, ladling a mix of fish and shellfish onto the toast in each bowl and covering with broth.

serves 6

Throughout Tuscany, a general rule prevails: fish and seafood are eaten by the sea and meat is eaten inland.

Firenze

Cinghiale in Umido

braised wild boar

As many people seem to be coming to Florence these days to visit the Prada outlet in nearby Montevarchi as to wander the halls of the Uffizi galleries to feast on Renaissance art. I've managed to avoid the outlet so far, but have eaten many wonderful meals at the divine Osteria di Rendola, Montevarchi's restaurant of choice for every food-loving Prada enthusiast.

This recipe comes from Francesco Berardinelli, the osteria's talented young owner and chef, who recommends pairing the strong flavor of the meat with a vintage bottle of Montalcino wine.

MARINADE

1 large carrot, peeled and thinly sliced

1 yellow onion, thinly sliced

1 celery stalk, thinly sliced

2 cups (16 fl oz/500 ml) dry red wine

½ cup (4 fl oz/125 ml) red wine vinegar

4 lb (2 kg) boneless wild boar meat from the rump, cut into 2-inch (5-cm) chunks

4 tablespoons (2 fl oz/60 ml) extra-virgin olive oil

salt to taste

1 yellow onion, chopped

1 carrot, peeled and chopped

1 celery stalk, chopped

2 cloves garlic, minced

3 fresh sage leaves, chopped

1 tablespoon finely chopped fresh flat-leaf (Italian) parsley, plus chopped parsley for garnish

1 cup (8 fl oz/250 ml) dry red wine

1 lb (500 g) plum (Roma) tomatoes, peeled, seeded, and chopped

1 fresh rosemary sprig

about 1 cup (8 fl oz/250 ml) beef or vegetable broth (page 247)

freshly ground pepper to taste

The day before serving the boar, make the marinade: In a bowl large enough to hold the meat, combine the carrot, onion, celery, wine, and vinegar. Rinse the meat well under running cold water and add to the bowl. Turn the meat to coat well, cover, and refrigerate overnight.

The following day, remove the meat from the marinade, discarding the marinade, and set aside. In a large frying pan over medium heat, warm 1 tablespoon of the olive oil. Add the meat and sprinkle generously with salt. Sauté the meat, stirring frequently, only long enough to draw out the liquid, about 5 minutes. This step removes any unpleasant gaminess. Using a slotted spoon, transfer the meat to a plate and set aside.

Rinse out the frying pan and return it to the stove over medium heat. Add the remaining 3 tablespoons olive oil and, when hot, return the meat to the pan. Brown it well on all sides, about 10 minutes.

Add the onion, carrot, celery, garlic, sage, and 1 tablespoon parsley to the pan. Sauté until the vegetables begin to soften and become fragrant, 2–3 minutes. Pour in the wine and simmer until most of the liquid evaporates, about 10 minutes.

Add the tomatoes and the rosemary sprig and simmer slowly, uncovered, until the meat is tender, about 2 hours, adding small amounts of the broth if the pan begins to dry out. Adjust the seasoning with salt and add pepper to taste.

Transfer to a deep bowl, discarding the rosemary. Sprinkle with parsley and serve immediately.

serves 6

Some of Tuscany's oldest and most interesting recipes spring from the hunting tradition.

La Caccia

For anyone who lives in the countryside of Tuscany, the beginning of hunting season cannot pass unnoticed. Weeks before the season officially opens and the first shot is fired, hunters begin to scour the woods and fields, accompanied by their faithful allies, sweet-tempered hounds wearing small bells around their necks. The patch of tamed wilderness surrounding my farmhouse yields to great stretches of wild fields, a tiny lake, and dense woods—a hunter's paradise. Thrush, pheasant, and hare live in the fields, and families of wild boar drink from the lake and sleep in the woods. Sometime in September, the season begins in earnest, and the fall air echoes with the sounds of the ancient sport.

In all honesty, I've yet to grow accustomed to the sound of gunfire ringing out at dawn on a Sunday morning, or to the sight of boar being chased by a group of men and dogs. Yet the rich culinary legacy inextricably tied to *la caccia* cannot be ignored. Some of Tuscany's oldest and most interesting recipes spring from the hunting tradition—bold-flavored dishes such as *cinghiale in umido,* wild boar braised in wine, broth, and tomatoes; pheasant, quail, and squab roasted with any combination of pancetta, sausage, mushrooms, and herbs; and *lepre in dolce e forte,* hare cooked in an aromatic mixture of spices, chocolate, nuts, and candied orange peel.

Arezzo

Anatra in Porchetta

duck in the style of porchetta

No one ever makes porchetta at home, for who has the need or resources to stuff a whole pig and roast it on a spit? That job is left to the experts, my favorite being the porchetta vendor who sets up shop at the Saturday open market in Greve in Chianti. Hunched over his table, with a crisp, open bread roll in one hand as he picks through bits of meat, herbs, and fat to construct the perfect panino, he has the wild-haired, thick-spectacled air of a mad, but brilliant, scientist.

Greve's other exceptional source for meats—both fresh and cured—is the esteemed shop of Falorni, where artisan butchers use quality cuts of meat from locally raised animals.

Duck, with its high fat content and flavorful meat, comes closest to mimicking the porchetta principle. Do as the aretini do and break up any leftover pieces of duck meat and stuffing to use as a sauce over homemade fresh pappardelle.

2 cloves garlic

3 fresh sage leaves, torn into pieces

leaves from 1 fresh rosemary sprig

6 oz (185 g) ground (minced) pork or 1 fresh Italian sausage, casing removed and meat crumbled

salt and freshly ground pepper to taste

1 duck, 5 lb (2.5 kg)

3 bay leaves

6 thick strips pancetta or fatty bacon, preferably unsmoked

1 tablespoon unsalted butter

¼ cup (2 fl oz/60 ml) extra-virgin olive oil

½ cup (4 fl oz/125 ml) dry red wine

❧ Preheat an oven to 450°F (230°C).

❧ On a cutting board, combine the garlic, sage, and rosemary and chop finely. Place the pork or sausage in a bowl, add the chopped herb mixture, and season with salt and pepper. Mix well.

❧ Rinse the duck and pat dry. Spoon the pork mixture into the cavity and insert 1 of the bay leaves. Cover the breast with the pancetta or bacon, overlapping the pieces. Tuck the wings behind the back, so they stay close to the body. Sew up the cavity, then draw the legs together and tie securely with kitchen string. Tie additional string around the body of the duck to secure the pancetta or bacon. Tuck the remaining 2 bay leaves under the kitchen string. Place the duck, breast side up, in a roasting pan.

❧ In a small pan, melt the butter with the olive oil, then pour evenly over the duck. Bake for 1 hour, rotating the duck completely in the fat twice during this period. Pour the wine over the duck and continue to roast, rotating the duck completely once more, until the pancetta or bacon and the duck skin are crisp and an instant-read thermometer inserted into the breast registers 175°F (80°C), about 45 minutes longer. Transfer the duck to a wooden carving board, tent loosely with aluminum foil, and let rest for 10–15 minutes before carving.

❧ Remove and discard the string and the bay leaves, including the leaf from inside the cavity. Using a spoon, scoop out the stuffing onto warmed individual plates, placing a small spoonful on each one. Carve the duck into 8 serving pieces and place 1 or 2 pieces on each plate. Serve immediately.

serves 4–6

Trota al Forno con Patate

oven-roasted trout with potatoes

Trout is the most common freshwater fish found in Tuscan fish markets. The clear, cold streams that course through the mountains in the Casentino above Arezzo have given Tuscany the lion's share of recipes for trout. To the north lies the town of Pontassieve, known for its soft, pleasing Chardonnays, ideal for pairing with the delicate flavor of this dish.

2 fresh rosemary sprigs

2 cloves garlic, minced

salt and white pepper to taste

1½ lb (750 g) new potatoes, peeled and thinly sliced

4 tablespoons (2 fl oz/60 ml) extra-virgin olive oil

2 tablespoons unsalted butter, cut into small pieces

4 small trout, ¾ lb (375 g) each, cleaned and filleted

☙ Preheat an oven to 375°F (190°C). Set aside 1 rosemary sprig and finely chop the leaves of the other. In a cup, combine the chopped rosemary and garlic. Season generously with salt and pepper.

☙ Oil a large baking pan. Arrange half of the potato slices in rows on the bottom, slightly overlapping the slices and the rows. Sprinkle evenly with one-third of the garlic mixture, drizzle with 1½ tablespoons of the olive oil, and dot with 1 tablespoon of the butter. Layer with the remaining potato slices, then top with another third of the garlic mixture and 1½ tablespoons of the oil and the remaining 1 tablespoon butter. Cover the dish and bake for 20 minutes. Uncover and continue to bake until the potatoes are almost tender, about 20 minutes longer.

☙ Remove from the oven and arrange the fish in a single layer on top of the potatoes. Drizzle with the remaining 1 tablespoon olive oil and sprinkle with the remaining garlic mixture. Lay the whole rosemary sprig on top. Return to the oven and bake until the fillets are opaque throughout, about 10 minutes. Remove from the oven and let rest for 10 minutes before serving directly from the baking pan.

serves 4

Pisa

Lepre in Dolce e Forte

hare cooked in sweet-and-sour sauce

Just outside the ancient walls of Pisa is San Rossore Park—dense woodlands woven with rivers and streams and bordered on the west by windswept dunes and Mediterranean coastline. I've spent days traversing the park on horseback, and its sheer wildness is astonishing. Boars peer out from under the wide branches of Mediterranean pines; deer bound fearlessly across the path; wild hare skitter through the underbrush.

The park was once the private reserve of the dukes of Savoy, hunting grounds for Italy's nobility. Hare caught there was often served with a sweet-and-sour sauce (or "sweet-and-strong," if you translate literally), a heady mixture of wine, fruit, herbs, and spices. The recipe, without much variation, appears throughout Tuscany wherever the hunting tradition flourishes. The dish is particularly good if made a day in advance and rewarmed before serving.

1 hare, 4 lb (2 kg)

2 cups (16 fl oz/500 ml) dry red wine

½ cup (4 fl oz/125 ml) red wine vinegar

1 cup (4 oz/125 g) chestnut flour or (5 oz/155 g) all-purpose (plain) flour

salt and freshly ground pepper to taste

4–5 tablespoons (2–2½ fl oz/60–75 ml) extra-virgin olive oil

2 oz (60 g) pancetta, diced

1 yellow onion, chopped

1 celery stalk, chopped

1 carrot, peeled and chopped

2 fresh sage leaves

1 fresh rosemary sprig

1 bay leaf

½ cup (4 fl oz/125 ml) chicken or vegetable broth (page 247)

SAUCE

½ cup (4 fl oz/125 ml) chicken or vegetable broth (page 247)

½ cup (4 fl oz/125 ml) red wine vinegar

1 tablespoon sugar

2 oz (60 g) unsweetened chocolate, grated

2 tablespoons raisins

2 tablespoons pine nuts

2 tablespoons finely chopped candied orange peel

½ teaspoon ground cloves

⅛ teaspoon freshly grated nutmeg

⚜ Cut the hare into 12 serving pieces: Remove the forelegs and hind legs and cut each into 2 pieces. Then cut the body into 4 sections of saddle or loin. Rinse the hare pieces well under running cold water, drain, and place in a bowl. Add 1 cup (8 fl oz/250 ml) of the wine and the vinegar. Turn the pieces to coat well. Cover and refrigerate overnight.

⚜ Pour the flour onto a plate and sprinkle with salt and pepper. Drain the meat and pat dry, then coat the pieces with the flour, tapping off the excess. In a large, heavy frying pan over medium heat, warm 4 tablespoons (2 fl oz/60 ml) of the olive oil. Add the pancetta and sauté until golden, about 7 minutes. Using a slotted spoon, transfer the pancetta to a plate.

⚜ With the frying pan still over medium heat, distribute the hare pieces in the pan. Brown well on both sides, about 10 minutes. Add the onion, celery, and carrot and sauté, stirring frequently, until the vegetables soften, about 5 minutes, adding 1 tablespoon oil if necessary to prevent sticking.

⚜ Add the sage, rosemary, and bay leaf, then pour in the remaining 1 cup (8 fl oz/250 ml) wine and deglaze the pan, scraping up any browned bits from the pan bottom. Reduce the heat to low, cover, and cook, adding the broth a little at a time as the liquid cooks away, until the hare is dark brown and the juices run clear when the hare pieces are pierced with a fork, about 2 hours.

⚜ While the hare cooks, prepare the sauce: In a saucepan over medium heat, combine the broth, vinegar, and sugar and heat, stirring, until the sugar dissolves. Add the chocolate, raisins, pine nuts, orange peel, cloves, and nutmeg and stir until the chocolate melts. Remove from the heat.

⚜ Once the hare has finished cooking, remove and discard the rosemary and bay leaf. Transfer the hare pieces to a warmed serving platter and keep warm. Using a hand blender, purée the contents of the pan. (Alternatively, pass the contents of the pan through a food mill fitted with the fine disk.) Add the purée to the sauce and return the saucepan to medium–low heat. Cook the sauce, stirring frequently, for 5 minutes to blend the flavors and heat through. Taste and adjust the seasoning. Spoon the sauce over the hare and serve at once.

serves 6

Lucca

Cotolette alla Pontremolese

veal cutlets with garlic and capers

The small town of Pontremoli is in the northernmost part of Tuscany, close to neighboring Liguria and isolated from the cypresses, vineyards, and olive groves that typify the Tuscan countryside. The town's extraordinary baroque cathedral and crumbling medieval architecture, as well as the surrounding rocky landscape, speak of another Tuscany, one worth exploring.

These cutlets flavored with garlic and capers are typical of the area's unpretentious cuisine. The rich sauce begs to be sopped up with good country bread.

⅓ cup (3 fl oz/80 ml) extra-virgin olive oil

1 yellow onion, chopped

1 clove garlic, minced

2 tablespoons chopped fresh flat-leaf (Italian) parsley

1 lb (500 g) tomatoes, peeled, seeded, and chopped, or 1 can (1 lb/500 g) chopped tomatoes

1 tablespoon capers, rinsed

2 olive oil–packed anchovy fillets

4 veal steaks, about 1½ lb (750 g) total weight and each ½ inch (12 mm) thick

❧ In a large frying pan, warm the olive oil over medium heat. Add the onion and sauté until soft, about 3 minutes. Add the garlic and parsley and continue cooking until the onion is translucent, about 3 minutes longer. Add the tomatoes, reduce the heat to low, and simmer gently until the sauce is quite thick, about 15 minutes. Stir in the capers and the anchovy fillets, breaking up the anchovies in the pan with a wooden spoon, and cook for 1 minute longer.

❧ Push the sauce to the side of the pan and lay the veal steaks in the pan. Cook until the steaks lose their raw color on the first side, about 5 minutes. Turn the steaks, spoon the sauce over the top, cover, and continue to cook until lightly browned on the second side, 4–5 minutes longer.

❧ Transfer the veal steaks to a warmed platter and spoon the sauce over the top. Serve at once.

serves 4

Firenze

Polpette al Pomodoro

meatballs in tomato sauce

In all my years in Tuscany, I have yet to be served spaghetti and meatballs. I have, however, eaten and made all manner of polpette *(meatballs). Although this is the classic recipe for* polpette, *there are infinite variations. Polpette can be made using anything from leftover roasted meat to vegetables or fish. Seasonings can include any combination of onions, garlic, mushrooms, herbs, spices, lemon, cheese, and nuts. The ingredients can be bound with milk-soaked bread, potatoes, rice, egg, or white sauce.*

MEATBALLS

2 slices day-old white bread, crusts removed, torn into pieces

½ cup (4 fl oz/125 ml) milk

1 lb (500 g) ground (minced) beef top round or sirloin

½ lb (250 g) ground (minced) pork

2 eggs, lightly beaten

2 cloves garlic, minced

1 tablespoon finely chopped fresh flat-leaf (Italian) parsley

2 teaspoons finely chopped fresh basil

¼ cup (1 oz/30 g) grated Parmesan cheese

1 teaspoon salt

1 cup (4 oz/125 g) fine dried bread crumbs (page 248)

vegetable oil for frying

SAUCE

2 tablespoons extra-virgin olive oil

2 cloves garlic, crushed

4 tomatoes, peeled, seeded, and chopped

salt and freshly ground pepper to taste

1½ teaspoons chopped fresh flat-leaf (Italian) parsley

❦ To make the meatballs, in a bowl, combine the bread and milk and let soak for 10 minutes. Squeeze out and discard the liquid from the bread, then place the bread in a bowl. Add the beef, pork, eggs, garlic, parsley, basil, Parmesan cheese, and salt. Using a wooden spoon or moistened hands, blend the ingredients into a homogeneous paste.

❦ Using your hands, form the meat mixture into compact 2-inch (5-cm) balls, then flatten the balls into thick patties about 1 inch (2.5 cm) thick. You should have about 16 meatballs. Spread the bread crumbs on a plate and, one at a time, coat the meatballs evenly with the crumbs.

❦ Pour the vegetable oil to a depth of about ½ inch (12 mm) into a large, heavy frying pan and place over medium heat. When the oil is hot, add the meatballs and fry, turning them every few minutes, until they are cooked through and a deep golden brown on both sides, about 10 minutes. (If desired, to test for doneness, cut into the center of a meatball.) Using a slotted utensil, transfer to paper towels to drain, topping with a second layer of towels to blot the excess oil. Keep the meatballs warm.

❦ To make the sauce, in another large frying pan, warm the olive oil over medium heat. Add the garlic and sauté until it becomes fragrant, about 2 minutes. Remove and discard the garlic. Add the tomatoes to the pan and cook uncovered, stirring frequently, until the sauce is thick, about 15 minutes. Season to taste with salt and pepper. Gently set the meatballs in the sauce and cook over low heat for another 5 minutes to blend the flavors.

❦ Spoon some of the sauce onto a warmed platter. Place the meatballs on top and cover with the remaining sauce. Sprinkle with the parsley and serve.

serves 4

Il Vino

The Tuscan year is inextricably bound to the ancient tradition of growing grapes and making wine, from early spring when the first tender vines are neatly tied down with willow branches through the first days of fall and the *vendemmia* when the sweet, heavy grape clusters are snipped off the vine and carted off to the wine press. Tuscans have a wonderful relationship with wine. It is as essential to a meal as olive oil, bread, and salt, and yet the drinking of wine in this region is refreshingly free of pomp and snobbery.

Historically, Chianti was the quintessential Tuscan wine: sturdy and inexpensive, sold in potbellied raffia-covered *fiaschi*. But this is no longer true. The past twenty-five years have brought a wine-making revolution to the entire region, with vintners experimenting with grape varietals and production methods and crafting truly world-class wines.

Chianti, still the best known of all Tuscan wines, is made from a mixture of grapes, the most dominant of which is the Sangiovese, local to Tuscany and thought to date back to Roman times. The Chiantis range from everyday *vini da tavola* to wonderfully rich and full-bodied vintages. Brunello di Montalcino is considered by many to be the greatest Tuscan red. It is a pure Sangiovese wine made in the warm, dry hills surrounding the town of Montalcino. Running a close second is Vino Nobile di Montepulciano, made from Sangiovese, Canaiolo, and other grapes, most frequently Mammolo, which gives the wine a lovely violet scent.

White wines from Tuscany tend to be light and drinkable and, except for the well-known Vernaccia di San Gimignano (made from the Vernaccia grape), are generally pressed from Trebbiano grapes.

Much of the recent excitement surrounding Tuscan wines stems from the advent of the so-called Super Tuscans, innovative, high-quality wines such as Tignanello, Sassicaia, and Ornellaia that have been created by some of the region's major wine makers.

Siena

Bistecchine di Maiale Ubriache

drunken pork chops

Tuscans are wonderfully poetic about their food. These flavorful pork chops are ubriache, *or "drunken," because they are cooked in wine.*

Drink the same young Chianti you use for the chops, and serve the meat with mashed potatoes and steamed brussels sprouts dressed with extra-virgin olive oil and freshly squeezed lemon juice.

4 center-cut pork chops, each 1 inch (2.5 cm) thick

1½ tablespoons freshly ground pepper

2 tablespoons fennel seed, crushed, plus 1 teaspoon whole seed

2 tablespoons extra-virgin olive oil

salt to taste

1 cup (6 oz/185 g) crushed canned plum (Roma) tomatoes with juice

½ cup (4 fl oz/125 ml) young red wine, preferably Chianti

❦ Generously season both sides of the pork chops with the pepper and the crushed fennel seed. In a frying pan large enough to hold all the chops, warm the olive oil over medium heat. Lay the chops in the pan, turn them over when the meat becomes white, and sprinkle with salt. Raise the heat to high and add the tomatoes and wine. After 1 minute, reduce the heat to medium, cover the pan, and let the chops and sauce simmer, turning once, until the chops are well browned on both sides and pale pink in the center, about 15 minutes.

❦ Transfer the chops to a warmed platter and cover them loosely with aluminum foil. Toss the 1 teaspoon whole fennel seed into the sauce and cook for an additional 5 minutes to blend the flavors. Spoon the sauce over the meat and serve immediately.

serves 4

Pollo al Finocchietto

roast chicken with fennel seed

Wild fennel, with its bright green, feathery leaves, clusters of sunny yellow flowers, and ribbed aromatic seeds, is one of the Mediterranean's oldest herbs. In ancient times, it was popularly known as l'erba buona, or "the good herb," and was prized for its medicinal qualities. This centuries-old recipe is still served all over Tuscany, and for good reason: the chicken is beautiful to look at and the anise-scented fennel seed wonderfully fragrant.

1 chicken, 3½ lb (1.75 kg)

salt and freshly ground pepper to taste

6 fresh sage leaves, torn into small pieces

2 tablespoons extra-virgin olive oil, plus extra for drizzling

2 oz (60 g) pancetta, cut into small cubes

2 teaspoons fennel seed, crushed

2 large cloves garlic, sliced

⚜ Preheat an oven to 375°F (190°C).

⚜ Rinse the chicken and pat dry. Sprinkle the cavity with salt, pepper, and the sage. Set aside.

⚜ In a frying pan over medium–high heat, warm the 2 tablespoons olive oil. Add the pancetta, 1 teaspoon of the fennel seed, and the garlic and sauté gently until the mixture is fragrant but not brown, about 3 minutes.

⚜ Using a slotted spoon, transfer the pancetta mixture to the chicken cavity. Set aside the oil from the pan for basting the chicken as it roasts. Tuck the wings behind the back, so they stay close to the body. Draw the drumsticks together and tie securely with kitchen string. Place the chicken, breast side up, in a roasting pan. Drizzle with olive oil and sprinkle with the remaining 1 teaspoon fennel seed.

⚜ Roast, basting occasionally with the reserved oil, until the exterior is a deep golden brown, the juices run clear when a thigh is pricked with a fork, and an instant-read thermometer inserted into the thigh registers 180°F (82°C), about 1 hour.

⚜ Transfer the chicken to a cutting board, tent loosely with aluminum foil, and let rest for 10 minutes. Transfer to a warmed platter, cut into serving pieces, and serve.

serves 4

Firenze
Fegatini alla Salvia

chicken livers with sage

*In Tuscany, chicken livers are traditionally cooked
quickly in olive oil. I prefer a Florentine friend's
recipe, which calls for cooking the livers slowly in butter, turning them a deep, rich brown on the outside
while keeping them softly pink inside. Soaking the
livers in milk gives them a sweet, fresh flavor. Sage is
commonly paired with all types of meat in Tuscany,
particularly liver. Accompany the livers with sautéed
spinach, chard, or broccoli rabe.*

*Recipes for both pork liver and veal liver are also
common in Tuscany. In Arezzo, pork livers are coated
with a mixture of crushed fennel seed, garlic, salt, and
pepper, wrapped in meshlike* rete di maiale, *"pork
caul fat" (*rete *means "mesh"), and then strung on
a stalk of fresh fennel, bathed in olive oil, and baked
in the oven. Once cooked, they are served immediately
or are conserved under olive oil or melted lard in
a glass or earthenware container.*

1 lb (500 g) chicken livers

about 2 cups (16 fl oz/500 ml) milk

⅓ cup (3 oz/90 g) unsalted butter

handful of fresh sage leaves

salt and freshly ground pepper to taste

❦ Trim away the membranes and connective tissue
from the livers, and rinse the livers in running cold
water. Place them in a small bowl and add milk to
cover. Cover and refrigerate overnight. When ready
to use the livers, drain them and wipe them dry with
paper towels.

❦ In a large frying pan over very low heat, melt
the butter. Add the livers and sage and cook gently,
turning occasionally, until the meat is a deep, rich
brown on the outside and tender pink on the inside,
8–10 minutes.

❦ Using a slotted spoon, lift the livers and sage leaves
out of the butter and distribute them evenly among
warmed individual plates. Serve immediately.

serves 4

Siena

Lesso con Salsa Verde

boiled beef and broth with green sauce

Tuscans do not make as big a production of lesso *as their neighbors in Emila-Romagna do. Although the dish is generally associated with cool weather, the* signora *who shared this recipe with me serves it even in the summer. She prepares it one day ahead (in the evening before or after dinner), lets it sit out all night, and serves it the following afternoon when her husband and grown children come home for* pranzo, *sparing herself having to cook in the midday heat, yet still providing a hearty meal.*

The broth from the lesso *is often boiled with tortellini or very fine egg noodles and served as a first course. The green sauce tastes best if made a day before the dish is served.*

BOILED MEATS

about 8 cups (64 fl oz/2 l) water

1 lb (500 g) beef brisket

½ lb (250 g) beef tongue

½ calf's foot, halved lengthwise

1 yellow onion, halved

1 celery stalk, including leaves

2 carrots, peeled and halved lengthwise

2 tomatoes, cored

salt to taste

SAUCE

leaves from 1 bunch fresh flat-leaf (Italian) parsley

handful of fresh basil leaves

1 clove garlic, chopped

3 olive oil–packed anchovy fillets

1 teaspoon capers, rinsed

yolk of 1 hard-boiled egg

½ carrot, peeled and chopped

⅓ celery stalk, chopped

2 tablespoons fresh bread crumbs (page 248)

1 tablespoon fresh lemon juice

½ cup (4 fl oz/125 ml) extra-virgin olive oil

♛ To prepare the meats, pour the water into a large stockpot. Add the brisket, tongue, and calf's foot, cover, and bring to a boil over high heat. Skim off any scum that forms on the surface, then add the onion, celery, carrots, and tomatoes and season with salt. Reduce the heat to low, cover, and simmer the meats gently until very tender, about 2 hours.

♛ While the meats are cooking, make the sauce: In a food processor, combine the parsley, basil, garlic, anchovy fillets, capers, egg yolk, carrot, celery, bread crumbs, lemon juice, and olive oil. Process until a paste forms, then transfer to a bowl.

♛ Remove the meats from the heat and set aside to cool. Remove the calf's foot and discard it.

♛ To serve, remove the skin, bones, and gristle from the tongue and discard. Cut the tongue across the grain into slices. Cut the brisket across the grain into slices. Skim any fat from the surface of the broth and strain the broth. Arrange the sliced meats on a warmed platter and ladle a little broth over the slices. Pass the sauce at the table.

serves 6

Grosseto

Spiedini di Anguilla Arrosta

roast eel kabobs

Old Tuscan cookbooks are filled with recipes for preparing eel, although I've only rarely seen it at fishmongers or on a restaurant menu. Eel fishing, raising, and cooking are still much alive in Orbetello, in the southern Maremma. The lagoons there are reputed to have the finest-quality eel in central Italy.

2 lb (1 kg) baby eels

2 tablespoons extra-virgin olive oil

2 cloves garlic, minced

2 tablespoons chopped fresh flat-leaf (Italian) parsley

juice of 1 lemon

salt and freshly ground pepper to taste

1 baguette, sliced ½ inch (12 mm) thick (20 slices)

16 bay leaves

1 cup (8 fl oz/250 ml) dry red wine

❦ Wearing rubber gloves and using a sharp knife, slit the skin around each eel's head. Holding the head, grasp the skin with a coarse-textured cloth and re-move from the eel by pulling it toward the tail. Discard the skin. Make a slit up the length of the eel and remove the viscera. Cut off the head. Wash the body thoroughly. Cut the eels crosswise into pieces 2 inches (5 cm) long. You should have 16 pieces.

❦ In a bowl, combine the oil, garlic, parsley, and lemon juice. Season with salt and pepper and mix well. Add the eel pieces and turn to coat well with the marinade. Cover and refrigerate for 2 hours.

❦ Preheat an oven to 375°F (190°C).

❦ Drain the eel. Thread a bread slice onto a metal or bamboo skewer, followed by a piece of eel, and then a bay leaf. Repeat until there are 4 pieces of eel on the skewer, then slip a slice of bread onto the end. Lay the skewer in a baking dish. Repeat to fill 3 more skewers, and add to the baking dish.

❦ Bake the eel, basting from time to time with the wine, until crisp, about 20 minutes. Turn the heat off and let the eel rest in the oven with the door closed for 15 minutes before serving. Transfer the skewers to a platter or individual plates and serve.

serves 4

Livorno

Spigola al Cartoccio con Salsa di Capperi

sea bass in parchment with caper sauce

The first time I ordered fish al cartoccio was because the woman at the table next to mine had ordered it. I had watched in fascination as the mysterious parcel was brought to her on a plate and she carefully unwrapped it using the tips of her fingers. Before even picking up her fork, she bent her head over the open package to peer inside and inhale a whiff of rising steam. It looked magical, dramatic even. The method is an old one, used primarily for cooking fish. The parchment holds in both the flavor and the juices of the fish, and the presentation is at once elegant and intriguing, but quite simple to execute.

1 tablespoon unsalted butter

1 tablespoon extra-virgin olive oil

2 cloves garlic, minced

2 tablespoons capers, rinsed

juice of ½ lemon

freshly ground pepper to taste

4 sea bass fillets, each about ½ lb (250 g) and 1 inch (2.5 cm) thick

salt to taste

handful of fresh basil leaves

❦ Preheat an oven to 425°F (220°C).

❦ In a small frying pan over medium heat, melt the butter with the olive oil. Add the garlic and sauté until fragrant, about 1 minute. Add the capers and cook for 1 minute longer. Remove from the heat, stir in the lemon juice, and season lightly with pepper.

❦ Cut 4 large rectangles of parchment (baking) paper or aluminum foil. Lay a fish fillet on each rec-tangle and sprinkle lightly with salt. Distribute the garlic–caper mixture over the fillets, then scatter a few basil leaves on top. Wrap each fillet in the paper or foil, bringing together the long edges and folding them over to seal well, then folding in the sides and sealing them. Transfer the parcels to a baking dish.

❦ Bake until the fish is opaque throughout, 10–15 minutes. To check for doneness, unwrap a parcel and pierce the fillet with a knife. Serve the fish fillets, still in their wrappers, on warmed individual plates.

serves 4

Lucca

Orata Grigliata con Finocchio Selvatico

grilled sea bream with wild fennel

As spring gives way to summer, I find myself longing for the sea. On such a day I might drive from Florence to Forte dei Marmi just to have lunch at Da Bruno, on the beach. Forte dei Marmi has the reputation of being Versilia's most elegant seaside town. The highlight of my meal would be a grilled sea bream. Orata comes from oro, or "gold," an allusion to the golden head of this beautiful fish. The meat is so tender and delicate that orata is nearly always prepared very simply, either roasted or grilled.

2 large tomatoes, cut into 1-inch (2.5-cm) wedges

¼ cup (2 fl oz/60 ml) extra-virgin olive oil

juice of ½ lemon

1 tablespoon finely chopped fresh flat-leaf (Italian) parsley

2 large cloves garlic, crushed

salt and freshly ground pepper to taste

2 sea bream, about 1½ lb (750 g) each, cleaned with heads and tails intact

small handful of fresh fennel leaves, plus chopped fennel leaves for garnish

1 long fresh rosemary sprig

☙ Prepare a medium-hot fire in a grill.

☙ Lightly oil the grill rack and arrange the tomato wedges on it. Grill, turning once, until they are dry but not leathery, 10–15 minutes on each side. Remove from the grill and set aside.

☙ While the tomatoes are on the grill, in a bowl, stir together the olive oil, lemon juice, parsley, garlic, salt, and pepper. Set aside. Rinse the fish and pat dry. Sprinkle the cavity of each fish with salt and stuff loosely with the handful of fennel leaves. Drizzle half of the seasoned olive oil over the fennel.

☙ Place the fish in 2 oiled grilling baskets. Grill, turning once, until opaque throughout, about 10 minutes on each side. Use the rosemary sprig to baste the fish with the remaining seasoned oil. Remove the fish from the basket and transfer to a warmed platter. Lay the grilled tomatoes over the fish. Scatter with the chopped fennel leaves and serve.

serves 4

Il Pescivendolo

I've learned more about cooking fish from Tuscany's fishmongers than from the scores of cookbooks lining my kitchen shelves. Livorno, Tuscany's largest city after Florence and Italy's second largest port after Genoa, is a treasure trove of seafood. Most of it is sold out of Livorno's beautiful nineteenth-century, cast-iron market, a replica of the Mercato Centrale in Florence. But unless you are lucky enough to live by the sea, buying fresh fish in the region requires some forethought. Except for a quite reputable fishmonger within the giant COOP supermarket in San Casciano, not far from my house, my nearest fish shop is twenty-five minutes away in Florence.

Many people, however, myself included, buy fresh fish from traveling fishmongers. On the same morning each week, my fishmonger drives his refrigerated truck into the small town of Impruneta, where he sets up shop in the main square next to the church. His counter is filled with mesh bags of tiny, sweet clams; shrimp (prawns) of various sizes; squid and cuttlefish, their sacs still filled with black ink; small, flat *sogliola* (sole), which he expertly fillets for my children; and an assortment of glorious, albeit expensive, catches like *orata* (sea bream) and *branzino* (sea bass). He never fails to ask me how I plan to cook what I buy—and to offer his own much-appreciated advice.

Arezzo

Coniglio in Salmì con Salsa di Funghi

marinated rabbit with wild mushrooms

Salmì is an ancient and popular way of cooking game, especially hare and rabbit. Recipes vary considerably, with some including chocolate and cream, and others more heavily spiced with a mixture of juniper berries, peppercorns, cloves, nutmeg, cinnamon, and herbs. Since the flavor of rabbit is less intense than that of its cousin, the seasonings in this recipe from Arezzo are more subtle as well. Chicken can be substituted for the rabbit; the total cooking time is 45 minutes.

1 oz (30 g) dried porcino mushrooms

¾ cup (6 fl oz/180 ml) warm water

1 rabbit, 3 lb (1.5 kg)

1 tablespoon butter

3 tablespoons extra-virgin olive oil

salt to taste

1 yellow onion, chopped

1 piece (3 oz/90 g) prosciutto, cut into small cubes

2 cloves garlic, minced

2 whole cloves

1 cinnamon stick, 3 inches (7.5 cm) long

½ cup (4 fl oz/125 ml) white wine

2 tomatoes, peeled, seeded, and chopped

1 fresh rosemary sprig

freshly ground pepper to taste

In a bowl, combine the porcini and warm water and let soak to rehydrate for 30 minutes.

Drain the mushrooms, reserving the soaking liquid, and squeeze out the excess moisture. Chop roughly and set aside. Filter the soaking liquid through a sieve lined with a paper towel and set aside.

Cut the rabbit into 12 serving pieces: Remove the forelegs and hind legs and cut each into 2 pieces. Then cut the body into 4 sections of saddle or loin. Rinse the rabbit pieces under running cold water and pat dry.

In a large frying pan over medium-high heat, melt the butter with the olive oil. When the mixture is hot, lay the rabbit pieces in a single layer in the pan, sprinkle with salt, and brown the pieces well on both sides, about 10 minutes.

Add the onion, prosciutto, garlic, cloves, and cinnamon stick to the frying pan and cook, stirring often, until the onion begins to soften, about 5 minutes. Add the wine and cook for 2 minutes to evaporate the alcohol.

Add the mushrooms and the tomatoes and stir to combine. Add the rosemary sprig, reduce the heat to medium-low, cover, and cook until the sauce is thick, about 30 minutes.

Stir in the reserved soaking liquid from the mushrooms, season with pepper, re-cover, and continue cooking until the rabbit has soaked up most of the herbed juices and is tender when tested with a fork, about 30 minutes longer.

Remove the rosemary sprig, cloves, and cinnamon and discard. Transfer the rabbit pieces to a warmed platter and serve immediately.

serves 4

Firenze

Salsicce con Fagioli all'Uccelletto

fresh pork sausages with cannellini in herbed tomato sauce

Florentines enjoy eating cannellini beans all'uccelletto, or "cooked in the manner of little birds," with garlic, sage, and tomatoes.

2 cups (14 oz/440 g) dried cannellini beans

4 cloves garlic

8 fresh sage leaves

1 tomato, cored and halved

salt and freshly ground pepper to taste

2 tablespoons extra-virgin olive oil

8 fresh Italian sausages, about 2½ oz (75 g) each

2 cups (12 oz/375 g) crushed canned plum (Roma) tomatoes with juice

pinch of ground red chile

꙼ Pick over the beans, discarding any grit or misshapen beans. Rinse well and place in a bowl. Add water to cover generously and let soak overnight.

꙼ The next day, drain the beans and place in a large saucepan with 7 cups (56 fl oz/1.75 l) water. Bring to a boil and add 2 of the garlic cloves, 4 of the sage leaves, and the tomato halves to the saucepan. Reduce the heat to a very gentle simmer and cook, uncovered, until the beans are tender, 1½–2 hours. Season with salt, then drain the beans. Discard the garlic, sage, and tomato.

꙼ Crush the remaining 2 garlic cloves. In a large frying pan, warm together the olive oil, the remaining 4 sage leaves, and the 2 crushed garlic cloves. Add the sausages and brown lightly on all sides, about 10 minutes. Add the beans, crushed tomatoes, and ground chile. Simmer, uncovered, stirring gently every so often, for about 15 minutes. Adjust the seasoning with salt and pepper.

꙼ Spoon the beans onto a warmed oval platter. Lay the sausages on top and serve.

serves 4

Arezzo

Pollo al Mattone

chicken cooked under bricks

The clay content of Tuscan soil makes the region's terra-cotta tiles and pottery some of the most prized in the world. Wherever terra-cotta bricks are made, this recipe for chicken, weighted with bricks as it cooks, is common. The weight keeps the chicken flat. The skin is wonderfully crisp and the meat tender and juicy.

1 chicken, 4 lb (2 kg)

¼ cup (2 fl oz/60 ml) plus 3 tablespoons extra-virgin olive oil

2 cloves garlic, crushed

1 dried hot chile, crumbled

salt and freshly ground pepper to taste

☙ Lay the chicken on its back. Separate the breast into halves by cutting down the center of the breast-bone. Turn the chicken, flatten, and, using the heel of your hand, crack the backbone. Turn the wings back and fold the tips under the breast. Make small slits on either side of the breast tips, then insert the ends of the drumsticks into each opening. Pour the ¼ cup (2 fl oz/60 ml) olive oil into a dish large enough to hold the flattened chicken, then add the garlic, chile, salt, and pepper. Lay the chicken in the marinade and turn to coat with the mixture. Cover and marinate for 1 hour at room temperature, turning the chicken from time to time.

☙ In a large, heavy frying pan over medium-high heat, warm the 3 tablespoons olive oil. When the oil is hot, remove the chicken from the marinade and lay it, skin side up, in the pan. Top with a heavy cast-iron frying pan and fill the pan with 2 stacked bricks or other weights. Reduce the heat to medium and cook for 15 minutes.

☙ Remove the weights, then transfer the chicken to a plate and drain off all but 1 tablespoon of the fat from the pan. Return the chicken to the pan, skin side down, and weight it down again. Continue to cook until the juices run clear from the thigh when pricked with a fork, 15–25 minutes longer.

☙ Transfer to a cutting board, cut into serving pieces, and divide among warmed individual plates.

serves 4

Firenze
Agnello in Umido
braised lamb

Since lamb is eaten infrequently in Tuscany, the number of recipes calling for it are far fewer than those for other meats. In the Mugello, it is braised with wine, tomatoes, garlic, and herbs, which form a thick, savory sauce. Serve the lamb with sautéed artichokes and a Chianti Rufina, which has a dense red color and fresh fruitiness that are clean and inviting.

2 cloves garlic

leaves from 1 fresh rosemary sprig

3 tablespoons extra-virgin olive oil

4 lb (2 kg) boneless lamb shoulder, cut into 2-inch (5-cm) chunks

salt and freshly ground pepper to taste

1 cup (8 fl oz/250 ml) dry white wine

1 lb (500 g) tomatoes, peeled, seeded, and chopped

❦ In a large, heavy pan over medium heat, warm together the garlic, rosemary, and olive oil.

❦ When the garlic begins to color, after about 2 minutes, working in batches, add the chunks of lamb and sauté, stirring frequently, until the meat is well browned on all sides, about 10 minutes. Season with salt and pepper.

❦ Return all the meat to the pan. Pour the wine over the meat and deglaze the pan, stirring with a wooden spoon to scrape up any browned bits on the pan bottom.

❦ When the liquid has reduced, after about 5 minutes, stir in the tomatoes. Bring to a simmer, then reduce the heat to medium-low and cook uncovered, stirring occasionally, until the sauce is thick, the meat is tender, and the flavors are blended, about 15 minutes.

❦ Transfer to a warmed platter or individual warmed plates and serve.

serves 6

In fact, the word arista *comes from the aristos, meaning "the best." These were the very words said to have been uttered by the Greek bishops present at Florence's council when they first tried the roasted pork—although in truth, the Italian writer Sacchetti had referred to roast pork as* arista *in a novel a century earlier.*

Arezzo is not generally considered one of Tuscany's premier wine-making provinces, but Podere il Bosco from Tenimenti Luigi D'Alessandro near Cortona is regarded as one of Italy's finest syrahs. Lightly peppery with hints of blackberries and red currants, it pairs beautifully with this elegant roast.

ARISTA

1 bone-in pork loin, 3 lb (1.5 kg)

3 cloves garlic

2 fresh rosemary sprigs

salt and freshly ground pepper to taste

¼ cup (2 fl oz/60 ml) extra-virgin olive oil

POTATOES

1 tablespoon unsalted butter

¼ cup (2 fl oz/60 ml) extra-virgin olive oil

3 lb (1.5 kg) baking potatoes, peeled and cut into 1-inch (2.5-cm) chunks

❦ Meanwhile, prepare the potatoes. In a large, heavy pan over medium heat, melt the butter with the oil. Add the remaining garlic-rosemary paste and the potatoes, toss the potatoes to coat them with the oil and the paste, and then sauté until golden, about 15 minutes. Remove from the heat.

❦ About 40 minutes before the pork is done, transfer the potatoes to the roasting pan to finish cooking with the meat.

❦ When the pork is ready, remove the roasting pan from the oven and transfer the pork to a carving board. Cut away the string and remove the bone. Slice the meat and arrange on a warmed platter.

❦ Stir the potatoes in the roasting pan to coat them with the juices, and then arrange on the platter with the sliced meat. Garnish with rosemary sprigs and serve immediately.

serves 4–6

Arezzo is renowned for porchetta, the roasted

Il Trippaio

My niece and nephew grew up in the heart of Florence, just steps away from the city's Mercato del Porcellino and its stalls filled with ceramics, embroidered linens, writing paper, and leather goods. In a corner of the market, the *trippaio*—"tripe man"—operates from a mobile cart that is inevitably surrounded by a small crowd of people (my niece and nephew usually among them) eating sandwiches—tripe sandwiches.

Tripe is the lining from one of the four chambers of a ruminant's stomach, usually a young ox. Florentines love the stuff. Although all tripe is edible, the most tender and subtly flavored type is the honeycomb tripe from the second chamber. The mobile tripe vendors cut the tripe into short strips and boil it in large vats of seasoned water. It is eaten plain on the spot stuffed into hard-crusted rolls, or it is brought home to be simmered with tomatoes and other vegetables, broth, and wine, or to be combined with onions, sweet peppers, and olives and then tossed with olive oil and lemon juice.

The name Porcellino acknowledges the large bronze statue of a wild boar that stands to one side of the lively commercial space. Legend has it that anyone who rubs the boar's snout will be assured of returning to Florence. His snout shines smooth and golden from the touch of countless tourists who have made their wishes.

Firenze

Peposo

peppery beef stew

This dish takes its name from the peppercorns, or granello di pepe, used to spice it. The stew comes from the hill town of Impruneta, just nine miles (15 km) from Florence and renowned for the quality of its cotto, or terra-cotta. Traditionally, the stew was baked in the same ovens in which the terra-cotta vases and tiles were fired.

I ate my first peposo at Pasquini, a tiny restaurant in Florence. It was wintertime, and the stew was so spicy and warming that I ate every last bite, mopping up the sauce with bread and accompanying it with a half carafe of fine house wine. The stew is remarkably effortless to make.

1½ lb (750 g) beef or pork stew meat, cut into large cubes

1 pork shank, about 2 lb (1 kg)

1⅓ cups (8 oz/250 g) chopped and drained canned plum (Roma) tomatoes

1 yellow onion, finely chopped

1 carrot, peeled and finely chopped

1 celery stalk, finely chopped

4 cloves garlic, crushed

1 bay leaf

2 cups (16 fl oz/500 ml) dry red wine

1 tablespoon peppercorns, lightly crushed

♛ Preheat an oven to 350°F (180°C).

♛ In a baking dish, combine the stew meat, pork shank, tomatoes, onion, carrot, celery, garlic, bay leaf, wine, and peppercorns. Mix well and add enough water just to cover the meat.

Livorno

Tonno alla Livornese

tuna with garlic, basil, and tomato

This sauce marries the best flavors of the Mediterranean: tomatoes, olives and olive oil, capers, garlic, and basil. It is a particular treat over fresh tuna.

6 tablespoons (3 fl oz/90 ml) extra-virgin olive oil

1 large yellow onion, chopped

3 cloves garlic, 2 minced and 1 crushed

1 lb (500 g) tomatoes, peeled, seeded, and chopped

8 fresh basil leaves

2 tablespoons chopped fresh flat-leaf (Italian) parsley, plus chopped parsley for garnish

4 tuna steaks, each about ½ lb (250 g)

salt and freshly ground pepper to taste

1 cup (5 oz/155 g) pitted brine-cured black olives

4 teaspoons capers, rinsed

☙ In a frying pan over medium heat, warm 3 tablespoons of the olive oil. Add the onion and sauté gently until it begins to soften, about 3 minutes. Add the minced garlic and sauté until golden, about 2 minutes longer. Stir in the tomatoes, basil, and 2 tablespoons parsley and cook uncovered, stirring occasionally, until thickened, about 15 minutes. Remove from the heat and pass through a food mill fitted with the medium disk. Set aside.

☙ In a frying pan large enough to hold the fish in a single layer, warm the remaining 3 tablespoons oil over medium heat. Add the crushed garlic and sauté until golden, about 2 minutes. Remove and discard the garlic clove. Lightly season the tuna steaks with salt and pepper and place in the pan. Raise the heat to medium-high and cook, turning once, until lightly browned on both sides, about 2 minutes. Pour the reserved sauce directly over the fish, reduce the heat to low, add the olives and capers, and cook until the sauce thickens, about 5 minutes.

☙ Transfer to warmed individual plates, sprinkle with parsley, and serve immediately.

serves 4

Siena

Faraona Ripiena

roasted guinea hen stuffed with sausage and mushrooms

Guinea fowl are beautiful speckled birds originally from West Africa and Egypt, which explains why they were once called Numidian or pharaoh's hens. Free-range guinea hens taste much like pheasant and must be matured for three or four days before cooking. Grain-raised hens resemble chicken in flavor and do not need to be matured.

In Tuscany, guinea hens and pheasants are used interchangeably in recipes. If they are unavailable, substitute chicken.

¼ lb (125 g) fresh button or cremini mushrooms, brushed clean and sliced

1 fresh Italian sausage, casing removed and meat crumbled

leaves from 1 fresh sage sprig, finely chopped

2 cloves garlic, minced

salt and freshly ground pepper to taste

1 guinea hen, 3½ lb (1.75 kg)

¾ cup (6 fl oz/180 ml) extra-virgin olive oil

½ cup (4 fl oz/125 ml) dry white wine

½ lb (250 g) fresh porcino mushrooms, brushed clean and sliced

2 cups (12 oz/375 g) peeled, seeded, and chopped fresh or crushed canned plum (Roma) tomatoes

♛ Preheat an oven to 375°F (190°C).

♛ In a bowl, combine the button or cremini mushrooms, sausage meat, sage, and half of the minced garlic. Season to taste with salt and pepper. Mix well.

♛ Rinse the guinea hen and pat dry. Season the cavity with salt and pepper, and fill it with the mushroom–sausage mixture.

♛ Truss the hen with kitchen string, then set on a rack inside a roasting pan. Pour ¼ cup (2 fl oz/60 ml) of the olive oil over the bird.

♛ Roast, basting frequently with the pan juices and the white wine, until the skin is crisp and the juices run clear when a thigh is pierced, about 55 minutes.

♛ Meanwhile, in a large frying pan over medium heat, warm the remaining ½ cup (4 fl oz/120 ml) olive oil. Add the remaining minced garlic and, as it begins to color, after about 1 minute, add the porcino mushrooms. Season with salt and pepper and sauté, stirring frequently, until the liquid released by the mushrooms has cooked off and the edges of the mushrooms are dark brown, about 10 minutes.

♛ Add the tomatoes to the frying pan and continue to cook, stirring occasionally, until the sauce is thick, about 20 minutes longer.

♛ Transfer the roasted guinea hen to a cutting board, tent loosely with aluminum foil, and let the hen rest for 10 minutes before carving.

♛ To serve, spoon out the stuffing and set aside. Carve the bird into 8 pieces. Spread the tomato sauce over a warmed platter, lay the pieces on top, and scatter the stuffing over the pieces. Serve immediately.

serves 4

Firenze

Calamari in Zimino

squid with spinach

In zimino refers to a particular sauce—a combination of spinach, tomatoes, and aromatic vegetables cooked with wine.

2 lb (1 kg) squid

2 lb (1 kg) spinach, stems removed

1 cup (8 fl oz/250 ml) water

salt to taste

⅓ cup (3 fl oz/80 ml) extra-virgin olive oil

1 yellow onion, chopped

1 small carrot, peeled and chopped

1 small celery stalk, chopped

2 cloves garlic, minced

1 tablespoon chopped fresh flat-leaf
(Italian) parsley

1 or 2 small dried hot chiles, crumbled

½ cup (4 fl oz/125 ml) dry white wine

¾ lb (375 g) tomatoes, peeled, seeded, and
coarsely chopped

❦ Clean the squid as directed on page 251. Cut the bodies crosswise into rings ¼ inch (6 mm) wide, and cut the tentacles into pieces 2 inches (5 cm) long.

❦ Stack 10 spinach leaves, roll up, and coarsely slice crosswise. Pour the water into a saucepan, place over medium heat, salt lightly, and add the spinach. Cover and cook until wilted, about 3 minutes. Drain well in a colander, pressing against the spinach with a wooden spoon to extract as much water as possible.

❦ In a frying pan over medium heat, warm the olive oil. Add the onion and sauté until soft, about 3 minutes. Add the carrot, celery, garlic, parsley, and chiles. Sauté, stirring frequently, until the garlic begins to color, about 4 minutes. Season with salt.

❦ Add the squid to the pan with the vegetables, douse with the wine, and cook until the squid is opaque, about 5 minutes. Add the spinach to the pan and stir well to coat it with the pan juices. Sauté until the flavors are blended, about 5 minutes. Stir in the tomatoes, season with salt, and reduce the heat to low. Cover and simmer gently until the stew is dark, about 30 minutes. Transfer to warmed individual wide, shallow bowls and serve.

serves 4–6

Grosseto

Triglie dell'Argentario

red mullet in white wine, garlic, and parsley

Triglie are beautiful fish whose silvery pink skins are speckled with red. Known in English as red mullets, they are a bit of work to eat (because of their many bones), but the extra effort is a small price to pay for the full flavor and strong, lean meat.

In Grosseto, the wine of choice—both for cooking and for serving with the fish—is Ansonica, a celebrated local white from a varietal of Sicilian origin.

3 cloves garlic

8 red mullets, ½ lb (250 g) each, cleaned,
with head and tail intact

salt to taste

3 tablespoons chopped fresh flat-leaf
(Italian) parsley

½ cup (4 fl oz/125 ml) extra-virgin olive oil

½ cup (4 fl oz/125 ml) dry white wine

juice of ½ lemon

2 lemons, cut into wedges

❦ Crush 1 garlic clove. Thinly slice the remaining 2 cloves. Rinse the fish and pat dry. Sprinkle the cavity of each fish with salt and divide the garlic slices and the parsley evenly among them.

❦ In a large frying pan over medium heat, warm the olive oil. Add the crushed garlic to the pan and sauté until it begins to color, about 2 minutes. Remove and discard the garlic.

❦ Lay the fish in the pan, pour in the wine, and let the alcohol bubble away for a couple of minutes. Turn the fish, reduce the heat to low, cover, and cook, shaking the pan from time to time, until opaque throughout, about 15 minutes longer.

❦ When the fish are ready, uncover, pour the lemon juice evenly over them, and then carefully transfer to a warmed platter. Garnish with the lemon wedges and serve at once.

serves 4

Firenze
Coniglio alla Cacciatora

hunter's style rabbit

Hunters hunt, yet they rarely cook. Usually it is the hunter's moglie *(wife) or* mamma *(if he's lacking the former) whose task it is not only to skin and draw the animal but also to cook it in a manner befitting her husband's or son's hard work. This is a common recipe throughout Tuscany. In the mountains, it would be served with polenta. You can also accompany it with crusty bread and broccoli rabe. The use of olives is typical of the neighboring region of Umbria, passed to Tuscany via the Valdarno, near Arezzo.*

1 rabbit, 3 lb (1.5 kg)

salt to taste

2 tablespoons (4 fl oz/60 ml) extra-virgin olive oil

1 yellow onion, sliced

2 cloves garlic, minced

2 large carrots, peeled and chopped

1 large celery stalk, chopped

½ cup (4 fl oz/125 ml) dry white wine

1 can (28 oz/875 g) plum (Roma) tomatoes, crushed, with juice

1 fresh rosemary sprig

2 tablespoons chopped fresh sage

1 bay leaf

1 cup (5 oz/155 g) pitted brine-cured black olives

freshly ground pepper to taste

❧ Cut the rabbit into 12 serving pieces: Remove the forelegs and hind legs and cut each into 2 pieces. Cut the body into 4 sections of saddle or loin.

❧ Rinse the rabbit pieces well and pat dry. Sprinkle lightly with salt.

❧ In a large frying pan over medium heat, warm 3 tablespoons of the olive oil. Add the rabbit and brown well on all sides, about 10 minutes. Transfer the rabbit pieces to a plate.

❧ Add the remaining 1 tablespoon oil to the same pan over medium heat, add the onion, and sauté until it begins to soften, about 3 minutes. Add the garlic, carrots, and celery and cook, stirring often, until tender, about 8 minutes.

❧ Raise the heat to high, pour in the wine, and deglaze the pan, scraping up any browned bits from the pan bottom. Cook the wine and pan juices until reduced by half, about 5 minutes. Add the tomatoes, rosemary, sage, and bay leaf and bring the mixture to a boil. Reduce the heat to low and return the rabbit pieces to the pan. Spoon the sauce over the meat, cover the pan, and cook gently, stirring and turning the pieces occasionally, until the meat is tender when prodded with a fork, about 45 minutes longer.

❧ Transfer the meat to a warmed serving platter and cover loosely with aluminum foil. Cook the sauce remaining in the pan over high heat until it thickens, 5–7 minutes.

❧ Remove and discard the bay leaf and rosemary sprig, then stir in the black olives. Season with salt and pepper, then pour the sauce over the meat. Serve immediately.

serves 4

Massa-Carrara

Vitello al Latte

veal braised in milk

In Italy, veal is milk-fed and the meat is a pale pink with no marbling. Gourmet butchers should be able to procure true milk-fed veal for you.

2 lb (1 kg) boneless veal cut from rump, in 1 piece

salt and freshly ground pepper to taste

½ cup (4 fl oz / 125 ml) extra-virgin olive oil

4 large carrots, peeled and finely chopped

1 cup (8 fl oz / 250 ml) beef or vegetable broth (page 247)

½ cup (4 fl oz / 125 ml) milk

❀ Compress the meat into a cylindrical shape and tie it with kitchen string at 1- to 2-inch (2.5- to 5-cm) intervals along its length. Combine equal portions of salt and pepper in a small bowl. Pat the mixture all over the surface of the meat.

❀ Pour the olive oil into a large saucepan and place over medium heat. Add the carrots and cook gently until they soften, 5–8 minutes.

❀ Add the veal and turn in the pan to flavor it on all sides. Pour in the broth, cover, and reduce the heat to medium-low. Cook, turning the meat from time to time, until the meat is slightly golden, about 45 minutes. Raise the heat to medium-high and lightly brown the meat on all sides, about 15 minutes. Reduce the heat to medium-low and pour in the milk. Re-cover and cook until the milk is absorbed, about 10 minutes, making certain the meat doesn't scorch.

❀ Transfer the meat to a carving board and let cool for 10 minutes. Snip and remove the strings. Cut the meat into slices ¼ inch (6 mm) thick. Pour the contents of the pan into a food mill fitted with the medium disk and purée.

❀ Reassemble the slices into the original cylindrical form, return to the pan, and baste with the purée; this infuses the meat with flavor and keeps it moist.

❀ Transfer the slices to a warmed platter and ladle the sauce over the top. Serve immediately.

serves 4

Agnello Arrosto

roasted lamb

Peer into the dining room of nearly any Tuscan house on Easter Sunday, and you will most likely see lamb being served. Spring is the only time lamb is regularly eaten in the region. It is the season when the animals are young and their meat is still tender and delicately flavored. Marinating the lamb, as is done in this recipe from Siena, softens the meat even more and saturates it with flavor. When roasted this way, the lamb is almost always served medium-rare, with the outer meat well browned and the inside a deep pink.

1 bone-in leg of lamb, 4 lb (2 kg)

½ cup (4 fl oz / 125 ml) white wine vinegar

¼ cup (2 fl oz / 60 ml) extra-virgin olive oil

2 cloves garlic, thinly sliced

leaves from 2 fresh rosemary sprigs, chopped

salt and freshly ground pepper to taste

1 cup (8 fl oz / 250 ml) dry white wine

¼ cup (2 fl oz / 60 ml) water

☙ Place the leg of lamb in a bowl and pour over the vinegar and olive oil. Turn to coat well. Cover and marinate for 2 hours at room temperature, turning the lamb from time to time.

☙ Preheat an oven to 450°F (230°C).

☙ Transfer the meat to a roasting pan, reserving the marinade. Pierce the meat at regular intervals with the tip of a knife. Insert the garlic slices into the slits. Add half of the rosemary and season with salt and pepper, then pour the marinade and the wine over the meat. Place in the oven and immediately reduce the heat to 325°F (165°C). Roast the leg, basting frequently with the pan juices, until medium-rare, or 140°F (60°C) on an instant-read thermometer, about 1 hour. Transfer the lamb to a carving board, tent with aluminum foil, and let rest for at least 10 minutes.

☙ Meanwhile, skim any fat from the juices remaining in the pan. Place the pan over medium-high heat, add the water, and deglaze the pan, stirring to scrape up any browned bits on the pan bottom.

☙ Scatter the remaining rosemary over the lamb. Carve the lamb and reheat the pan juices if necessary. Serve the lamb drizzled with the pan juices.

serves 4

Grosseto

Sogliola alla Boscaiola

fillet of sole with mushrooms

Seafood and mushrooms are not an uncommon pairing in Tuscany. The word boscaiolo *means "woodsman," and anything cooked* alla boscaiola, *in woodsman style, typically includes mushrooms. Substitute 1½ pounds (750 g) sole fillets if small sole are not available.*

3 tablespoons unsalted butter

3 tablespoons extra-virgin olive oil

1 small yellow onion, thinly sliced

salt and freshly ground pepper to taste

4 small sole, cleaned, skinned, and head and tail removed

1 lb (500 g) mixed fresh mushrooms such as portobello, porcino, and/or cultivated white, brushed clean and thinly sliced

½ cup (4 fl oz /125 ml) dry white wine

♕ Preheat an oven to 375°F (190°C).

♕ In a frying pan over low heat, melt 1 tablespoon of the butter with 2 tablespoons of the olive oil. Add the onion and sauté, stirring frequently, until translucent, about 6 minutes. Remove from the heat. Spread half of the onion slices evenly over the bottom of a baking dish large enough to accommodate the fish in a single layer. Drizzle with the remaining 1 tablespoon olive oil and season with salt and pepper. Lay the fish over the onions. Cut the remaining 2 tablespoons butter into small pieces and use to dot the fish. Bake for 10 minutes.

♕ While the fish is baking, add the mushrooms to the pan holding the remaining onions, season with salt and pepper, and sauté over medium-high heat until the mushrooms soften and expel their liquid, about 10 minutes.

♕ Remove the fish from the oven, spoon the mushroom mixture evenly over them, pour the wine evenly over the surface, and return the dish to the oven. Bake until the fish is opaque throughout and the wine has evaporated, about 5 minutes longer. Transfer to a warmed platter and serve.

serves 4

I Funghi Porcini

It was late spring, and my family had barely moved into the farmhouse we had spent three years restoring. Most mornings found our gardener, Silvano, hard at work trying to tame our wild patch of land into something resembling a garden. The past few days it had rained, but now that the air was warm and sweet, he was nowhere to be found.

Silvano reappeared after a few days, on his face an equal mixture of chagrin and triumph and in his arms a gift: a handwoven wicker basket, lined with bright green fern leaves and filled with porcini he had gathered himself. They had large, smooth, pale brown heads and thick, bulbous stems and would have cost a small fortune at the market.

Of course, Silvano was generous, but not so generous that he would ever tell me where exactly he had found the porcini or allow me to accompany him on a mushroom-hunting expedition. The hunting of porcini (and of truffles even more so) is generally a secretive and solitary affair.

We feasted on the mushrooms that night. For the first course, I sliced the stems thinly, sautéed them in garlic, parsley, and white wine, and tossed them with fresh *tagliolini*. The glorious caps I spiked with slivers of garlic and mint-scented *nepitella,* then sprinkled with salt and pepper and grilled like steaks.

Porcini are most popular in central and northern Italy, and the largest body of recipes using the mushrooms comes from the north, but Tuscans do love their porcini and eat them whenever they can. These woodland mushrooms grow in the spring and fall, when the weather is warm and damp, and are often found in the vicinity of chestnut trees. They are also perhaps the world's best drying mushrooms. Whole porcini are cut into slices, dried, and sold in small (not inexpensive) cellophane packages. Their musky earthiness is a wonderful addition to pasta sauces and risottos or can deliver a welcome boost of flavor to the more subtle flavors of most cultivated mushrooms.

Firenze
Baccalà coi Porri

salt cod with leeks

That Florence has very few fish dishes it can call its own is not surprising. Today, the city is an hour's drive from the sea; in the fifteenth century, when the port town of Livorno was under its dominion, the trip took ten hours, far too long for something as perishable as fresh fish. Dried salt cod provided a practical and economical solution for il venerdì di magro, *the meatless Friday meal that is part of Catholic tradition. Of all the various* baccalà *preparations, this is my favorite. The subtle sweetness of the leeks softens the weightier flavor and texture of the cod.*

2 lb (1 kg) salt cod

vegetable oil for frying

1 cup (5 oz/155 g) all-purpose (plain) flour

salt and freshly ground pepper to taste

3 tablespoons extra-virgin olive oil

2 cloves garlic, crushed

6 leeks, white part and 1 inch (2.5 cm) of the green, thinly sliced

1 cup (6 oz/185 g) crushed canned plum (Roma) tomatoes with juice

1 lemon, cut into wedges

♛ Combine the salt cod in a large bowl with water to cover generously. Cover the bowl and refrigerate for 48 hours, changing the water 8 times during that period. Drain the salt cod and remove the bones. Cut into large pieces and pat dry with paper towels.

♛ Pour the vegetable oil to a depth of about ½ inch (12 mm) into a large, heavy frying pan and place over medium-high heat until hot but not smoking. Meanwhile, pour the flour onto a plate and season with salt and pepper. Coat the fish pieces in the flour, tapping off the excess.

♛ When the oil is ready, working in batches, slip the fish pieces into the pan and fry, turning once, until opaque on both sides, about 6 minutes total. Do not worry if the fish sticks; it will be broken up in the sauce. Using a slotted utensil, transfer to a plate.

♛ In a pan large enough to hold the fish pieces in a single layer, warm the olive oil over medium-low heat. Add the garlic and sauté until golden and fragrant, about 2 minutes. Remove and discard the garlic. Add the leeks to the pan and season with salt. Sauté gently until the leeks have softened but not browned, about 10 minutes. Add a little water as necessary to prevent the leeks from sticking. Add the tomatoes and cook for 5 minutes. Raise the heat to medium, arrange the fried salt cod and any accumulated juices on top of the leeks and tomatoes, and cook, turning the cod pieces occasionally, until the cod is well flavored with the sauce, about 15 minutes.

♛ Transfer the salt cod and leeks to warmed individual plates, garnish with the lemon wedges, and serve at once.

serves 6

Cod for baccalà is pulled from icy seas in the coldest months.

Firenze

Bistecca alla Fiorentina

florentine steak

Bistecca alla fiorentina *is the exception to the general rule that although Tuscans eat meat often, the portions are relatively small. These steaks are gargantuan—each one large enough for two generous portions. Traditionally, the meat came from the now-dwindling herds of Chianina cattle that graze in Val di Chiana, between Arezzo and Florence.*

Today, any high-quality beef is used, but the cooking of the meat is still subject to a few easy, but stringent, rules. Each steak, for two people, must weigh between 1¼ and 1¾ pounds (625 and 875 g), be about one inch (2.5 cm) thick, and contain its T-bone, fillet, and tenderloin. You are never asked how you'd like your meat cooked, for an authentic bistecca *is well browned on the outside and blood red inside—no exceptions. A fresh juniper branch is typically added to the coals to scent the meat.*

1 T-bone or porterhouse steak, cut from the rib with the bone, 1½ lb (750 g)

2 tablespoons extra-virgin olive oil

salt and freshly ground pepper to taste

lemon wedges

❦ Take the meat out of the refrigerator about 2 hours before cooking it. Prepare a medium-hot fire in a grill.

❦ Rub the meat on both sides with the olive oil. (Do not add any salt at this point.) Using your hands or a pair of tongs so as not to pierce the meat, set the meat on the grill rack about 5 inches (13 cm) above the coals. Cook until browned and juicy on the first side, 5–7 minutes. Turn the meat (without piercing it) and sprinkle with salt. Cook on the second side until browned and juicy, 5–7 minutes longer. Then turn the meat over once again and sprinkle with salt.

❦ Transfer the steak to a cutting board and season generously with pepper. Garnish with lemon wedges and bring to the table on the board.

serves 2

CONTORNI

For Tuscans, the connection between l'orto ~ the garden~ and the table is direct and strong.

Preceding pages: This shimmering olive grove lies south-east of Pisa, on the arable plain beside the river Arno. The silvery-leaved trees are as elemental to Tuscany's landscape as their fruity oil is to the Tuscan cuisine. **Above top:** A dark plume of cypress punctuates the countryside near Volterra. **Above:** Not all of Tuscany's onion plants are grown for eating. Ornamental onions are prized for the superb flower heads atop tall sturdy stalks. When dried, they lose their oniony smell but retain their fine form, making them ideal for long-lasting arrangements. **Right:** At an open-air *mercato,* long tables are laden with a bounti-ful harvest, from green beans and tomatoes to zucchini (courgette) flowers and squashes.

IN THAT GRAND OPERA that constitutes a full-scale Tuscan meal—*antipasto, primo, secondo,* and *dolce*—*contorni,* or vegetable side dishes, are the supporting players, appearing at the table along with the meat or fish course. In restaurants and trattorias, *contorni* rarely automatically accompany a main dish. Instead, they are ordered individually and brought to the table on separate plates.

In many cultures, the side dish is either treated as a decoration and left on the plate or dutifully eaten with about as much enthusiasm as one would show for a handful of vitamins. Not so in Tuscany, where the connection between the garden and the table is direct and strong. *Contorni,* despite their relatively humble place in the grand scheme of a meal, are about *verdure* (vegetables) and by inference about the land and the particular gifts each season brings. A look at Tuscan *contorni* is a look into the Tuscan garden.

We had only the tiniest vegetable garden the first year my husband, our two children, and I came to live in the small farmhouse we had spent three years bringing back to life. It seemed a miracle in itself that we had finally tamed the wild grasses and thickets of tangled vines threatening to engulf the little house and devour it whole. And although we were delighted with the handful of herbs and scattering of lettuces growing in the farmhouse *orto,* we were far from self-sufficient, and feeding *la famiglia* generally required a trip or two each week to the market.

I had lived in Tuscany before but never as a bona fide homeowner, never with a kitchen of my own, and never with two children whose bellies I was obliged to fill at regular intervals throughout the day. I tried every nearby marketing venue available to me. There were many: the Saturday morning *mercato* in the triangular "square" in Greve, the Sunday market in Panzano (a bit of a journey, although I couldn't imagine a more beautiful one), the wonderful food shops lining San Casciano's cobblestoned main *strada,* and the cramped "supermarket" and handful of stores scattered along the narrow streets of Impruneta. But it was on a hike through the woods above my house and across acres of vineyards and olive groves to the village of Mercatale Val di Pesa that I wandered into paradise.

I had heard about a local family of *contadini* (farmers) growing vegetables on several acres of farmland bordering the town. I kept expecting to stumble upon the place, but somehow it had eluded me.

Dietro al bar—"behind the bar"—my neighbor Bea told me. I had never noticed the narrow arched passageway carved into the pale ocher wall abutting the *caffè.* I followed it into a small inner courtyard and through a green iron gate that opened onto a sprawling patchwork of summer vegetables and flowers. A lanky man in overalls and a charcoal gray beret was tilling the soil along a row of pole beans. He looked up, smiled, and motioned in the direction of an old barn. Inside, a row of tables was heaped with the morning's harvest, everything from great bunches of spinach and chard to neatly rounded piles of *pomodori,* eggplants (aubergines), peppers (capsicums), and potatoes.

I didn't expect the *contadini*—two brothers and one of their wives—to be well into their seventies and early eighties, and I never imagined they would be so willing to share not only the fruits of their magnificent garden,

but also generations worth of culinary wisdom on the subject of cooking *la verdura.*

I was familiar with the handful of standard trattoria side dishes that appears on menus virtually year-round: spinach or Swiss chard sautéed with garlic and olive oil; *patate arroste,* oven-roasted potatoes seasoned with rosemary or other herbs; and tender cannellini beans cooked with garlic, sage, and peppercorns, then doused with fruity green olive oil. These I had both eaten and cooked at home. But there were "mystery vegetables," too: fava (broad) beans still in their woolly green pods; *cardi,* or "cardoons," whose gray-green weathered stalks and prickly leaves made them look anything but edible; and *finocchio,* or "fennel," which I had eaten but hadn't the faintest idea how to cook. These grew in the garden of the *contadini* as well, and I was going to need a bit of help and guidance to learn to make friends with them.

"*Eh … qui ci vuole un po' di lavoro … ma vale la pena*"—"Ah … these take a bit of work … but it's worth it"—the *signora* explained, handing me a giant bunch of silvery green cardoons that I was instructed to clean (no small task), boil, and then sauté with tomatoes and aromatic herbs. They certainly required more attention than I was used to giving Tuscan vegetables, but soon I was captivated by the delicate flavor of this somewhat rougher cousin of the noble artichoke.

The *contadini* were not my only teachers. As I grew more comfortable and courageous in my kitchen, I rarely passed up an opportunity to experiment with unusual vegetables and cooking methods. I traveled to the Paterna agricultural cooperative in the Valdarno, near Arezzo, to see Tuscany's famed *zolfini* beans growing and learn how to cook them *al fiasco.* We stripped away the straw covering of the wine flask, dropped the beans in one by one (there is no quicker way), pushed a couple of unpeeled cloves of garlic, a few peppercorns, and a sprig of sage through the narrow

Left: The highlight of a visit to the port city of Livorno is a shopping excursion to the historic 1895 covered market at the Scali Saffi, which houses the stalls of nearly two hundred vendors. Local seafood dominates, of course, but almost every imaginable edible delight of the Tuscan palate can be found there as well. **Below:** Globe eggplants (aubergines), sliced thickly, are ideal for the grill. **Below bottom:** In Siena, a streetside niche invites passersby to pause and reflect for a moment.

bottleneck, and doused the beans with olive oil and water. Finally the bottle was sealed with a wad of flax and set in the hearth surrounded by a bed of embers. Hours later, we uncorked the bottle and shook the steaming beans into a bowl. It was an exquisitely picturesque—and delicious—culinary moment.

On a day trip to Pistoia, a charming medieval town at the foot of the Apennines, halfway between Florence and Viareggio, I wandered out of the town's hushed, dimly lit *duomo,* past a beautiful glazed terra-cotta rendering of the Madonna and child by della Robbia, and into a bright, busy market square called La Sala.

On one of the tables, wedged between a mountain of spring artichokes and the last of winter's fennel bulbs were what looked to me like clumps of blue-green sea grass. By now I had become an intrepid shopper: *"Che cosa sono … e come si cucinano?"* "What are these," I asked, "and how do you cook them?" *"Agretti,"* the vendor answered. "Boil them in salted water for ten minutes, then dress them with lemon juice and olive oil … *sono buoni."*

Left: Braids of onions brighten a pale wall. **Above top:** From May to October, seekers of good health make their way to northern Tuscany, to take the curative waters of Montecatini Terme, Italy's famous spa. The thermal springs arise from subterranean sources in the Valdinievole, "Valley of Mists," which lies west of Pistoia. **Above:** In bas-relief, a merciful angel proffers a goblet of wine.

Below: Most villages and towns in Tuscany hold weekly market days, when the frugal shopper can find the freshest produce *a buon mercato,* "at a good price." **Below bottom:** Many Tuscan households rely on homegrown vegetables to augment their market purchases. This well-worn doorway attests to frequent to-and-fro between kitchen and garden. **Right:** A *motorino* makes quick work of a trip to the *mercato,* and the handlebars do efficient double duty in carrying home sacks of produce.

I wasn't exactly inspired by their name, which roughly translated means "little sour things," but by now I felt too far into the transaction to walk away without buying some to bring home. And they were good—tart and green, tender to the bite but still firm. Yes, they *were* slightly sour, but in a pleasant way, just like the *amarognolo* (bitterness) of radicchio, which my taste buds had slowly learned to appreciate (so much so that there are usually at least two varieties growing in my vegetable garden at any one time). Alongside the marbled pink-and-white heads of *radicchio di Chioggia* (the most widely exported variety), there is usually a patch of my favorite salad radicchio (sold in markets as *radicchio scoltellato*), which grows in small deep burgundy and forest green florets.

Nearly a decade has passed since I happened upon the *contadini* in Mercatale. Every year they threaten to retire, but their green gate continues to open onto a paradise of the simplest, most elemental sort. Our own garden has come fully to life, and although we are still nowhere near self-sufficient, we too have fallen in step with the seasons, and our daily table bears the signs of its bounty, from spring's pale green spears of asparagus to winter's heavy squash and the deep green, crinkled leaves of Tuscan black cabbage.

Grosseto

Cipolle alla Maremmana

baked stuffed onions

*In the Maremma, onions are traditionally stuffed
with a mixture of sausage and ground (minced) beef
seasoned with nutmeg, cinnamon, and cloves. But
once on my way to visit the Giardino dei Tarocchi—
a whimsical garden near the medieval walled village
of Capalbio and filled with monumental sculptures
influenced by the pictorial symbols on tarot cards—
I ate onions stuffed with herbed goat cheese. It was
a delicious combination and decidedly lighter
than its classic forebears.*

4 red (Spanish) onions, unpeeled

2 tablespoons extra-virgin olive oil

salt to taste

STUFFING

3 oz (90 g) fresh goat cheese

1 tablespoon chopped fresh herb such as
tarragon, mint, or basil

freshly ground pepper to taste

1 egg, lightly beaten

❦ Preheat an oven to 250°F (120°C).

❦ Slice the onions in half lengthwise and place
them, cut side up, on a baking sheet. Drizzle lightly
with the olive oil and sprinkle with salt. Bake until
wilted and soft, 1½–2 hours.

❦ While the onions are baking, prepare the stuffing:
In a small bowl, combine the goat cheese, herb, pepper, and 1 tablespoon of the beaten egg (reserving
the remainder for another use) and mix until the
ingredients are well blended.

❦ Remove the onions from the oven and raise the
oven temperature to 375°F (190°C). When the
onions are cool enough to handle, remove the heart
of each onion with a spoon (a grapefruit spoon
works beautifully), leaving ½-inch (12-mm) walls
and the base intact. Generously fill the onions with
the cheese mixture.

❦ Return the baking sheet to the oven and bake
until the centers have risen and are golden, about
30 minutes. Remove from the oven and let cool for
10 minutes. Transfer to a warmed platter and serve.

serves 4

Livorno

Gurguglione

vegetable stew

*Here is Elba's version of ratatouille, or peperonata,
as it is called elsewhere in Tuscany. Traditionally
the recipe calls for green peppers, although I prefer
the sweeter flavor of red or yellow. Gurguglione
is delicious hot, warm, or cold and makes a perfect
accompaniment to a simple roast chicken or fish.
Use the leftovers as a sauce for pasta or spooned
on top of soft polenta.*

*The dynamic pace of wine making on the Tuscan
mainland has not yet hit Elba, where the tempo
remains much slower. Wines are still made pretty
much as they always have been, with Acquabona's
Elba Bianco a nice clean white to pair with the
warm summer flavors of this stew.*

6 tablespoons (3 fl oz/90 ml) extra-virgin
olive oil

1 large red (Spanish) or yellow onion, sliced

2 large eggplants (aubergines), cut into
1-inch (2.5-cm) cubes

2 tablespoons chopped fresh basil

1 tablespoon finely chopped fresh flat-leaf
(Italian) parsley

2 red, yellow, or green bell peppers (capsicums),
seeded and cut into 1-inch (2.5-cm) squares

2 zucchini (courgettes), cut into large chunks

¾ lb (375 g) tomatoes, peeled, seeded,
and chopped

salt and freshly ground pepper to taste

❦ In a large frying pan over medium heat, warm the
olive oil. Add the onion and sauté until soft and fragrant, about 5 minutes. Add the eggplants, basil, and
parsley, mix well, cover, and cook, stirring occasionally, until the eggplants are soft, about 15 minutes.

❦ Add the bell peppers and zucchini and sauté until
they begin to soften, about 5 minutes.

❦ Stir in the tomatoes, season with salt and pepper,
cover partially, and simmer until the vegetables are
soft, 10–15 minutes.

❦ Transfer to a serving bowl and serve at once, or let
cool and serve warm or at room temperature.

serves 4–6

L'Orto

Give most people a postage stamp–sized piece of land and what will they do? Plant a few shrubs or rosebushes, seed a tiny patch of grass, tame it into something that neither offends nor astonishes the eye? Not a Tuscan. With a speck of earth, whether it's just beyond the doorstep or a narrow strip of land beside some nearby train tracks, the Tuscan will plant a vegetable garden.

In the spring, the garden will be a sea of shelling peas, fava (broad) beans, cutting lettuces, and onions. In a spot all their own are the *carciofaia* and *asparagiaia*—artichoke and asparagus patches—the artichokes blossoming like flowers among the silvery spiked leaves, the asparagus spears shooting out of the soil toward the sun.

In summer, the *orto,* however small, will be in all its wild glory: a tangle of tomatoes, basil, parsley, zucchini (courgettes), cucumbers, green beans, eggplants (aubergines), peppers (capsicums), and chiles. Typically, a few grapevines will be climbing their way up a rough trellis, and some plump melons will be trailing across the earth if there's room. Cabbage, especially Tuscany's deep green *cavolo nero,* and radicchio are the mainstays of the winter garden, the only vegetables hardy enough to survive the icy layer of frost that settles on their leaves each night.

In rural areas, where whole hillsides are dotted with grapevines and olive groves, there is always a spot set aside (usually quite close to the house) for the vegetable garden. Traditionally, the *orto* yielded enough food to render a household almost entirely self-sufficient. Even now, most people (myself included) plant more than they ever eat of the things they especially love. Tomatoes are canned for sauce; zucchini and lettuces are given to friends who don't have gardens.

Nature has been generous to Tuscany. Fruits and vegetables seem just to want to spring from its rich brown soil. And to the Tuscan eye, a warm tomato fresh from a summer garden is every bit as beautiful as a rose.

Firenze

Piselli Freschi con Pancetta

spring peas with pancetta

Tucked in a tiny alleyway, steps from the Ponte Vecchio, is the tiny Buca dell'Orafo, one of my favorite trattorias in Florence. Crowded with tables, the walls plastered with oil paintings by local artists, it is the type of place that serves peas only when they are in season—freshly shelled, gently cooked until tender, and sweet as springtime itself. Florentines often serve peas with roasted meats, such as pork or lamb.

Although it takes many rows of pea vines to produce an appreciable amount of peas, there is nothing more beautiful in a spring garden than the delicate green vines laden with plump pods. Likewise, shelling a huge pile of bright green pods to end up with a rather small bowl of peas is well worth the time and effort—there is simply no better way to eat them.

4 lb (2 kg) English peas

3 oz (90 g) pancetta, finely cubed

2 cloves garlic, crushed

1 cup (8 fl oz/250 ml) water

salt and freshly ground pepper to taste

❧ Shell the peas and set them aside in a bowl. You should have about 4 cups (1¼ lb/625 g).

❧ In a heavy saucepan over low heat, warm the pancetta. When it begins to sweat its fat, after about 4 minutes, add the garlic and cook, stirring often, until the garlic is lightly golden and the pancetta is soft but not browned, about 1 minute.

❧ Stir in the peas, pour in the water, cover, and cook over low heat, stirring occasionally, until the peas are tender but not mushy, about 10 minutes. Season with salt and pepper (use salt sparingly, as the pancetta is already quite salty). Transfer to a warmed serving bowl and serve at once.

serves 4–6

Stufato di Baccelli

braised fava beans

The word baccelli, *as fava beans are generally called in Tuscany, literally means "pods," but the term typically is used for the green beans inside. Young, tender beans are commonly eaten raw with pecorino cheese, but as the pods mature on the plant, the beans become larger and their skins thicken, making them better suited for braising than for eating out of hand. Some home cooks peel away the outer skin of the beans if it is particularly thick. Others add a tablespoon of sugar to the broth to sweeten the beans, while still others substitute a little water and a few coarsely chopped tomatoes for the broth.*

¼ cup (2 fl oz/60 ml) extra-virgin olive oil

3 oz (90 g) pancetta, cubed

1 small red (Spanish) onion, chopped

2 lb (1 kg) shelled fava (broad) beans (4 lb/2 kg unshelled beans), peeled (page 246)

salt and freshly ground pepper to taste

1 tablespoon tomato paste

1 cup (8 fl oz/250 ml) chicken or vegetable broth (page 247), or as needed

2 teaspoons sugar

2 tablespoons finely chopped fresh flat-leaf (Italian) parsley

☙ In a saucepan over medium heat, warm the olive oil. Add the pancetta and sauté until light golden, about 6 minutes. Add the onion and sauté until soft, about 4 minutes. Add the beans, season with salt and pepper, and cook, stirring occasionally, until brown spots appear on the beans, about 10 minutes.

☙ In a cup, stir the tomato paste into the 1 cup (8 fl oz/250 ml) broth and add to the beans.

☙ Add the sugar and parsley to the pan, cover partially, and cook until the liquid has reduced by half and the beans are tender, 15–20 minutes longer, adding more broth if needed to prevent scorching.

☙ Transfer to a warmed serving bowl and serve immediately.

serves 4–6

Le Fave

For some people, spring is when the hedgehog first shows his face or when the lilacs begin to bloom. For me, it is when baskets of unshelled fava (broad) beans appear at the market.

Although there is nothing particularly exotic about *fave*, known also in Tuscany as *baccelli*, I had never tasted them until my first Tuscan spring. My husband's mother grew them in her vegetable garden—the pods were longer than my opened hand, thick and fuzzy as peaches, the beans inside tender and thin skinned.

She would open a bottle of white wine—it was always cool rather than refrigerator cold—pile the beans on the table, and set out a round of fresh *marzolino*, a tender spring cheese made from sheep's milk. As we shelled the beans, we would pop them into our mouths, alternating them with slivers of cheese and sips of wine.

For guests, we would prepare a proper salad, shelling the beans into a bowl with small pieces of cheese, a generous dousing of olive oil, and lots of black pepper. When the beans were larger and their skins thicker, we'd braise them with pancetta and onions. But I still like best the simplicity of shelling and eating them at the table.

Firenze

Fagottini di Melanzane Ripieni di Scamorza Affumicata

grilled eggplant stuffed with smoked scamorza

Most scamorza cheese comes from Molise and Abruzzo, but it is sold in cheese shops throughout Tuscany and appears frequently on restaurant menus, especially in preparations such as this one. The cheese, made from cow's milk, is easily recognizable: its pear shape is tied at the top with a piece of twine, and its rind is an ivory color when the cheese is fresh and a pale brown when it is smoked.

2 large eggplants (aubergines)

salt

3 tablespoons extra-virgin olive oil, plus oil for frying

2 cloves garlic, crushed

2 cups (16 fl oz/500 ml) tomato purée

salt and freshly ground pepper to taste

½ lb (250 g) smoked scamorza cheese

handful of fresh basil leaves

⅓ cup (1½ oz/45 g) grated Parmesan cheese

❦ Remove the green top from each eggplant where the stem was attached. Cut the eggplant lengthwise into slices ¼ inch (6 mm) thick, discarding the first and last slices (which are primarily the outer purple skin). Sprinkle the eggplant with salt and place in a colander for 30–60 minutes to drain off any bitter juices. Rinse the eggplant slices and pat dry.

❦ Meanwhile, in a small saucepan over low heat, warm together the 3 tablespoons olive oil and the garlic. When the garlic is pale gold on all sides, after about 2 minutes, discard it. Add the tomato purée to the oil, season with salt and pepper, and simmer uncovered, stirring occasionally, until thickened, about 15 minutes. Remove from the heat; set aside.

❦ Preheat an oven to 400°F (200°C). Lightly oil a 9-inch (23-cm) square baking dish.

❦ Cut the scamorza cheese into finger-sized rectangular pieces that are as long as the eggplant slices are wide. Cut as many pieces of cheese as you have eggplant slices.

❦ In a large frying pan over medium heat, warm about 2 tablespoons olive oil. In batches, fry the eggplant slices, turning once, until lightly golden on both sides but not fully cooked, about 10 minutes total. (The eggplant will finish cooking in the oven.) Add more olive oil to the pan as needed to prevent the slices from sticking.

❦ Lay a piece of cheese and a couple of basil leaves crosswise at the center of each eggplant slice, then roll up the eggplant slice like a cigar. Place the eggplant rolls, seam side down, in a single layer in the prepared baking dish.

❦ Bake the eggplant rolls until tender but still firm, about 10 minutes. Remove from the oven, spoon the tomato sauce over the top, and sprinkle with the Parmesan cheese. Return to the oven and bake until the Parmesan is golden and the tomato sauce is bubbling, 3–5 minutes.

❦ Serve at once, either directly from the dish or on warmed individual plates.

serves 4

Lucca

Patate all'Ortolano

braised potatoes

I had never actually appreciated the wonder of new potatoes until my gardener, Silvano, planted a bushel of tubers one year. They slept in the dark soil throughout the cold winter, but as soon as the pale spring sun began to warm the ground, they sent up leafy green shoots that filled with pale blue flowers. In late spring, when the plants began to wither, Silvano and I headed into the garden with shovels and spades, turning up the soil to discover an underground forest of potatoes with wispy yellow skins and wonderfully moist and flavorful flesh.

¼ cup (2 fl oz/60 ml) extra-virgin olive oil

2 cloves garlic, minced

4 large fresh sage sprigs

1½ lb (750 g) new potatoes, peeled and cut into 1-inch (2.5-cm) dice

¾ lb (375 g) tomatoes, peeled, seeded, and coarsely chopped, or 1½ cups (9 oz/280 g) crushed canned plum (Roma) tomatoes with juice

salt and freshly ground pepper to taste

❧ In a frying pan over medium heat, warm the olive oil. Add the garlic and sage and sauté until fragrant but not browned, about 1 minute.

❧ Add the potatoes to the pan, stir to coat in the oil, and sauté just until they begin to color, 5–7 minutes.

❧ Pour in the tomatoes, season with salt and pepper, cover partially, and cook, stirring occasionally, until the potatoes are tender, about 15 minutes.

❧ Transfer to a warmed serving bowl and serve immediately.

serves 4

Firenze
Asparagi in Salsa Gialla

asparagus in yellow sauce

Asparagus is one of the first harbingers of a Tuscan spring. Outdoor markets usually offer a few varieties, from thick, juicy spears to thin, elegant ones to the wispy bundles of wild shoots gathered in the woods and used in omelets. Restaurants tend to use stocky spears when serving asparagus whole, reserving the thinner shoots for pasta sauces and risottos. This fresh and easy dish is the humble ancestor to that staple of French haute cuisine, asparagus with hollandaise.

1½ lb (750 g) asparagus spears

1 extra-large hard-boiled egg, peeled

5 tablespoons (2½ oz/75 g) unsalted butter

1 teaspoon fresh lemon juice

2 teaspoons finely chopped fresh flat-leaf (Italian) parsley

salt and freshly ground pepper to taste

❦ Bring a large saucepan three-fourths full of salted water to a boil. Cut off the tough white ends of the asparagus spears. If the spears are thick, using a vegetable peeler, pare away the tough outer skin of each spear to within about 2 inches (5 cm) of the tip, so that the entire spear will be tender and wholly edible once it is cooked. Using kitchen string, tie the asparagus into a bundle.

❦ When the water is boiling, add the asparagus bundle, tips up, and cook for 4–6 minutes, depending on the thickness of the asparagus you are using. The asparagus should remain bright green and be firm but tender. Drain well and remove the string. Arrange the asparagus on a serving platter so that their tips overlap.

❦ Meanwhile, separate the cooked white of the egg from the yolk. Pass the egg white through a fine-mesh sieve or mash finely with a fork, and set aside. In a small frying pan over medium heat, melt the butter. With the back of a fork, mash the yolk into the melted butter, then stir to make a paste. There may be small lumps. Add the lemon juice, stirring constantly.

❦ Pour the sauce over the asparagus tips. Sprinkle with the egg white, parsley, salt, and pepper, and serve immediately.

serves 6

Arezzo

Sformato di Spinaci

spinach timbale

This is one of the few Tuscan recipes that come from the kitchens of noblemen rather than those of humble peasants. It is most popular in Arezzo, where it is made with any one of a number of different vegetables, from spinach, chard, or artichokes to zucchini (courgettes) or cardoons. At home, sformati are usually made in ring molds and sliced at the table; at restaurants, chefs often make them in individual ramekins. A light tomato sauce looks beautiful spooned on top.

WHITE SAUCE

4 cups (32 fl oz/1 l) milk

1 cup (8 fl oz/250 ml) chicken or meat broth (page 247)

5 tablespoons (2½ oz/75 g) unsalted butter

5 tablespoons (2 oz/60 g) all-purpose (plain) flour

salt and freshly ground pepper to taste

½ cup (2 oz/60 g) grated Parmesan cheese

pinch of freshly grated nutmeg

2 lb (1 kg) spinach, stems removed

3 whole eggs plus 1 egg yolk, well beaten

¼ cup (1 oz/30 g) grated Parmesan cheese

salt and freshly ground pepper to taste

boiling water, as needed

To make the white sauce, pour the milk and broth into a saucepan and place over medium heat until small bubbles appear along the edges of the pan. In another saucepan over low heat, melt the butter. Slowly add the flour and, using a whisk, stir continuously until the mixture thickens and smells faintly of biscuits but does not brown, 2–3 minutes. Slowly add the hot milk and broth, whisking constantly. Season with salt and pepper. Cook over low heat, stirring occasionally, until a creamy sauce forms, about 10 minutes. Reduce the heat to very low and cook the sauce, whisking occasionally, for 2 minutes longer. Remove from the heat and stir in the Parmesan cheese and nutmeg. You should have about 4½ cups (36 fl oz/1.1l). Set the sauce aside, stirring occasionally to prevent a skin from forming.

Preheat an oven to 325°F (165°C). Generously butter a 6-cup (48-fl oz/1.5-l) ring mold.

Place the spinach in a saucepan with only the rinsing water clinging to the leaves, cover, and cook until tender, 4–8 minutes. Check the pan from time to time and add a bit of water if needed to prevent scorching. Drain and rinse under running cold water to cool completely. Form the spinach into a ball and squeeze forcefully to remove as much water as possible. Finely chop the spinach, then squeeze again to force out any additional water and transfer to a bowl.

Add the white sauce, eggs, and Parmesan to the spinach and mix well. Season with salt and pepper. Pour the mixture into the prepared mold. Place the mold in a roasting pan and pour boiling water into the pan to reach three-fourths of the way up the sides of the mold.

Bake the mold until a toothpick inserted into the center comes out dry, about 1 hour. Remove the mold from the water bath and allow the timbale to cool for 10 minutes.

Run a knife around the inside edge of the mold, invert a serving plate on top of the mold, and invert the mold and plate together. Lift off the mold. Cut the timbale into wedges to serve.

serves 4–6

Firenze

Fagioli all'Olio

white beans with olive oil and herbs

Florentines take their white beans seriously. Historically, the beans were the "poor man's meat" and an indispensable item in every pantry. But more importantly—much more importantly—they have always been one of the vehicles for that most prized of all local ingredients: olio nuovo, new olive oil. The operative principles for cooking white beans are time (lots of it), temperature (a low simmer), and olive oil (the very best available). Freshly shelled cannellini beans have a wonderfully buttery texture. They can be prepared the same way, but omit the overnight soaking and reduce the cooking time to about 45 minutes.

2 cups (1 lb / 500 g) dried cannellini beans

8 cups (64 fl oz / 2 l) water

2 tablespoons extra-virgin olive oil, plus oil for drizzling

2 cloves garlic, unpeeled

4 or 5 fresh sage leaves

a few peppercorns

salt and freshly ground pepper to taste

♛ Pick over the beans, discarding any grit or misshapen beans. Rinse well, place in a large bowl, and add water to cover generously. Let soak overnight.

♛ The next day, drain the beans and place them in a heavy soup pot. Add the water, 2 tablespoons olive oil, garlic, sage, and peppercorns, cover, and bring to a simmer over medium heat. Reduce the heat so that the water simmers very gently and cook for 1½–2 hours. The beans are ready when the skins are tender and the interiors are soft. Season with salt three-fourths of the way through the cooking time.

♛ Remove from the heat and allow the beans to cool for 1 hour in the water in which they cooked. Before serving, drain the beans and place in a serving dish. Alternatively, gently reheat, drain, and place in a warmed dish. Drizzle abundantly with olive oil and season with salt and pepper.

serves 4–6

Siena

Carciofi Scazzottati

sautéed artichokes with tomato and white wine

Until I came to Tuscany, every artichoke I had ever eaten was the size of a grapefruit. Little did I know about tiny purple-tinged artichokes whose undeveloped centers hid no furry choke, but only a tender, edible heart. Few places celebrate the artichoke better than Tuscany. During the height of the season, most vegetable shops offer several varieties, some suitable for eating raw, others for cooking, all so gorgeous that I set their long stems in water as if they were flowers and keep them on the kitchen counter until they are needed for something more than their beauty.

10 baby artichokes

¼ cup (2 fl oz/60 ml) extra-virgin olive oil

½ small yellow or red (Spanish) onion, chopped

1 clove garlic, minced

5 fresh basil leaves

½ teaspoon fresh nepitella (page 249) or thyme leaves

¼ cup (2 fl oz/60 ml) dry white wine

1 cup (8 fl oz/250 ml) tomato purée

salt and freshly ground pepper to taste

Trim and slice the baby artichokes as directed on page 246.

In a frying pan over medium heat, warm the olive oil. Add the onion and sauté until it begins to soften, about 3 minutes. Add the garlic, basil, and *nepitella* or thyme and cook, stirring frequently, until the garlic has softened, about 2 minutes longer.

Drain the artichokes, add them to the pan, and cook, stirring occasionally, for 2 minutes. Add the white wine, raise the heat to high, and cook until the alcohol evaporates and the wine reduces, about 5 minutes. Stir in the tomato purée, season lightly with salt, and then reduce the heat to low. Cover and cook until the artichokes are tender when pierced with a fork, about 15 minutes. If the pan begins to look dry during cooking, add a bit of water.

Uncover and season with salt and pepper. Transfer the artichokes to a serving dish and serve hot or at room temperature.

serves 4–6

Insalate e Erbe Selvatiche

It took me awhile to realize what they were doing, those occasional solitary figures I'd see walking along country roads, heads bowed, large bags in tow, stooping every so often to pull up something from what for all the world looked to me like a field of native grasses.

I then discovered that they were gathering *insalate e erbe selvatiche* (wild lettuces and herbs), things like *erba cipollina*, bright green chives that sprout each spring from the tilled soil between the rows of grapevines; borage, with its pale blue flowers and furry cucumber-scented leaves used in stuffed pastas and savory herb pies; and my favorite, *nepitella,* or calamint, a small-leaved herb, traditionally added to the garlic and olive oil in which porcino mushrooms are sautéed.

An *insalata di campo* is a salad made from greens growing wild in untended fields or along the rough edges of cultivated farmland. The leaves tend to be much tougher than garden lettuces, although wonderfully flavorful. Most common is wild arugula (rocket), with leaves smaller and much more peppery than its cultivated cousin; various types of chicory whose bitter leaves are a Tuscan favorite; lemony sorrel; and dark green, tangy mâche.

Lucca

Rigatini

white beans with broccoli rabe

DOLCI

Most dolci are linked to certain times of the year, to specific holidays, to time-honored rituals.

Preceding pages: Pomegranates that feel heavy in the hand promise an abundance of sparkling ruby seeds bursting with juice. **Above top:** As the Arno flows through Florence, it passes under the venerable Ponte Vecchio, which was first constructed by the early Romans and rebuilt many times since, following repeated destruction by wars and floods. **Above:** When perfectly ripened, late-summer figs make a simple yet sensuous dessert. **Right:** An extravagant bouquet of cones irresistibly draws the eye to the billows of creamy gelati.

WHAT I LOVE about Tuscan desserts is their simplicity, their lack of pretension, and a certain ephemeral quality that comes from the fleetingness with which they appear on the culinary horizon, shine brightly and deliciously, and then—poof!—disappear for another year. Most regional *dolci* are associated with specific times in the calendar. Every holy day has something sweet to say for itself, every season its own particular treats.

In February, during *carnevale,* a four-week period of revelry ending on the day before Lent, pastry shops are filled with trays of *schiacciata alla fiorentina,* a golden yellow cake dusted with confectioners' (icing) sugar. It couldn't come at a better time of year. The city's streets are bathed in soft gray light, the trees are leafless, and wherever you look, the warm, buttery glow of a *caffè* beckons you in from the cold for a cup of bittersweet *cioccolata calda* (hot chocolate) topped with a pillow of whipped cream and accompanied with a slice of that wonderful cake.

Nowhere in Tuscany is *carnevale* celebrated with more liveliness and spirit than in the

al gusto di
FRAGOLA

al gusto di
CREMA

al gusto di
STRACCIATELLA

Below: At one time considered a rustic spirit, grappa has evolved into a sophisticated, yet potent after-dinner liquor. Grappa improves with aging, either in the bottle for seven to eight months or in small wooden casks for three to five years. **Below bottom:** The Madonna and child watch over the everyday doings on Siena streets. **Right:** Sited in an emerald park just south of the hill town of Montepulciano, the exquisitely proportioned Church of the Madonna di San Biagio is built of creamy yellow travertine. The architectural composition is based on a Greek cross, with the central dome and campanile gracefully fitted into the cruciform plan.

strawberry itself. They require little or no adornment and are usually simply sprinkled with sugar or scattered over a dish of creamy vanilla ice cream.

Although not everyone would agree with me, the passage from late summer to autumn is perhaps the loveliest time of the Tuscan year. It is a period of bounty, of ripeness and abundance. Grapes hang lush and sweet in the vineyards, and whatever isn't made into wine is baked into *schiacciata all'uva,* a wonderfully bready cake studded with wine grapes and fresh rosemary. Glossy brown chestnuts encased in prickly outer shells begin to fall from leafy branches. The hearth, dormant during the heat of the summer, crackles back to life, and chestnuts are laid atop a bed of embers to roast, scenting the air with their sweet earthiness.

With a rapidity that always seems to catch one unawares, fall gives way to Christmas, and holiday sweets line the windows of pastry shops, some in all their naked splendor, others wrapped and ribboned to be offered as gifts. Siena is acknowledged as having the finest

Tuscan Christmas sweets, from *ricciarelli,* almond cookies whose preparation dates back to the Medicis, to its most famous dessert, *panforte,* a rich, dense, flat cake laden with honey, nuts, candied fruits, and spices. But it is panettone, a dome-shaped yeast cake with golden raisins and citrus peel, that reigns as Tuscany's most common Christmas cake. Its primacy is surprising, for it is neither Tuscan (its origins are in northern Italy) nor homemade (a handful of commercial bakeries have all but cornered the panettone market). Nonetheless, if you spend any amount of time in Tuscany during the holiday season, expect to be offered a slice of the golden cake.

One of my favorite ends to a Tuscan meal isn't sweet at all. Not far from my house, on a cobblestoned pedestrian street in the town of San Casciano, is a small, utterly simple *osteria* called Caffè del Popolano. It serves an outrageously creamy *panna cotta* (cooked cream) bathed in warm chocolate sauce, and platefuls of the ubiquitous (and thoroughly delicious) *biscottini di Prato* (small almond biscotti) to dip

into tumblers of amber-colored *vin santo,* Tuscany's famed dessert wine.

Despite such riches, I can never get past the cheese list. Or the wine list. If there is any better end to a meal than a glass of ruby-hued, velvety Brunello di Montalcino and a plate of handcrafted Tuscan pecorino cheeses accompanied with chestnut honey, fig jam, or piquant fruit mustard (candied fruits covered with spiced honey and white wine), I have yet to taste it. My current favorite is *buccia di rospo,* a densely flavored pecorino that takes its name (literally, "toad's skin") from its admittedly unattractive dull brown, warty-looking rind.

Of course, if I can get someone to share a wedge of cheese and a dessert, all the better. For I am what is known in Tuscany as a *buona forchetta*—"a good fork"—meaning I eat a lot and with great enthusiasm. In other cultures this appellation might be the source of some embarrassment, but in Tuscany it is offered as the highest compliment, and one that guarantees you'll be invited back for lunch, dinner, or a homespun Tuscan *dolce* and a glass of sweet *vin santo.*

Left: A young enthusiast of *dolci* is wonder-struck by towers of *panforte,* Siena's "strong bread" generously studded with nuts and candied fruits. **Above top:** Sweet *vin santo* is a specialty of Tuscany, usually served with hard almond cookies for dipping in the "holy wine." The grapes are first dried on cane mats for several months, to concentrate their sugars. **Above:** *Biscotti di Prato,* also known as *cantuccini,* are the traditional accompaniment to *vin santo.* The city of Prato lays claim to originating the recipe, but the *biscotti* can be found in nearly every Tuscan town.

Lucca

Torta di Riso

rice custard cake

It is not unusual for rice to be used in Tuscan sweets. At breakfast time, Florentine caffè sell budino di riso, rice simmered in milk and butter, then mixed with custard and baked inside a small, oval pastry shell. The Garfagnana, an agricultural area of Lucca, is known for this dense golden torta, which is more of a rice custard than a cake. The deep red cherry compote offsets the flavors beautifully.

The compote can be made 2 days in advance and kept covered in the refrigerator. Bring the compote to room temperature before serving.

CHERRY COMPOTE

1 lb (500 g) dark sweet cherries, stems removed, pitted, and halved

1 tablespoon unsalted butter

1 tablespoon sugar

¼ cup (2 fl oz/60 ml) vin santo

1 teaspoon almond extract (essence)

CAKE

semolina flour for dusting pan

½ cup (3½ oz/105 g) short-grain white rice

2 cups (16 fl oz/500 ml) milk

7 eggs

1 cup (8 oz/250 g) plus 2 tablespoons sugar

1 teaspoon rum

½ teaspoon grated lemon zest

½ teaspoon grated orange zest

☙ To make the compote, in a nonaluminum saucepan over high heat, combine the cherries, butter, and sugar and cook, stirring occasionally, until the fruit has begun to soften, 3–5 minutes. Remove from the heat and stir in the *vin santo* and almond extract.

☙ Return the compote to medium-low heat and cook, uncovered, until the alcohol has evaporated, about 2 minutes. Remove from the heat and set aside.

☙ Preheat an oven to 375°F (190°C). Lightly butter a 9-inch (23-cm) round cake pan, then dust with semolina flour, tapping out the excess.

☙ To make the cake, fill a saucepan three-fourths full with lightly salted water and bring to a boil over high heat. Add the rice, reduce the heat to medium-high, and boil for 10 minutes. The rice should be plump. Drain well and spread evenly on the bottom of the prepared pan. Set aside.

☙ In a saucepan over medium heat, warm the milk until small bubbles appear along the edges of the pan. Meanwhile, in a bowl, using an electric mixer, beat together the eggs and sugar until a creamy pale yellow and thick, about 5 minutes. Add the rum and the citrus zests and mix well to combine.

☙ While stirring constantly, slowly pour ½ cup (4 fl oz/125 ml) of the warm milk into the egg mixture. Stir the remaining milk into the egg mixture, then pour the contents of the bowl into the saucepan. Place over low heat and heat gently, stirring continuously, until a custard forms that is thick enough to coat the back of a spoon, about 10 minutes. Do not allow it to boil.

☙ Pour the custard evenly over the cooked rice.

☙ Bake until a toothpick inserted into the center of the cake comes out clean, 45–60 minutes. Transfer to a wire rack and let cool in the pan for 30 minutes, then invert onto a serving plate and lift off the pan. Let cool to room temperature.

☙ To serve, cut into wedges. Spoon the compote over each serving.

serves 6

The little-visited Garfagnana is home to sprawling chestnut groves and nearly forgotten stone hamlets.

Firenze

Schiacciata alla Fiorentina

florentine carnival cake

During the Renaissance, Florentines were enthusiastic celebrants of carnevale. Creative energies—of the men at least—were rarely channeled into culinary endeavor. Instead they penned poetry and songs that relied on crude double entendres for effect, and then roamed in masquerade serenading ladies who listened from open windows. Today, carnival is celebrated primarily by children, who parade through town in costume.

This cake appears in pastry shops throughout Florence in late-winter carnival season. There are a few variations worth noting: A pinch of saffron is sometimes added to the batter to bring a bit of color and a touch of exotic flavor. Pastry shops occasionally cut the schiacciata through the middle, filling it with whipped cream or custard. Making this cake with lard, as is traditional, gives it a wonderfully tender texture, but butter is a fine substitute.

SPONGE

1 cake (1 oz/30 g) fresh yeast or 2½ teaspoons (1 envelope) active dry yeast

1 cup (8 fl oz/250 ml) lukewarm water (110°F/43°C)

½ teaspoon granulated sugar

3 cups (12 oz/375 g) cake (soft-wheat) flour

DOUGH

½ cup (4 oz/125 g) lard or unsalted butter

1 teaspoon salt

4 eggs

½ cup (4 oz/125 g) granulated sugar

½ teaspoon grated orange zest

½ teaspoon grated lemon zest

1½ teaspoons vanilla extract (essence)

1½ cups (6 oz/185 g) cake (soft-wheat) flour

confectioners' (icing) sugar for dusting

⚜ To make the sponge, in a small bowl, sprinkle the yeast over the lukewarm water and stir gently. Stir in the granulated sugar and let the mixture stand until creamy, about 5 minutes.

⚜ In a large bowl, mound the flour and make a well in the center. Pour the yeast mixture into the well. Stir in a circular motion, incorporating all of the flour until well mixed. Cover the bowl with a kitchen towel and set in a warm place to rise until the sponge has doubled in volume, about 1 hour.

⚜ Butter a 13-by-9-inch (33-by-23-cm) baking pan.

⚜ To make the dough, in a small saucepan over low heat, melt the lard or butter with the salt, then remove from the heat and let cool for 10 minutes.

⚜ In a bowl, using an electric mixer, beat together the eggs and the granulated sugar until light yellow. Stir in the citrus zests and vanilla.

⚜ Add the egg mixture to the sponge, stirring vigorously with a wooden spoon to mix thoroughly. Stir in the cooled lard or butter. Add the flour, 2 tablespoons at a time, incorporating each new addition fully before adding the next. The resulting batter will be rather thick and sticky, more like a bread dough than a cake batter. Pour the batter into the prepared pan, cover with a kitchen towel, and let the batter rise until almost doubled in volume, about 1 hour.

⚜ Preheat an oven to 375°F (190°C).

⚜ Remove the towel and bake the cake until the surface is a soft gold, 30–35 minutes. Transfer to a wire rack and let cool completely.

⚜ Just before serving the cake, using a fine-mesh sieve, heavily dust the top with confectioners' sugar. Cut into squares to serve.

serves 12

Siena

Pere al Vino Bianco Dolce

pears poached in sweet white wine

Fruit and wine have always been a popular pairing in Tuscany—ripe fresh peaches and wine in the summertime and pears gently poached in wine during cooler weather. The train from Florence to Venice passes through the flatlands that extend alongside the Po River and its miles of commercial pear groves, with the trees trained to grow almost like grapevines. In Tuscany, the trees are left to grow freely, their full branches bejeweled with lush fruit in a scene that looks every bit like the background of a Botticelli painting.

2 cups (16 fl oz/500 ml) sweet white wine

½ cup (4 oz/125 g) sugar

3 tablespoons fresh lemon juice

4 firm pears such as Bartlett (Williams'), peeled, halved, and cored

4 fresh mint sprigs

In a wide, shallow nonaluminum pan over medium heat, combine the wine, sugar, and lemon juice. Bring to a simmer, stirring until the sugar has dissolved completely.

Lay the pear halves in the simmering liquid, cover, and gently cook the pears until just tender, about 20 minutes. The timing will depend upon the ripeness of the fruit.

Using a slotted spoon, carefully transfer the pear halves to an attractive serving bowl.

Raise the heat to high and boil the liquid in the pan vigorously until it is reduced to about 1 cup (8 fl oz/250 ml) thick syrup, about 10 minutes.

Spoon the syrup over the pears. Garnish with the mint sprigs and serve immediately.

serves 4

Firenze

Salame di Cioccolato

chocolate refrigerator cake

When a working mother volunteers to bring a dolce to a kids' event, whether a birthday party or a holiday happening, it's a safe bet she'll bring one of these sausage-shaped cakes. The bambini *love it, and it requires no cooking for the busy mom. Although not at all traditional, a slice of "chocolate salami" à la mode is delicious—you could even make ice-cream sandwiches.*

40 *chocolate wafer cookies, 10 oz/315 g total weight*

¼ *cup (2 oz/60 g) unsalted butter, melted and cooled*

¼ *cup (2 oz/60 g) sugar*

⅓ *cup (2 oz/60 g) pine nuts, lightly toasted*

½ *cup (4 fl oz/125 ml)* vin santo

♛ In a food processor, working in batches if necessary, process the cookies until they are reduced to fine crumbs.

♛ With all the crumbs in the food processor, add the butter, sugar, pine nuts, and *vin santo*. Pulse until all the crumbs are well moistened and the pine nuts are evenly distributed.

♛ Lay a large sheet of plastic wrap on a work surface. Transfer the cookie mixture onto the sheet in a mound. Pick up the sides of the plastic and compress the crumbs tightly, forming a compact log or "salami" about 3½ inches (9 cm) in diameter. Wrap tightly in the plastic and refrigerate for at least 2 hours or for as long as overnight.

♛ To serve, unwrap the log and, using a long serrated knife, cut it into slices ½ inch (12 mm) thick.

serves 10

Pisa

Crostata con la Marmellata di Albicocche

apricot jam tart

Peek into the pantry of any Tuscan home and you are likely to find a few jars of marmellata fatta in casa—*"homemade jam"—made from apricots, blackberries, currants, strawberries, or any fruit that was in abundance during the season. Some of the jam ends up on bread at breakfast, but it is just as commonly used in jam tarts. My garden is filled with blackberries and currants, and my cupboards are stocked with their jam. Last year my friend Margi brought me a giant basket of apricots from her orchard, and nearly all of the jam I made from her gift has ended up in* crostate.

3 cups (12 oz/375 g) cake (soft-wheat) flour

¼ cup (2 oz/60 g) sugar, plus sugar for dusting

½ teaspoon grated lemon zest

⅛ teaspoon salt

½ cup (4 oz/125 g) unsalted butter, cut into ½-inch (12-mm) cubes and chilled

1 whole egg, plus 1 egg yolk

2 cups (1¼ lb/625 g) homemade or premium-quality apricot jam

❧ In a food processor, combine the flour, ¼ cup (2 oz/60 g) sugar, lemon zest, and salt. Process to combine. Remove the top from the processor and distribute the butter evenly into the flour mixture, coating all the pieces lightly with flour to prevent the blades from getting clogged. Replace the top. Pulse 6 times, or until the flour resembles coarse crumbs. Add the whole egg and the egg yolk through the feed tube and pulse again until the dough just comes together in a very rough mass. Do not allow it to form a ball. (Alternatively, in a large bowl, combine the flour, sugar, lemon zest, and salt. Add the butter and, using your fingers, work the butter into the flour until the mixture resembles coarse crumbs. In a small bowl, using a fork, beat the egg and egg yolk, and then pour into the flour-butter mixture and lightly beat with the fork until the dough comes together in a rough mass.) Transfer the dough to a large, heavy-duty lock-top plastic bag and press together to form a ball. Flatten into a disk and refrigerate for 30 minutes.

❧ Preheat an oven to 375°F (190°C). Butter a 9-inch (23-cm) tart pan with a removable bottom.

❧ Divide the dough in half. On a lightly floured work surface, roll out half of the dough into an 11-inch (28-cm) round about ⅛ inch (3 mm) thick. Drape the round over the rolling pin and carefully ease it into the prepared pan, pressing it into the bottom and sides. (Alternatively, roll out the dough between 2 sheets of plastic wrap, peel off the top sheet, and use the other sheet for transferring the pastry round to the pan.) Fold the pastry overhang back into the rim to reinforce the sides. Spread the jam in the lined pan, and smooth the surface with the back of a spoon or a rubber spatula.

❧ Roll out the remaining dough into a 10-inch (25-cm) round about ¼ inch (6-mm) thick. Using a sharp knife or pastry wheel, cut the dough into strips ½ inch (12 mm) wide. Lay half of the strips across the jam, spacing them about ¾ inch (2 cm) apart. Lay the remaining strips on the diagonal on top of the first ones, to form a diamond pattern. Press the ends of the strips to the edge of the bottom crust, allowing a bit of slack to account for shrinkage.

❧ Bake the tart until the crust is golden brown, about 20 minutes. Transfer to a wire rack and let cool completely. Dust the surface of the tart with sugar and serve.

serves 6

Il Vin Santo

The ritual is almost always the same: dinner plates are cleared from the table and replaced by a bowl of almond biscotti and a tray bearing tiny glasses and a small bottle of *vin santo*.

This so-called holy wine is an amber dessert wine with a slightly caramel flavor laced with hints of almond and fig. A bottle of quality *vin santo* (the only kind worth drinking) will bear a vintage date on its label and a rather high price tag that is justified by the tremendous amount of time and effort that goes into making the wine.

In the fall, the best white wine grapes, usually Malvasia and Trebbiano, are hung or laid on rush mats to dry in large, airy rooms or barns. Powdered sulfur set out in small dishes near the grapes is burned to keep them from molding as they dry. In late winter, the semidry grapes are pressed and then allowed to ferment in small oak or chestnut barrels called *caratelli*. The barrels are sent to the *vinsantaia*, an attic or other place where the wine will be exposed to the great fluctuations in temperature necessary for making fine *vin santo*. The sweet wine is left to age three to four years, and occasionally longer, before being bottled.

Firenze

Cantuccini

almond biscotti

Although delicious right out of the oven, traditionally cantuccini are left to harden for three days, turning them into the perfect cookie for dipping into a glass of vin santo.

2 whole eggs, plus 1 egg yolk

¾ cup (6 oz/185 g) sugar

2½ cups (10 oz/315 g) cake (soft-wheat) flour

1 teaspoon baking powder

1 teaspoon salt

1½ teaspoons grated lemon zest

1 cup (5½ oz/170 g) almonds, toasted and coarsely chopped

2 tablespoons milk

❧ In a bowl, using a fork, beat together the whole eggs, egg yolk, and sugar until light and creamy. Pour the flour into a mound on a work surface. Add the baking powder, salt, and lemon zest and stir briefly. Make a well in the center of the mound and add the egg mixture. Using the fork, swirl the mixture, slowly incorporating the flour from the sides of the well. Add the almonds and knead to distribute evenly. The dough will be sticky. Spoon into a large, heavy-duty plastic bag and refrigerate for 1 hour.

❧ Preheat an oven to 375°F (190°C). Line a baking sheet with parchment (baking) paper.

❧ Snip a large corner off the bag containing the dough. Squeeze the dough onto the lined baking sheet, making 2 logs each about 2 inches (5 cm) wide and 12 inches (30 cm) long. (Alternatively, roll the dough into 2 logs on a floured work surface.) Space them far apart, as they will expand in the oven. Brush the top of each log with the milk. Bake the logs until light gold, about 25 minutes. Remove from the oven and reduce the temperature to 275°F (135°C). Let the baked dough cool for 5 minutes.

❧ Transfer the logs to a cutting board and, using a long serrated knife, cut crosswise into slices ¾ inch (2 cm) wide. Place the slices on the baking sheet and bake until golden, about 30 minutes longer. They will be quite dry. The biscotti can be stored in an airtight container for up to 1 week.

makes 24–30 cookies

Pistoia

Focaccia Dolce di Ciliege e Mandorle

baked custard with cherries and almonds

I ate this dessert one spring at a friend's house in Pistoia. We picked the cherries from a tree in her garden, and her mother turned our bounty into this delicious focaccia.

2 lb (1 kg) sweet cherries such as Bing or Tartarian

4 eggs

¾ cup (6 oz/185 g) granulated sugar

1 tablespoon vin santo

1 cup (8 fl oz/250 ml) milk

¾ cup (4 oz/125 g) all-purpose (plain) flour

⅓ cup (1½ oz/45 g) slivered blanched almonds

confectioners' (icing) sugar for dusting

♛ Remove the stems and pits from the cherries. Preheat an oven to 375°F (190°C). Lightly butter a 10-inch (25-cm) shallow baking dish or pie pan.

♛ In a large bowl, using a whisk, beat together the eggs and granulated sugar until creamy. Add the *vin santo* to the milk, then stir into the egg mixture. Slowly incorporate the flour, stirring constantly. Let the batter rest for 15 minutes.

♛ Place the cherries in the bottom of the prepared dish or pan. Pour the batter through a fine-mesh sieve held over the cherries. Sprinkle the almonds evenly over the top.

♛ Bake for 10 minutes. Reduce the heat to 350°F (180°C) and continue to bake until golden and glossy, about 30 minutes longer. Transfer the custard to a wire rack and let cool for 10 minutes. Using a sieve, dust the surface of the custard with the confectioners' sugar. Cut into wedges and serve warm.

serves 6

Grosseto

Fichi alla Contadina

candied figs

I had never seen, much less eaten, a fresh fig until I went to Italy in my late teens. My boyfriend in Florence had a house on the edge of town with a tiny, well-tended garden crowded with herbs, cutting lettuces, tomatoes, and one generous fig tree. Figs, like olives and grapes, are part of the ancient culinary heritage of the Mediterranean. The trees grow in orchards and gardens all over Tuscany, but they thrive on hillsides in the wild as well, seeming to require nothing more than what is provided by Mother Nature.

In late summer, fresh figs are often paired with salami as an antipasto. In this recipe, the figs are baked, which gives them a luscious texture and a wonderful caramel flavor. They are delicious served whole with a dollop of mascarpone cheese or drizzled with heavy (double) cream. You can also try removing the stems, stirring the cooked fruit, and then using it as a base for homemade ice cream or to dress up a simple cake.

1 cup (8 oz/250 g) plus 1 tablespoon sugar

24 figs

1 tablespoon honey

juice of ½ lemon

½ cup (4 fl oz/125 ml) vin santo

⚜ Preheat an oven to 375°F (190°C).

⚜ Select a square baking pan large enough to accommodate the figs snugly. Line the bottom with parchment (baking) paper, then spread the 1 cup (8 oz/250 g) sugar over the paper. Wipe the figs clean and arrange, stem end up, on the sugar. Drizzle the honey and lemon juice evenly over the figs. Sprinkle with the remaining 1 tablespoon sugar.

⚜ Bake until the sugar caramelizes, about 30 minutes. Remove from the oven. Dip a pastry brush into the *vin santo* and drizzle it over the hot figs. Return the pan to the oven for another 5 minutes to evaporate the alcohol. Let cool completely.

⚜ Divide among individual dessert plates, drizzle with the liquid remaining in the pan, and serve.

serves 6

Torta di Mele con Pinoli e Uvetta

apple torte with pine nuts and raisins

This is my favorite Tuscan cake, in part because the house smells so divine while it bakes, and in part because others seem to love it as much as I do.

2 large Golden Delicious apples

juice of ½ lemon

3 eggs

1½ cups (12 oz/375 g) sugar, plus sugar
for dusting

½ cup (4 oz/125 g) unsalted butter, melted
and cooled

½ cup (4 fl oz/125 ml) milk

1 teaspoon vanilla extract (essence)

1 cup (4 oz/125 g) cake (soft-wheat) flour

1 teaspoon baking powder

⅛ teaspoon salt

1 teaspoon grated lemon zest

⅓ cup (2 oz/60 g) raisins, soaked in warm
water for 30 minutes

¼ cup (1¼ oz/37 g) pine nuts

♛ Preheat an oven to 375°F (190°C). Lightly butter a 10-inch (25-cm) springform pan, then dust with flour, tapping out the excess.

♛ Peel the apples, halve and core them, and then slice thinly. Place in a bowl and toss with the lemon juice to prevent discoloration. Set aside.

♛ In a bowl, using a whisk, beat together the eggs and 1½ cups (12 oz/375 g) sugar until creamy. Stir in the butter, milk, and vanilla. Sift the flour into a separate bowl, and stir in the baking powder, salt, and lemon zest. Using a wooden spoon, gradually incorporate the egg mixture. Drain the raisins and add to the batter along with the pine nuts. Pour the batter into the prepared pan. Arrange the apple slices in concentric circles over the surface.

♛ Bake until a toothpick inserted into the center of the cake comes out clean, about 45 minutes. Transfer to a wire rack to cool completely, then release the pan sides and slide the cake onto a serving plate. Dust the surface of the cake with sugar. Cut into wedges to serve.

serves 8

Pisa

Sorbetto di Cocomero alla Menta

watermelon and mint sorbet

Two Tuscan summertime favorites—sorbetto and cocomero—are combined in this refreshing dessert. If I had to pick one scene that typifies a sultry Tuscan summer night, it would be a brightly lit watermelon stand surrounded by a crowd of people. During July and August, the stands crop up everywhere—in city squares, along boulevards leading out of town, at the sea, in the countryside.

Of course, you can buy a whole melon from one of the vendors to take home, but the main reason for stopping is to stand at the counter and eat an ice-cold slice right on the spot. Interestingly, only children eat the melon out of hand. Adults use knives, but not forks, politely cutting bite-sized pieces, then popping them into their mouths with their hands.

3½-lb (1.75-kg) piece watermelon

1 cup (8 fl oz/250 ml) water

½ cup (4 oz/125 g) sugar

20 fresh mint leaves

❦ Cut away the rind and remove any seeds from the watermelon. Cut the melon flesh into chunks. In a food processor or blender, working in batches, purée the flesh. You should have 5 cups (40 fl oz/1.1 l). Transfer the watermelon purée to a bowl, cover, and refrigerate to chill well.

❦ In a small saucepan over high heat, combine the water and the sugar and bring to a boil, stirring to dissolve the sugar. Reduce the heat to low and simmer, stirring occasionally, until the sugar has dissolved and a syrup has formed, about 4 minutes. Remove the pan from the heat, add the mint leaves, and let cool completely.

❦ Scoop out and discard the mint leaves, then stir the syrup into the chilled watermelon purée.

❦ Return the bowl to the refrigerator for 1 hour. Freeze the mixture in an ice-cream maker according to the manufacturer's instructions.

makes 2 qt (2 l); serves 8

Il Gelato

If there's anything better than a gelato on a sweltering Mediterranean day, I can't imagine what it could be (except perhaps a thick wedge of cold watermelon). Tuscany is home to many famous *gelaterie*, but my very favorite gelato, and one that typifies all that is wonderful about Italian ice cream, comes from Bar Italia in the town of Impruneta, just five minutes from my house.

In the window of the bar is a small placard stating *produzione propria*, or "made on the premises," a sign to look for if you want the real thing. As my young son once pointed out, what makes a good gelato is that "every flavor tastes like what it is. *Gelato di fragola* tastes more like strawberries than like ice cream."

Bar Italia offers an ever-changing variety of flavors, ranging from a heavenly *cioccolatte* scattered with bits of dark chocolate to a mouth-puckeringly tart lemon *sorbetto*. An order of one "scoop" can be made of up to three flavors, so a customer's curiosities can be satisfied without gorging. There are many irresistible combinations. Try mixing the rich, cream-based gelati like *gianduia* (chocolate with hazelnut) or *cocco* (coconut) with a light, refreshing sorbet such as *frutti di bosco* (wild berries).

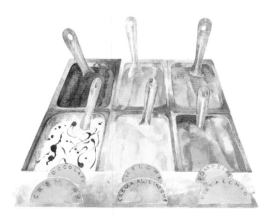

Lucca

Bruciate Ubriache

drunken chestnuts

Roasting chestnuts is one of my family's favorite cold-weather activities. Pairing chestnuts with fennel dates back to medieval times, when a handful of wild fennel seed was thrown into the water in which chestnuts were boiling, infusing the nuts with a mild anise flavor and the house with an enticing fragrance. This recipe from the mountains of the Garfagnana calls for another famous cold-weather staple, grappa, a fiery, translucent, uniquely Italian spirit made from distilled vinacce, *the grape skins and seeds left over from the wine-making process. Serve with small glasses of grappa, if desired.*

2½ lb (1.25 kg) chestnuts in the shell

2 teaspoons fennel seed, crushed

2 cups (16 fl oz/500 ml) grappa

¼ cup (2 oz/60 g) superfine (caster) sugar

❦ Preheat an oven to 375°F (190°C).

❦ Cut a small X into the curved side of each chestnut shell (this keeps them from bursting as they roast). Spread the chestnuts in a baking pan and sprinkle with the fennel seed.

❦ Roast until dark and puffed out, about 30 minutes. Remove from the oven. When the chestnuts are cool enough to handle, using a sharp paring knife and starting at the X, peel away the hard outer shell and the slightly fuzzy inner skin from each nut.

❦ In a saucepan, combine the shelled chestnuts and the grappa and set aside to soak for 1 hour.

❦ Cover the saucepan and place over low heat. Warm the alcohol but do not allow it to boil. Remove from the heat and transfer the chestnuts and grappa to a heatproof serving bowl. Using a long kitchen match and extreme caution, ignite the liquid. The alcohol will burn off quickly and the flames will die out. Sprinkle the sugar evenly over the chestnuts.

❦ Divide the chestnuts among goblets or small dessert bowls and serve at once.

serves 6

Firenze

Zuppa Inglese

tuscan-style trifle

Literally "English soup," zuppa inglese is not a soup, of course, but a dessert so named because of its resemblance to English trifle. Homemade with high-quality ingredients, it is not only delicious but also a perfect primer on standard dessert-making techniques. Those who lack the time to make the cake can use store-bought sponge cake (cut into ¼-inch/ 6-mm strips) or ladyfingers, also known as savoiardi.

CAKE

3 eggs, separated

½ cup (4 oz/125 g) sugar

1 teaspoon minced lemon zest

¼ teaspoon cream of tartar

¼ teaspoon salt

¾ cup (3 oz/90 g) cake (soft-wheat) flour

1 teaspoon baking powder

CUSTARD

2 cups (16 fl oz/500 ml) milk

4 egg yolks

½ cup (4 oz/125 g) sugar

1 tablespoon all-purpose (plain) flour

1 teaspoon minced lemon zest

1 teaspoon vanilla extract (essence)

1 cup (8 fl oz/250 ml) rum or cherry brandy (optional)

2 cups (16 fl oz/500 ml) heavy (double) cream

❧ Preheat an oven to 350°F (180°C). Lightly butter a 9-inch (23-cm) round cake pan, then dust with flour, tapping out the excess.

❧ To make the cake, in a bowl, using an electric mixer, beat together the egg yolks and sugar until pale and creamy, 5 minutes. Stir in the lemon zest.

❧ In another bowl, using clean beaters, beat the egg whites until frothy. Add the cream of tartar and salt and continue to beat until stiff peaks form.

❧ Add one-third of the egg whites to the egg yolk mixture and stir until fully incorporated. Add the remaining egg whites and fold in gently just until combined. Sift the flour and baking powder over the top and fold it into the batter until fully incorporated. Pour the batter into the prepared pan.

❧ Bake until golden, about 25 minutes. Transfer to a wire rack and let cool in the pan for 5 minutes. Invert onto the rack and let cool for at least 3 hours.

❧ To make the custard, in a saucepan over medium heat, warm the milk until small bubbles appear along the edges of the pan. In a bowl, using an electric mixer, beat together the egg yolks and sugar until light and creamy. Sprinkle in the flour and beat until the mixture is pale yellow and thick, about 5 minutes. Slowly pour in the warm milk while stirring constantly with a wooden spoon. Pour the contents of the bowl into the saucepan, place over low heat, and stir in the lemon zest. Heat gently, stirring continuously, until the mixture is thick enough to coat the back of the spoon, about 5 minutes. Do not allow it to boil. Pour the custard through a fine-mesh sieve placed over a bowl. Stir in the vanilla. Cover the bowl with plastic wrap, pressing it directly onto the surface of the custard. Set aside to cool.

❧ To assemble the trifle, using a serrated knife, cut the cake into slices ¼ inch (6 mm) thick. Line an 8-cup (64–fl oz/2-l) dessert bowl with a layer of the slices, trimming them as necessary to fit the bowl. Douse the cake layer with one-third of the rum or brandy, if using, then spread with one-third of the custard. Repeat to make 2 more layers. Cover and refrigerate for 2–3 hours.

❧ In a bowl, whip the cream until stiff peaks form. Remove the trifle from the refrigerator. Spoon the cream attractively over the top and serve.

serves 6

La Merenda

The traditional system of Tuscan meals—*colazione* (breakfast), *pranzo* (lunch), and *cena* (dinner)—is punctuated by two additional appointments, one in the morning at around 10:30 and the second in the afternoon, usually around 4:00. These little gastronomic breaks in the day are known as *merende,* which, roughly translated, means "snacks," though in truth they have none of the casual randomness I've always associated with eating between meals.

The morning *merenda* is the only chance a school-age child has to bring something to eat from home, since school lunches are full-scale meals complete with first course, meat, vegetable, and fruit. My kids bring the same things their friends do: a piece of *schiacciata* fresh from the bakery or a small sandwich of bread and Nutella (a much-beloved chocolate-hazelnut spread—the Italian response to peanut butter) and sometimes fruit, such as a couple of tangerines or plums, a handful of cherries or grapes, or whatever is in season and travels well in their backpacks.

My children's afternoon *merenda* is almost always at home, except when I am persuaded to stop at the neighborhood *bar* for a gelato, a slice of Florentine carnival cake, or a wedge of blackberry jam torte, depending on the weather and the season. The reigning *merenda* of choice at my home is the same as it has been in Tuscan homes for centuries, *pane e olio* (bread and olive oil). I provide the bread (usually toasted), two plates, a tiny saucer of salt, and a bottle of fruity green olive oil. They do the rest. Packaged sweet snacks have all but replaced another favorite Tuscan *merenda—* sliced country bread dipped in wine and sprinkled with sugar.

Generally speaking, it is children who have *merenda.* Adults treat themselves to a *spuntino,* a term that means more or less the same thing, though it is more likely to include something like a wedge of cheese, a handful of olives, or a few slices of cured meat. This adult snack is usually accompanied by an appropriately grown-up beverage—an *espresso,* a cup of tea, or a glass of wine.

Siena

Castagnaccio

chestnut flour cake

It is said that the recipe for castagnaccio *is as old as the Tuscan mountains upon which the chestnut trees grow. Some say it originated in Siena.*

¾ cup (4½ oz/140 g) dried currants or raisins

2½ cups (10 oz/315 g) chestnut flour

¼ teaspoon salt

1½ cups (12 fl oz/375 ml) water

5 tablespoons (2½ fl oz/75 ml) extra-virgin olive oil

leaves from 2 fresh rosemary sprigs

12 walnut halves, broken into pieces

⅓ cup (2 oz/60 g) pine nuts

In a small bowl, combine the currants or raisins with warm water to cover. Let soak for 20 minutes. Preheat an oven to 400°F (200°C). Butter a 9-by-13-by-2-inch (23-by-33-by-5-cm) baking pan.

In a large bowl, stir together the flour and salt. Add the water in a steady stream, stirring constantly with a wooden spoon to prevent any lumps from forming. Stir in 2 tablespoons of the olive oil and then allow the batter to rest in the bowl for at least 15 minutes or up to 25 minutes. It will be very thin and aromatic.

In a small frying pan over medium heat, warm the remaining 3 tablespoons olive oil. Add the rosemary leaves and heat until they are fragrant but not brown, about 1 minute. Remove from the heat, then lift out the rosemary with a spoon. Reserve the rosemary and the oil separately.

Drain the currants or raisins and stir them into the batter. Pour the batter into the prepared pan. Sprinkle the sautéed rosemary and the nuts evenly over the surface. Using a pastry brush, spread the reserved oil evenly over the surface.

Bake until the crust is dark but not burned and a wooden skewer inserted into the center of the cake comes out clean, 30–45 minutes. Transfer the pan to a wire rack and let cool completely. Serve the cake directly from the pan.

serves 6

Siena

Gelato di Vin Santo

vin santo ice cream

A twentieth-century addition to Tuscan cuisine, this recipe was passed to me by a friend who had eaten it at a wine maker's estate outside the beautiful hill town of Montepulciano. Serve it with light, buttery cookies—not cantuccini di Prato (the Tuscan cookies usually associated with vin santo), which are too hard for this delicate gelato.

2 cups (16 fl oz/500 ml) heavy (double) cream

2 cups (16 fl oz/500 ml) milk

4 egg yolks

¾ cup (6 oz/185 g) sugar

¼ cup (2 fl oz/60 ml) vin santo

❦ In a saucepan over medium heat, combine the cream and milk and heat until small bubbles appear along the edges of the pan.

❦ Meanwhile, in a bowl, using an electric mixer, beat together the egg yolks and sugar until the mixture is thick and a creamy pale yellow. Whisking continuously, slowly add ½ cup (4 fl oz/125 ml) of the warm milk-cream mixture to the eggs. Then pour the resulting mixture into the saucepan with the remaining milk and cream. Place over low heat and heat gently, stirring continuously, until the mixture is thick enough to coat the back of a spoon, about 8 minutes. Do not allow it to boil.

❦ Pour the mixture through a fine-mesh sieve placed over a bowl. Stir in the *vin santo,* cover, and refrigerate to chill thoroughly.

❦ Freeze the mixture in an ice-cream maker according to the manufacturer's instructions. Transfer to an airtight container and chill in the freezer for 1 hour before serving.

makes about 1 qt (1 l); serves 4

The finest vin santo is laced with hints of almond and fig.

Firenze

Quaresimali

lent alphabet cookies

Every Florentine over the age of thirty-five remembers looking for the first letter of his or her name in the pile of alphabet cookies known as quaresimali *at the local pastry shop. The chocolate-brown cookies were eaten during the forty days of Lent and were made with very little sugar or fat, in keeping with the abstemious nature of the religious period.* Quaresimali *have gone somewhat out of fashion, and when you find them, they are usually made from a slightly richer recipe, like the one here.*

½ cup (4 oz/125 g) unsalted butter, at room temperature

¾ cup (6 oz/185 g) sugar

1 egg

1 teaspoon vanilla extract (essence)

1¾ cups (9 oz/280 g) all-purpose (plain) flour

½ teaspoon grated orange zest

½ teaspoon salt

¼ cup (¾ oz/20 g) unsweetened cocoa powder

❦ In a large bowl, using an electric mixer, beat together the butter and sugar until creamy. Add the egg and vanilla and beat until light and fluffy. Stir in the flour, orange zest, salt, and cocoa until well combined. Transfer the dough to a sheet of plastic wrap, shape into a ball, and flatten to a disk. Wrap well and refrigerate until very firm, about 2 hours.

❦ Preheat an oven to 350°F (180°C). Line 2 baking sheets with parchment (baking) paper.

❦ On a work surface, place the dough disk between 2 sheets of plastic wrap. Roll out ⅛ inch (3 mm) thick. Using a sharp knife, cut out letters 2 inches (5 cm) tall. Using a metal spatula, transfer the letters to the prepared baking sheet, spacing them about 2 inches (5 cm) apart. Place the sheet in the freezer for 10 minutes before baking. Gather the dough scraps and refrigerate if too soft to roll easily, then roll out and cut more cookies.

❦ Bake until firm to the touch, 10–12 minutes. Transfer to a wire rack to cool on the pan for 2 minutes, then transfer the cookies to the rack and let cool completely. Store in an airtight container at room temperature for up to 1 week.

makes about 36 cookies

I Pinoli

Scattered throughout the Tuscan country-side, especially in the untamed woods near the sea in the Maremma, are Mediterranean pine trees. Unlike their rigidly angular alpine cousins, these trees have thick trunks, gnarled sprawling limbs, and great wide tops, which together make them look a bit like giant green mushrooms leaning into the elements. Not only are they graciously beautiful, but nestled among their scented needles are dusky brown pinecones loaded with ivory-hued nuts.

Pine nuts find their way into both sweet and savory Tuscan recipes. They are used with fresh basil and olive oil in making pesto, a Ligurian specialty, and are sprinkled into pasta or meat sauces. The nuts are also scattered atop the fragrant chestnut flour batter used to make *castagnaccio* and are incorporated into many tortes and cakes.

A favorite pastime of grade-school children is to hand-harvest pine nuts. They pry open the petals of the pinecones, pull out the *pinoli* still in their pale brown shells, and then use small stones to crack open the shells gently without damaging the sweet nutmeats inside.

Massa-Carrara

Torta di Ricotta

ricotta tart

Ricotta, although called a cheese, is actually a by-product of the cheese-making process. In Tuscany, it is fashioned from the whey left over from making the region's famous pecorino, or sheep's milk cheeses. When very fresh, it is eaten plain or lightly seasoned with olive oil. It is also used as a pasta filling, in vegetable pies, and in this delicately textured torte.

Pasta frolla is the typical pastry dough used throughout Italy. It is slightly sweeter than pie dough—almost like a sugar cookie. The sugar in the dough makes it somewhat sticky and difficult to handle. Chilling the dough eases rolling it out and lifting it to line the pan.

In Siena, ricotta tarts are sometimes covered with toasted almonds and walnuts, then dusted with powdered sugar and cocoa. The tart is also lovely paired with a fruit compote and a glass of vin santo.

PASTRY

1½ cups (6 oz / 185 g) cake (soft-wheat) flour

⅓ cup (3 oz / 90 g) sugar

6 tablespoons (3 oz / 90 g) unsalted butter, melted and cooled

½ teaspoon grated lemon zest

⅛ teaspoon salt

1 whole egg, plus 1 egg yolk

FILLING

⅓ cup (2 oz / 60 g) raisins

1¼ cups (10 oz / 315 g) ricotta cheese

2 eggs

⅓ cup (3 oz / 90 g) plus 1 tablespoon sugar

1 tablespoon cake (soft-wheat) flour

1 teaspoon grated lemon zest

1 teaspoon vanilla extract (essence)

To make the pastry, in a large bowl, mound the flour and make a well in the center. Add the sugar, butter, lemon zest, and salt to the well. In a small bowl, using a fork, beat the whole egg and egg yolk, and then pour into the well. Lightly beat the mixture in the well with the fork, then slowly incorporate the

flour in a circular motion until well mixed and a rough dough has formed. Dust your hands with flour and knead the dough briefly in the bowl until it forms a large ball.

Flatten the ball into a thick disk, place in a heavy-duty lock-top plastic bag, and refrigerate for 1 hour.

Preheat an oven to 375°F (190°C). Lightly butter a 9-inch (23-cm) springform pan, then dust with flour, tapping out the excess.

Begin to make the filling by placing the raisins in a small bowl with warm water to cover. Let soak for 20 minutes, then drain.

In a bowl, using an electric mixer, beat together the ricotta, eggs, and sugar until the mixture is evenly blended.

Sift the flour into the bowl. Add the drained raisins, lemon zest, and vanilla to the bowl. Stir to mix well. Set the filling aside.

On a floured work surface, roll out the dough into an 11-inch (28-cm) round about ⅛ inch (3 mm) thick. Drape the round over the rolling pin and carefully ease it into the prepared pan, pressing it into the bottom and sides. (Alternatively, roll out the dough between 2 sheets of plastic wrap, peel off the top sheet, and use the other sheet for transferring the pastry round to the pan.)

Pour the ricotta mixture into the lined pan. Trim the edges of the dough, then crimp lightly to form an attractive rim around the filling.

Bake until the top of the cake is a soft yellow and not quite set in the center, 30–45 minutes. Transfer the pan to a wire rack and let cool for 15 minutes.

Release the sides of the pan and use a long metal spatula to transfer the tart to a serving plate. Serve at room temperature.

serves 6

Pisa

Pesche al Vino Rosso

peaches in red wine

In Tuscany, June brings the year's longest days, the first warm nights of summer, and fireflies flickering in and out of the garden. Meals reflect the desire to play outside rather than labor in the kitchen. I can think of no dessert that better expresses the mood and flavors of the season than fresh peaches in chilled wine. It is a standard all over the region.

6 ripe but firm peaches

1 bottle (24 fl oz/750 ml) young red Chianti, chilled

⅓ cup (3 oz/90 g) sugar

☙ Using a paring knife, peel the peaches. If they resist easy peeling, bring a saucepan three-fourths full of water to a boil, add 2 peaches, blanch for about 20 seconds, and then immediately immerse the peaches in cold water. Remove from the water and, using the knife, slip the skins from the peaches. Repeat with the remaining peaches.

☙ Cut the peaches in half and then into slices, allowing them to drop into a bowl. Add the wine and sugar, stir gently, cover, and refrigerate for 1–2 hours.

☙ To serve, ladle the peaches and wine into small shallow bowls or wineglasses.

serves 6

Every holy day – and there are scores of them – promises a special sweet to mark the occasion.

Pistoia

Croccante

hazelnut brittle

Fairs and festivals abound in Tuscany, where nearly any occurrence is an excuse for a celebration. Streets fill with processions, the night sky glitters with fireworks, and traveling vendors set up stands offering everything from roasted chickens and sausages to chocolates, nougats, and crunchy, sweet brittle made with toasted nuts. Many of the vendors come from Lamporecchio, a town famous for croccante. *Try eating the brittle broken over vanilla ice cream or with a glass of sweet wine.*

1 lb (500 g) hazelnuts

vegetable oil for oiling marble slab and tools

3½ cups (1¾ lb/875 g) sugar

2 tablespoons water

☙ Preheat an oven to 400°F (200°C).

☙ Spread the nuts on a baking sheet. Toast, shaking the pan occasionally, until the nuts are evenly toasted and a light shade of brown, 7–8 minutes. While the nuts are still warm, place in a kitchen towel. Rub the towel vigorously to remove most of the skins.

☙ Lightly oil a marble slab or a baking sheet with vegetable oil. If using a baking sheet, refrigerate for 15 minutes.

☙ Pour the sugar into a heavy-bottomed saucepan and place over medium heat. Heat the sugar for 1 minute, shaking the pan occasionally. Add the water to the center of the pan and stir gently until the sugar dissolves and becomes syrupy, about 8 minutes. Continue cooking over medium heat, stirring constantly, until the mixture turns a warm copper color, about 8 minutes.

☙ Using a lightly oiled wooden spoon, quickly stir in the toasted nuts all at once, taking care to coat them evenly with the syrup. Remove from the heat and pour the mixture onto the marble slab or chilled baking sheet. Using an oiled metal spatula, spread it evenly about ½ inch (12 mm) thick. Allow to cool for 5 minutes. Oil the blade of a sharp knife and use to cut the brittle into jagged bits. Wrap in cellophane and then brown paper, or place in an airtight container. Store at room temperature for up to 1 week.

serves 10

Pistoia

Fragole in Coppa

strawberries with custard

Fragoline di bosco, *wild strawberries that grow in the Apennines above Lucca and Pistoia, taste like the essence of springtime. Here, cultivated strawberries are soaked in rum and dressed with a lovely custard.*

2 pt (1 lb/500 g) strawberries, stems removed, sliced lengthwise

¼ cup (2 fl oz/60 ml) rum

1 cup (8 fl oz/250 ml) milk

2 egg yolks

¼ cup (2 oz/60 g) sugar

2 teaspoons all-purpose (plain) flour

½ teaspoon grated lemon zest

½ teaspoon vanilla extract (essence)

whipped cream for serving

☗ Place the strawberries in a bowl, add the rum, and mix gently. Cover and set aside at room temperature or in the refrigerator for 3–4 hours but no longer.

☗ In a saucepan over medium heat, warm the milk until small bubbles appear along the edges of the pan. In a bowl, beat the egg yolks and the sugar until light and creamy. Sprinkle in the flour and beat until the mixture is pale and thick, about 5 minutes. Slowly pour in the warm milk, stirring constantly. Pour the contents of the bowl into the saucepan, place over low heat, and stir in the lemon zest. Heat gently, stirring continuously, until the mixture is thick enough to coat the back of a spoon, about 5 minutes. Do not allow to boil. Pour the custard through a fine-mesh sieve placed over a bowl. Stir in the vanilla. Cover with plastic wrap, pressing it directly onto the surface of the custard. Set aside to cool.

☗ Divide half of the strawberries among 4 goblets and top with the custard, dividing it evenly. Top with almost all of the remaining berries, reserving some for garnish. Cover and refrigerate for about 2 hours. Just before serving, top with whipped cream and garnish with the reserved berries.

serves 4

La Frutta

My first summer in Florence I remember having dinner at a small trattoria and watching in amazement as the man at the next table was brought a whole peach on a plate and a knife. With the precision of a surgeon, he sliced the velvet skin from the fruit in one long strip, then slowly ate the peach, wedge by perfectly cut wedge. I had never eaten fruit with such care, and except for the occasional bowl of wild berries, I had never seen, much less ordered, fruit for dessert at a restaurant.

Fruit is not eaten casually in Tuscany. It appears less often as a between-meals snack than as a full-fledged dessert at the end of a simple lunch or dinner. Springtime is for cherries and strawberries, often tossed with sugar and lemon, or scattered over vanilla ice cream, and for tart, apricot-hued medlars. Summer brings apricots, plums, peaches, and melons, although cantaloupe is served at the beginning of a meal with slices of cured prosciutto, rather than as dessert. Plump, tart gooseberries and delicate red currants are made into jams and tortes. Sweet black and green figs ripen in late summer and are eaten at the end of a meal or at the beginning with slices of mild salami. Harvest season brings grapes (lushly flavorful and full of seeds), pears, apples, and chestnuts, and winter delivers glossy persimmons and juicy tangerines.

Perhaps the Tuscan reverence for fruit can be explained by the fact that it is typically exceptional. The quality stems from two simple facts: first, fruit is generally eaten only in season, with locally grown fruit, denoted by the word *nostrale,* almost always preferred over something shipped from a distant continent; and second, Tuscans are far more concerned about how a fruit tastes than what it looks like, and will regard with suspicion anything that looks unnaturally perfect. In fact, children are told that an orchard apple lightly pecked at by a bird is likely to be far sweeter than the untouched (and presumably less ripe) fruits from the same tree. The bird knows better than the eye.

Firenze

Schiacciata all'Uva

flat bread with wine grapes and rosemary

On the road from Florence to Greve is a speck of a town called Falciano, home to three restaurants, a few terra-cotta factories, and one bar. *The* bar *is nicknamed* I Ladri *(The Thieves) because everything sold in the town seems to cost twice as much as it does anywhere else. Every fall I happily plunk down a small fortune for a delicious* schiacciata all'uva, *a sweet, chewy flat bread dotted with wine grapes and rosemary. The herb may seem an odd ingredient to find in a dessert, but the piney taste lends a surprisingly pleasant note, adding an element of intrigue to otherwise predictable flavors. Wine grapes are generally smaller than table grapes, with dense skins and tart seeds. You can substitute table grapes, which will eliminate the seeds but also some of the flavor.*

At our house, we tend to eat schiacciata all'uva *for* merenda, *though I have seen people serve it for breakfast and also for dessert with glasses of sweet wine.*

1 cake (1 oz/30 g) fresh yeast or 2½ teaspoons (1 envelope) active dry yeast

1 cup (8 fl oz/250 ml) lukewarm water (110°F/43°C)

½ teaspoon plus 1 tablespoon sugar

4½ cups (22½ oz/700 g) all-purpose (plain) flour

5 tablespoons (2½ fl oz/75 ml) extra-virgin olive oil

1 teaspoon salt

¾ lb (375 g) red wine grapes

leaves from 2 fresh rosemary sprigs

sugar for dusting

⚜ In a small bowl, sprinkle the yeast over the lukewarm water and stir gently. Stir in the ½ teaspoon sugar and let the mixture stand until creamy, about 5 minutes.

⚜ In a large bowl, mound the flour and make a well in the center. Pour the yeast mixture and 4 tablespoons (2 fl oz/ 60 ml) of the extra-virgin olive oil into the well and sprinkle in the salt. Stir in a circular motion, slowly incorporating all of the flour until the ingredients are well mixed and a rough dough has formed.

⚜ Turn the dough out onto a lightly floured work surface and knead until smooth and soft, about 10 minutes. If the dough is very sticky, add small amounts of flour as you work the dough. Shape the dough into a ball and place it in a well-oiled bowl. Turn to coat with oil, cover the bowl with a damp kitchen towel, and set in a warm place to rise until the dough has doubled in volume, about 1 hour.

⚜ Preheat an oven to 375°F (190°C). Oil a 9-by-13-by-2-inch (23-by-33-by-5-cm) baking pan.

⚜ Punch down the risen dough. Return it to the floured surface and knead it for another 10 minutes. Divide the dough in half. Roll out half of the dough into a size that roughly matches the size of the prepared pan. Transfer the rolled-out dough to the prepared pan and scatter one-half of the grapes and one-third of the rosemary leaves evenly over the surface. Sprinkle with the 1 tablespoon sugar.

⚜ Roll out the second half of dough on the floured surface into a sheet of the same size and lay it on top of the grape-and-herb-covered dough. Cover evenly with the remaining grapes and rosemary and drizzle with the remaining 1 tablespoon extra-virgin olive oil. Cover the pan with a damp kitchen towel and set in a warm place to rise until the dough has doubled in volume, about 30 minutes.

⚜ Bake until a soft gold on top, 30–35 minutes. Remove the pan from the oven and transfer to a wire rack to cool until warm. Remove the bread from the pan, dust the surface with sugar, and cut into squares to serve. The bread can be stored, well wrapped, for up to 2 days and reheated or served at room temperature.

serves 12

From late summer to autumn, grapes hang lush and sweet in the vineyards, awaiting the harvest.

Arezzo

Panna Cotta

cooked cream with caramel sauce

Panna cotta is an old-fashioned Tuscan dessert enjoyed throughout the region. I remember eating a particularly delicious version at a restaurant near the Piazza Grande, in Arezzo. The town sits at the foot of the Casentino, the most mountainous part of Tuscany and the area from which the famed Arno River springs. Arezzo is the birthplace of several of the great names of the Renaissance, including Piero della Francesca and Giorgio Vasari. The town is well worth a trip to see the restored della Francesca frescoes or to hunt for treasures at the monthly antique fair.

Remember that the cooked cream must be made the day before serving, so that it can set fully in its mold.

COOKED CREAM

2 tablespoons cold water

2 teaspoons unflavored gelatin

2 cups (16 fl oz/500 ml) heavy (double) cream

¾ cup (6 oz/185 g) sugar

1 teaspoon vanilla extract (essence)

CARAMEL SAUCE

1 cup (8 oz/250 g) sugar

⅓ cup (3 fl oz/80 ml) water

1 teaspoon sweet white wine

¼ cup (2 fl oz/60 ml) heavy (double) cream

½ teaspoon unsalted butter

❦ To make the cooked cream, pour the water into a heatproof glass or metal bowl. Sprinkle the gelatin over the water and let stand for 10 minutes, without stirring, to soften. Bring a small saucepan half filled with water to a gentle simmer, and set the bowl of gelatin over, not in, the water. Stir until the gelatin dissolves, no more than 1 minute. Remove the bowl from the saucepan.

❦ In a heavy saucepan over medium heat, combine the cream and sugar. Heat, stirring, until the sugar has dissolved; do not allow to boil. Remove from the heat and add the vanilla and the gelatin mixture, whisking until well combined. Pour into a 7-inch (18-cm) ring mold, cover, and refrigerate overnight.

❦ To make the caramel sauce, in a heavy-bottomed saucepan over low heat, combine the sugar, water, and wine and heat, stirring frequently and being careful the mixture doesn't boil, until the sugar has dissolved. Raise the heat to medium and bring to a boil. Do not stir, but swirl the pan from time to time. If sugar crystals form on the sides of the pan, brush them down with a wet pastry brush. Watch the mixture carefully, making sure it does not burn. Once the mixture begins to turn amber, after about 8 minutes, remove from the heat and stir in the cream. It will bubble vigorously and splatter (you may want to use oven mitts to protect your hands).

❦ When the cream is well incorporated into the caramel sauce, beat in the butter. If any bits of hard caramel appear, return the pan to medium heat and stir until they melt. The caramel should be slightly warm or at room temperature when served.

❦ To unmold the cooked cream, immerse the base of the mold in hot water for 15 seconds. Run a knife between the side of the pan and the firmed cream, then repeat for the inner ring. Invert a serving plate over the mold and invert the mold and the plate together. Lift off the mold and spoon some of the sauce over the top. Serve the remaining sauce in a bowl at the table.

serves 6

Siena

Panforte

spiced fruit cake

Panforte is rarely made at home, since the bakers in Siena make it so well, but this recipe is worth trying for the dense rich cake it produces.

1 cup (8 oz/250 g) granulated sugar

½ cup (6 oz/185 g) honey

1 lb (500 g) assorted chopped candied fruits such as pear, apricot, and citron but no apple

¼ cup (1½ oz/45 g) candied orange peel, chopped

1 cup (5½ oz/170 g) blanched almonds, coarsely chopped

½ cup (2 oz/60 g) cake (soft-wheat) flour

½ teaspoon each salt, crushed coriander seed, and ground cinnamon

¼ teaspoon ground mace

confectioners' (icing) sugar for dusting

❧ Preheat an oven to 375°F (190°C). Lightly butter a 10-inch (25-cm) springform pan, then dust with flour, tapping out the excess.

❧ In a large saucepan over medium heat, combine the granulated sugar, honey, and 2 tablespoons water and bring to a simmer, stirring to dissolve the sugar. Simmer until a thick syrup forms, 5–10 minutes. Do not allow the syrup to caramelize. Remove from the heat.

❧ Immediately stir in all the candied fruits and the nuts until well blended. Sift in the flour and add the salt, coriander, cinnamon, and mace. After the mixture has cooled, moisten your hands with water and use them to combine the ingredients well. The dough will be stiff and sticky. Transfer to the prepared pan, patting down with your fingers.

❧ Bake until dark golden, about 40 minutes. Transfer to a wire rack and let cool completely. Remove the pan sides and slide the cake onto a serving plate.

❧ Just before serving, using a fine-mesh sieve, dust the top of the cake with confectioners' sugar. To serve, cut into wedges with a very sharp knife.

serves 12

GLOSSARIO

The following entries cover key Tuscan ingredients and basic techniques called for throughout the book. Look for Tuscan and other Italian ingredients in Italian delicatessens, specialty-food stores, and well-stocked supermarkets. For information on items not found below, please refer to the index.

ANCHOVIES

Blended into a sauce or draped over a salad, tiny *acciughe,* also known as *alici,* appear widely in Italian cooking. Whole anchovies layered with salt have the best flavor of the preserved products. Buy them in bulk or in 1- to 2-pound (500-g to 1-kg) tins. Anchovy fillets in olive oil are commonly available in tins, but look for the higher-quality anchovies packed in glass jars. Anchovy paste lacks the depth of flavor of whole anchovies but is convenient for subtly boosting the flavor of soups and sauces. As a general rule, 1 teaspoon anchovy paste is equivalent to 1 anchovy fillet.

TO PREPARE WHOLE SALTED ANCHOVIES, rinse gently under running cold water. If a less assertive flavor is desired, soak for 10 minutes before proceeding. Scrape the skin away with the tip of a knife and cut away the dorsal fin. Press the anchovy open, flattening it carefully from head to tail end. Lift away the backbone, then cut the anchovy into 2 fillets. Rinse again, then dry on paper towels. The fillets can be used immediately or placed in a glass or other nonaluminum container, covered with olive oil, and refrigerated for up to 2 weeks.

ARTICHOKES

These Mediterranean natives, called *carciofi,* are cultivated for their thistlelike flowers, which are harvested before they bloom. The bud has thick, dark green, thorn-tipped leaves enclosing a tender, paler heart. Artichokes available in Tuscany range from large, weathered globe artichokes, or *mamme,* to small green-and-purple specimens, called *morellini,* eaten raw in *pinzimonio* and salads.

TO PREPARE ARTICHOKES, add the juice of 1 lemon to a bowl of cold water. Trim the stem from each artichoke, leaving 1 inch (2.5 cm) intact. Peel off the outer leaves until you reach the tender yellow and purple-tinged inner leaves. Lay the artichoke on its side and cut off the tough green tops of the leaves until only the tender, edible portion remains. Cut the artichoke in half lengthwise. If there are fibrous hairs surrounding the heart (this is the choke), run the tip of a small paring knife between the heart and the hairs, then scoop out the hairs with a spoon. Drop the halves into the lemon water. To slice the artichoke, thinly slice each half lengthwise and drop the slices into the lemon water. Drain well before using.

BEANS

Tuscans are known throughout Italy, and beyond it, for their creative uses of beans. Look in Italian markets for dried beans imported from Italy. Good-quality canned beans are a convenient alternative to cooking dried beans, especially in dishes that do not require long cooking to meld flavors. For every ⅔ cup (4½ oz/ 140 g) dried beans or 2 cups (14 oz/440 g) cooked beans in a recipe, substitute one 15-ounce (470-g) can. Rinse the beans well with cold water and drain before using.

CANNELLINI Ivory-colored beans with a fluffy texture, much-loved cannellini are most often served warm, drizzled with the finest Tuscan olive oil. If necessary, Great Northern beans can be used in their place.

BORLOTTI Similar to cranberry beans, these popular Italian beans sport an attractive pink-beige background speckled with maroon. Mild-flavored *borlotti* appear in soups, particularly *pasta e fagioli* and minestrone.

FAVA Slipped from their large pods, pale green fava (broad) beans resemble lima beans but have a slightly bitter flavor. Tuscans call them *baccelli* and enjoy them in the spring, at their tender best, served raw with young pecorino cheese. Fresh and dried fava beans are very different in flavor and should not be substituted for each other in recipes.

TO COOK DRIED BEANS, keep in mind that as a general rule beans triple or nearly triple in volume when cooked. Rinse dried beans well and pick them over to remove any bits of grit or misshapen beans. Soak overnight in cold water to cover by 3 inches (7.5 cm). Alternatively, bring to a boil, then remove from the heat, cover, and let stand for 1 hour. Remove and discard any beans that float. Drain the beans, transfer to a large pot, and cover with at least 4 inches (10 cm) of water or broth. Bring the beans to a boil, skimming off the foam that rises to the surface. Cover partially and simmer gently until tender, 1½–2½ hours, depending on the variety and age of the beans.

TO PREPARE FRESH FAVA BEANS, wear kitchen gloves, if desired, to prevent irritation of the skin. Fava beans are easily popped from their pods, but the beans, especially older ones, require peeling, as the thin skin covering each bean can be tough and bitter. To peel them easily, blanch the shelled beans in boiling water for about 1 minute. Drain, cool slightly under cold water, and then simply pinch each bean to slip it from its skin.

BORAGE

Borragine, which thrives in central and northern Italy, has mint-shaped leaves with tiny hairs and a distinctive cucumber scent. Finely chopped, the leaves add a distinctive note to salads or ravioli filling.

BREADS

There is a saying in Italy reserved for complimenting a particularly kindhearted person—*buono come il pane,* "good like bread." Eaten every day, basic bread varies from region to region in its shape and flavor, but traditional specialties, still made by hand, are enjoyed throughout the country.

CIABATTA Named for its long and flat "slipper" shape, *ciabatta* has a porous, chewy texture and a light, crisp crust dusted with flour. The roughly shaped loaves belie

BROTHS

Tuscans are the soup makers of Italy, and if there isn't a *zuppa* or *minestra* bubbling away on the stove, there's very often a *brodo,* or "broth," of one type or another slowly simmering for later use in soups or for cooking gnocchi. Meat and chicken broths can be stored for up to 5 days in the refrigerator, the vegetable broth for 3 days. All of the broths can be frozen for up to 2 months. When a recipe calls for a light broth, skim all fat from the surface of the broth and discard, then dilute the broth in a ratio of 3 parts broth to 1 part water.

CHICKEN BROTH

1 stewing chicken, 3–4 lb (1.5–2 kg)

3 qt (3 l) water

3 carrots

2 small yellow onions

1 large celery stalk with leafy tops, cut into 1-inch (2.5-cm) lengths

handful of fresh flat-leaf (Italian) parsley sprigs

3 peppercorns

1 bay leaf

1 teaspoon coarse salt

❧ Rinse the chicken under running cold water. In a stockpot, combine the chicken with the remaining ingredients except the salt. Bring almost to a boil, skimming off any froth on the surface. Add the salt, reduce the heat to low, cover partially, and simmer for 1 hour, continuing to skim any froth from the surface.

❧ Remove from the heat and let cool, then strain through a colander lined with cheesecloth (muslin) and placed over a large bowl. Cover and refrigerate until chilled or as long as overnight. Lift off and discard the solidified fat on the surface before using. *Makes about 2½ qt (2.5 l)*

MEAT BROTH

½ stewing chicken, about 2 lb (1 kg)

2 lb (1 kg) bone-in beef such as short ribs

3 qt (3 l) cold water, or as needed

1 large yellow onion, unpeeled

2 whole cloves

3 large celery stalks with leafy tops, cut into 1-inch (2.5-cm) lengths

2 large carrots

1 bunch fresh flat-leaf (Italian) parsley

1 very ripe tomato, cored

2 bay leaves

coarse salt to taste

❧ Rinse the chicken under running cold water. In a stockpot, combine the chicken and beef with the 3 qt (3 l) water. Bring to a boil over low heat, skimming off any froth that forms on the surface. Simmer, partially covered, for 1 hour, continuing to skim any froth from the surface.

❧ Cut the onion in half and insert a clove into each half. Add the onion halves and all the remaining ingredients to the stockpot. If much of the water has evaporated, add more water as needed to maintain the original level. Cover partially and simmer over low heat for 2 hours.

❧ Remove from the heat and let cool, then strain through a colander lined with cheesecloth (muslin) and placed over a large bowl. Cover and refrigerate until chilled or as long as overnight. Lift off and discard the solidified fat on the surface before using. *Makes about 2½ qt (2.5 l)*

VEGETABLE BROTH

3 tablespoons extra-virgin olive oil

1 large yellow onion, coarsely chopped

2 large carrots, halved lengthwise and cut into 1-inch (2.5-cm) lengths

2 large celery stalks with leafy tops, cut into 1-inch (2.5-cm) lengths

2 large cloves garlic, crushed

1 leek, including 2 inches (5 cm) of the pale greens, sliced

1 teaspoon plus 2 tablespoons coarse salt

1 large fennel bulb, including leaves, halved

1 large, very ripe tomato, cored

1 potato, halved

4 fresh sage leaves, torn in half

2 bay leaves, torn in half

5 peppercorns

2 qt (2 l) plus 1 cup (8 fl oz/250 ml) water

❧ In a stockpot over medium heat, warm the oil. Add the onion and sauté until soft, about 5 minutes. Add the carrots, celery, garlic, leek, and 1 teaspoon salt. Sauté, stirring often, until the vegetables begin to soften, about 3 minutes.

❧ Add the fennel, tomato, potato, sage and bay leaves, peppercorns, and 2 tablespoons salt to the stockpot. Raise the heat to high, cover, and bring to a boil. Reduce the heat to medium-low, cover partially, and simmer for 45 minutes.

❧ Remove from the heat and let cool, then strain through a colander lined with cheesecloth (muslin) and placed over a large bowl. *Makes about 6 cups (48 fl oz/1.5 l)*

a delicate flavor well suited to the breakfast table. They are popular sliced horizontally and used for sandwiches.

COARSE COUNTRY BREAD Freshly baked in a wood-burning oven, Italian country bread has a thick and chewy crust enveloping a tender and moist crumb. In Tuscany, loaves of *pane toscano,* made without salt, complement perfectly the assertive flavors of the region's cuisine. The classic loaf is white, but darker whole-wheat (wholemeal) versions are also sold.

FRUSTA A long, slim loaf commonly used for making *crostini, frusta* resembles the baguette of neighboring France. *Filone,* a similar bread, may also be used. If both are unavailable, buy the most slender baguette available.

TO MAKE BREAD CRUMBS, trim off the crust of stale bread. Tear the remaining interior into large pieces and place in a blender or food processor. Pulse to the desired fineness. For toasted crumbs, toast them in a 325°F (165°C) oven or in a heavy frying pan over low heat, stirring frequently, until dry and lightly golden.

BROCCOLI RABE

Related to mustard and turnips, this dark green vegetable resembles thin stalks of broccoli topped with jagged leaves and tiny bud heads. It is also known as broccoli raab, *rapini,* or rape.

BROTHS See box, page 247.

CAPERS

The unopened flower buds of a trailing shrub, *capperi* have a piquant flavor enjoyed throughout the Mediterranean. Capers packed in sea salt retain their intense floral flavor and firm texture, but brined capers are more commonly available. Those labeled nonpareil are smaller than the distinctly large capers sold in Italian markets. Rinse both salted and brined capers before using. When buying salted capers, check that the salt is dry and white; they can be kept in the refrigerator for up to 1 year.

CHEESES

Italy's diverse cuisine draws inspiration from special cheeses created in each region. Some of the world's most admired cheeses come from Tuscany, as well as from areas to its north and south.

AGED PECORINO A piquant sheep's milk cheese with a dry, grainy texture well suited to grating. Italians generally refer to all sheep's milk cheeses as pecorino, but many consider *pecorino toscano* to be the most flavorful and luxurious, which has led to its name being protected by law.

FRESH RICOTTA As its name implies, ricotta is made by "recooking" the whey left after the making of other cheeses. Outside Italy, ricotta is primarily made from cow's milk, but traditional Italian ricotta comes from the milk of sheep, water buffalo, or goats. In Tuscany, it has a dry texture and a sweet nuttiness. For a similar flavor, look for goat's milk ricotta made by small cheese producers. If using commercial cow's milk

ricotta, drain in a sieve for 30 minutes to rid it of excess moisture before using. Filled pasta dishes and simple desserts highlight the cheese's soft texture, snowy color, and fresh flavor.

MARSCARPONE Extremely rich, creamy smooth cheese with a soft texture and a sweet-tart flavor similar to that of Devonshire cream. A specialty of Lombardy, the double-cream cow's milk cheese appears in both sweet and savory recipes.

PARMESAN The king of cheese, Parmesan is fashioned into large wheels and aged for 1 to 3 years to develop a complex, nutty flavor and firm texture. "Parmigiano-Reggiano" stenciled on the rind ensures that the cheese is a true Parmesan made in Emilia-Romagna. Its dry, granular character makes it ideal for grating over pasta or shaving over antipasti and salads. It is also included on most cheese plates. Grana padano, a hard grating cheese, resembles Parmigiano-Reggiano and is often used in its place.

SCAMORZA A *pasta filata* (spun or pulled) cheese, scamorza is slightly drier, chewier, and more sharply flavored than mozzarella. Scamorza is sometimes smoked.

CHESTNUT FLOUR

This extremely fine flour, milled from sweet, starchy chestnuts, thickens sauces and is used in many traditional desserts. The best *farina di castagne* comes from the Garfagnana area, north of Lucca. Chestnuts from high-altitude forests are dried slowly on straw mats over smoldering wood, lending a smoky flavor to the flour. Store chestnut flour in the refrigerator to prevent rancidity.

CUTTLEFISH

Abundant in the waters of the Mediterranean, the cuttlefish is flatter, thicker, and meatier than its close relative, the squid. Cuttlefish ink, the dark brown sepia that once provided pigment for artists, has a more mellow flavor and more velvety texture than squid ink and is preferred for sauces. The ink is available frozen, in small plastic packages. If a cuttlefish is particularly large, it requires pounding to tenderize the meat before cooking. Squid can be used in place of cuttlefish, although squid ink is no substitute for the rich, flavorful cuttlefish ink. To clean cuttlefish, follow the directions for cleaning squid (page 251).

FENNEL

A native of the Mediterranean region, fennel is appreciated for its delicate anise flavor. Although in southern Italy the seeds, stalks, and leaves of wild fennel are often used in recipes, Tuscans prefer *finnochio* with its pale green and white bulb, layered much like celery.

HARE

Although often confused with rabbit, hare belongs to another genus. Unlike their burrowing cousins, hare build their nests aboveground, are generally large, and have longer ears and hind legs. Their meat is darker than that of rabbit and has a more pronounced flavor. Hare weighing less than 6 pounds (3 kg) are ideal for roasting, while larger hare are best for stews and terrines. Hare is available from fine butchers by special order and by mail order from companies specializing in game.

MUSHROOMS

The most beloved of all Tuscan mushrooms are porcini. These plump, full-flavored wild mushrooms, also known as cèpes or boletes, resemble cremini mushrooms because of their brown caps but have thicker, meatier stems. Porcini are sold dried as well as fresh. *Ovoli,* another prized mushroom, have brilliant orange caps and pale cream stems. They are sliced and featured raw in salads. Cremini mushrooms, also known outside Italy as Italian brown and common brown mushrooms, are firmer and more flavorful than their close relative, the white button mushroom. Allowed to mature, cremini grow into large, dark brown portobellos, appreciated for their meatiness and smoky flavor.

NEPITELLA

Mint-scented *nepitella (Calamintha nepeta)* is an Italian herb whose earthy, minty flavor complements porcino mushrooms perfectly. The decorative herb is known as catmint and calamint in English but should not be confused with wild mint. Before adding *nepitella* to a dish, rub it between your fingers to release its flavor. To replace it in a recipe, use two-thirds marjoram or summer savory and one-third mint, adding the former at the beginning of cooking and the latter at the end.

OLIVES

The primary use of olives in Tuscany is for the making of the region's prized olive oil. A variety of olives is used in Tuscan cuisine. Those picked unripe retain their green color, while those harvested later in the year become increasingly black as they ripen. Olives are typically cured in brine, oil, or lye or are dry-salt-cured and packed in oil, vinegar, or brine. Two especially popular types suitable for use in the recipes in this book are plump, tart, green Sicilian olives and smooth, nutty black olives from Gaeta.

ONIONS, SWEET

Tuscan cooks favor sweet onions, and one variety that has recently gained fame in the region is the *cipolla di Tropea,* named for a seaside town in Calabria. Small and oblong shaped, they are eaten fresh rather than dried. Vidalia or Maui onions, which are in season in spring and early summer, can be substituted, as can Walla Walla, another crisp and sweet variety, which comes to market in summer and early fall.

PANCETTA

This flavorful unsmoked bacon derives its name from *pancia,* Italian for "belly." After being cured with salt and perhaps a selection of spices that may include black pepper, cinnamon, clove, nutmeg, or juniper berries, the flat cut of belly pork is rolled into a tight cylinder. When the cylinder is cut, the slices of pancetta display a distinctive spiral of lean, satiny meat and pure white fat. Chopped and cooked in a little olive oil, pancetta serves as a flavor enhancer for a wide variety of soups, sauces, fillings, and side dishes. Sliced, it can be draped over lean meat and poultry before roasting.

PASTA See box, page 250.

PINE NUTS

Umbrella-shaped stone pines grow throughout the Mediterranean, and their long, slender seeds are high in oil and delicately flavored. Appearing in recipes both savory and sweet, *pinoli* (sometimes spelled *pignoli*) are especially popular in sauces, stuffings, rice dishes, and desserts. As with all nuts, toasting enhances their flavor.

POLENTA

Both cornmeal and the thick, porridgelike dish made from it, polenta is endlessly versatile. Soft polenta serves as a base for a hearty sauce, an accompaniment to roast meat or poultry, or a simple meal on its own with a swirl of Gorgonzola cheese. If spread in a pan and cooled, polenta becomes firm enough to cut and grill, layer like lasagne, or fry until crisp for serving with savory spreads.

PROSCIUTTO

This high-quality air-cured Italian ham has a silken texture and a sweet, almost fruity flavor. The hams are made according to a painstaking process that includes the careful raising of select pig breeds, the slow curing of the hams with minimal salt, and the gentle drying of them in breezes that have traveled over fragrant forests and meadows. Exceptional are hams from Parma, in Emilia-Romagna, considered to be the best, and from San Daniele, in Friuli, recognized by their flatter shape. Prosciutto from Tuscany is denser and more assertive in flavor. *Prosciutto crudo* refers more specifically to this cured and aged raw ham, while *prosciutto cotto* is a mildly cured cooked ham.

RABBIT

Classic Tuscan recipes for rabbit, or *coniglio,* include stewing with wine and olives and braising for a hearty sauce to serve with tagliatelle. Prized rabbits are fed fresh herbs to flavor their flesh. These farm-raised rabbits have fine, lean white meat that is less gamy than that of wild rabbits, although some cooks prefer the latter for their richer flavor. Smaller rabbits, between 2 and 2½ pounds (1 and 1.25 kg), are tender enough to be used in any recipe for chicken. Older and larger rabbits, especially those hunted in the wild, need the tenderizing power of slow, moist cooking in stews and braises.

RED MULLET

Highly valued in the Mediterranean, red mullet is a brilliant crimson fish with fine, sweet flesh. It is often cooked whole and uncleaned, as the liver is considered a delicacy. For the best flavor and texture, look for smaller fish, under 10 inches (25 cm) long. Small red snapper or bluefish may be substituted.

PASTA

Pasta has become a staple in the Tuscan diet only in the last fifty years, with penne being the preferred shape, followed closely by tagliatelle. There are two basic categories: fresh pasta *(pasta fresca)* made by hand and dried pasta *(pasta secca)* formed mechanically. Soft-wheat flour gives fresh pasta its silky texture, while a harder variety of wheat flour, durum semolina, lends dried pasta its toothsome firmness.

DITALI Literally "thimbles." A hollow, curved macaroni cut shorter than elbows.

FARFALLE Gathered and pinched to resemble bow ties or "butterflies." Large *farfallone* are coated in sauce, while the smaller ones, *farfallette* and *farfalline,* are added to soups. Also excellent in cold salads.

FUSILLI Spirals that twist like corkscrews or "springs." Their many curves are ideal for trapping chunky or thick, creamy sauces.

LINGUINE Long, flat noodles, ⅛ inch (3 mm) wide, that evoke "tongues." Both fresh and dried linguine are used.

PAPPARDELLE Ribbons of homemade egg pasta, ½–1 inch (12 mm–2.5 cm) wide, cut by hand, with either straight or sawtooth edges. The large, silky surface absorbs delicate butter and cream sauces well.

PENNE Relatively short, straight tubes cut diagonally at both ends, resembling the pointed, hollow nibs of pens or "quills." The smooth versions of this versatile dried pasta are ideal for creamy sauces, and the ridged ones take to coarser sauces.

RIGATONI Large, hollow tubes with grooves running their length. Their chewy texture can hold up to thick meat sauces and baking.

SPAGHETTI Long, round, thin "strings." One of the most common dried pastas in Italy and best when served with simple olive oil or tomato sauces.

TAGLIATELLE Flat ribbons of fresh egg pasta, ¼ inch (6 mm) wide, tagliatelle are traditionally served with Bolognese meat sauce.

TO PREPARE PASTA DOUGH, using the quantities specified in an individual recipe, pour the flour in a mound onto a wooden or marble work surface. Make a well in the center and sprinkle with the salt. Break the eggs into the center of the well, add the olive oil (if called for in the recipe), and lightly beat with a fork. Swirl the egg mixture in a circular motion, incorporating the flour from the sides of the well, until a rough mass forms. Shape the rough mass into a ball and set on top of the remaining loose flour. Use both hands to work the flour into the dough until the dough just barely stops sticking to your fingers. Clean the work surface; wash your hands and dry well. Dust the work surface lightly with flour and knead the dough until smooth and elastic, 6–8 minutes, adding flour if the dough is sticking to your hands. If rolling out the dough by hand, wrap tightly in plastic wrap and let rest for 20 minutes or for up to 3 hours.

TO ROLL OUT PASTA DOUGH, divide the dough into 2 or 3 pieces. To roll out by hand, place 1 piece on a floured work surface. Using a rolling pin and beginning at the center of the dough, roll the pin away from you. Rotate the dough and then roll again. Continue to roll out and rotate the dough—turning the dough over and dusting it with flour occasionally to prevent it from sticking—until the dough is smooth and has reached the desired thickness.

To roll out with a machine, use the dial to set the rollers to the widest opening and dust with flour. Flatten the dough and insert into the rollers while turning the handle of the machine. Fold the dough into thirds, dust with flour, and feed through the rollers again. Repeat the process several times, then adjust the dial to reduce the distance between the rollers and roll out the dough without folding it. Continue to feed the dough through the rollers—moving the dial each time to narrow the gap between the rollers—until the rollers are at the last setting.

Repeat the hand or machine rolling with the remaining dough and let the dough rest on floured, clean kitchen towels for 15 minutes. Place on a floured work surface and cut as directed in individual recipes with a fluted or straight-edged pastry wheel.

RICE

Although famous for its pasta, Italy is also Europe's largest rice producer. Many varieties of rice are eaten in the country, and northern Italians especially prize high-quality rice for preparing risotto. One of the best-known varieties is Arborio, cultivated in Lombardy's low-lying Po Valley. Carnaroli's longer, half-tapering shape, uniform cooking, and firmer texture make it a favorite for risottos and rice salads. The most prized rice is Vialone Nano. Polished by a special mechanical mortar and pestle, its grains emerge covered with powdery starch that results in the creamiest risotto of all. There are four commercial categories of Italian rice designating the size of the grains, from smallest to largest: *comune, semifino, fino,* and *superfino.* Look for *fino* or *superfino* on the label when choosing rice for risotto.

SALT

At key points along the Mediterranean coast, where sea water can be trapped and evaporated, pyramids of salt rise high. Made in limited quantities, this sea salt is naturally dried by the wind and bleached by the sun and, unlike refined table salt, contains no additives to make it flow freely. Naturally present minerals give it a rich, mellow flavor. Although most sea salts have coarse crystals, fine-grained versions are also available. The large flakes of kosher salt, another type of coarse salt created for the preparation of meat according to Jewish dietary laws, have a more complex, less salty flavor than table salt.

SALT COD

Cod salted and dried in the cold sea breezes of Scandinavia is one of the most celebrated products in Europe. Salt cod, known as *baccalà* in Italy, is an important ingredient throughout the Mediterranean, especially during Lent. Reconstituted, it has a robust flavor and firm texture that many prefer over fresh cod. Available filleted and unfilleted, with or without skin, salt cod is sold in bulk and in small wooden boxes. Look for white flesh, with a silvery sheen, that has not discolored with age.

SAUSAGES

In Tuscany, sausages are available fresh and aged. The latter are typically similar to salamis, with *salsicce di cinghiale* (wild boar sausage) a particular favorite. Unlike in southern Italy, where fresh sausages, usually pork, are commonly flavored with fennel seed or chile, fresh pork sausages in Tuscany are usually seasoned primarily with salt and pepper. Outside of Italy, the two fresh Italian varieties most readily available are a spicy (hot pepper) version and a mild, so-called sweet version. Whole fennel seed frequently appears in both. These sausages may be used in recipes in this book.

SEA BREAM

Abundant in the Mediterranean waters, sea bream has snow-white, lean, flaky flesh highly prized throughout Italy. Although bones are more easily removed from larger fish, the flavor and texture of the smaller ones are better. The porgy, a related species found in the waters off the eastern coast of the United States, can be used as a substitute.

SQUID

Well known by its Italian name, *calamari,* squid are cephalopods whose mild, sweet flesh complements the flavors of a wide range of dishes. With a tendency to toughen when overheated, squid should be cooked only briefly, no more than a few minutes or simmered gently for 30 minutes to 1 hour.

TO CLEAN SQUID, pull the head and tentacles from the body pouch, then discard the clinging innards. Just below the eyes, cut off the tentacles and reserve them, discarding the eye portion. Squeeze the cut end of the tentacles to expel the hard, round beak, discarding it. Pull out and discard the long, transparent quill from inside the body pouch. Rinse the pouch and tentacles thoroughly under running cold water and peel the gray membrane from the pouch, using a paring knife to scrape off any clinging bits. Cut the body or leave whole as directed in individual recipes.

TOMATOES

An abundance of *pomodori* flourish in Tuscan gardens: sweet, tiny cherry tomatoes; firm, juicy salad tomatoes; pear-shaped plum tomatoes; and *pomodori fiorentini,* with thick, pleated skins, used for sauces. Follow the lead of Italian cooks, avoiding fresh tomatoes in winter and using instead high-quality canned tomatoes. Home-grown tomatoes often do not need peeling, as they lack the thicker skins developed for commercial shipping. For smooth, delicate sauces and soups, however, always peel and seed tomatoes.

TO PEEL AND SEED A FRESH TOMATO, trim away the stem and cut a shallow X at the blossom end. Immerse the tomato in a large pan of boiling water and blanch until the peel begins to curl away from the X, about 20 seconds. Transfer to a bowl of ice water to cool. Peel away the skin with your fingers or a small paring knife. To extract the watery pulp and seeds, cut the tomato in half crosswise and, working over a bowl, squeeze each half gently, easing out any recalcitrant seed sacs with a fingertip.

TRUFFLES

Both black and white truffles are pricey elements of the Italian table. The esteemed—and more expensive—white truffle has a cult following drawn to its penetratingly earthy, woodsy flavor and its exceptional fragrance. Connoisseurs favor those found near the town of Alba, in Piedmont, declaring them the most intensely flavored. Black truffles are primarily from Umbria, but small pockets of them are also found in Tuscany. Although not as highly prized as their white cousins, black truffles are nonetheless luxurious treats.

WILD BOAR

Cinghiale, or wild boar, appears on menus throughout Italy but is especially loved in Tuscany, where priests bless both wine and boar on festival days and entire restaurants are dedicated to the art of cooking the meat. Wild boars roam freely in central Italy's forests, where their diet is rich in fruits and nuts. Their dark red and distinctly scented meat is leaner but more richly flavored than pork. Wild boar meat is available by special order at fine butchers and by mail order from companies specializing in game and exotic meats. Wild boar meat must be cooked thoroughly; never serve it rare.

ZUCCHINI FLOWERS

The large, golden blossoms of the prolific zucchini (courgette) vine serve as tasty vessels for a wide variety of meat and cheese fillings. Italians also enjoy them battered and fried, stirred into a frittata, or tossed with pasta and fava (broad) beans. Female flowers often c ome still attached to tiny baby zucchini, but the larger male flowers on stems are best for stuffing.

ACKNOWLEDGMENTS

Lori De Mori offers *mille grazie* and huge appreciation to Christine Bruscagli for her unfailing hard work, friendship, and culinary expertise; Riccardo Bruscagli for sharing literary tidbits and gastronomic reminiscences; Jason Lowe for his fabulousness both as a photographer and as a person; Hannah Rahill, Judith Dunham, George Dolese, Sharon Silva, Noel Barnhurst, and Marleen McLoughlin for their enormous contributions to this collaborative effort; Maureen and Eric Lasher, wonderful agents and friends; the Capezzana winery for so generously opening up their home; and Julien and Michela for being their own wondrous selves.

Noel Barnhurst wishes to thank his assistant, Noriko Akiyama. George Dolese wishes to thank Leslie Busch, food stylist, and Elisabet der Nederlanden, food styling assistant, for their stellar work in preparing the food for photography. Thanks also go to Robert Raasch for the generous use of his fine collection of Tuscan ceramics.

Jason Lowe wishes to thank Lori De Mori for being welcoming and for sharing a new view of modern Tuscany; Gaye Allen for her support on both sides of the pond; and his daughter, Rae, for being delicious.

Weldon Owen thanks Desne Border for her invaluable research for the caption text and for contributing her proofreading skills and Thy Tran for contributing her culinary expertise to the writing of the glossary text. We also thank Linda Bouchard for her expert computer layout and production, Jamie Leighton for her design assistance, Ken DellaPenta for indexing the book, and Cecilia Brunazzi for her translation services. Special thanks to the owners and staff of the Capezzana winery for their warm and generous hospitality.

Time-Life Books is a division of Time Life Inc. Time-Life is a trademark of Time Warner Inc. and affiliated companies.

TIME LIFE INC.
President and CEO: Jim Nelson

TIME-LIFE TRADE PUBLISHING
Vice President and Publisher: Neil Levin
Vice President, Content Development: Jennifer Pearce
Executive Editor: Linda Bellamy
Director of Design: Tina Taylor
Project Manager: Jennifer L. Ward

WILLIAMS-SONOMA INC.
Founder and Vice-Chairman: Chuck Williams
Book Buyer: Cecilia Michaelis

WELDON OWEN INC.
Chief Executive Officer: John Owen
President: Terry Newell
Chief Operating Officer: Larry Partington
Vice President International Sales: Stuart Laurence
Creative Director: Gaye Allen
Associate Publisher: Hannah Rahill
Managing Editor: Judith Dunham
Copyeditor: Sharon Silva
Designers: Colin Wheatland, Sarah Gifford
Production Director: Stephanie Sherman
Production Manager: Chris Hemesath
Editorial Assistant: Donita Boles
Consulting Editor: Norman Kolpas
Prop and Style Director: George Dolese
Calligrapher: Jane Dill

THE SAVORING SERIES
conceived and produced by Weldon Owen Inc.
814 Montgomery Street, San Francisco, CA 94133
Telephone: 415-291-0100, Fax: 415-291-8841

In collaboration with Williams-Sonoma Inc.
3250 Van Ness Avenue, San Francisco, CA 94109

Separations by Colourscan Overseas Co. Pte. Ltd.
Printed in Singapore by Tien Wah Press (Pte.) Ltd.

Savoring® is a registered trademark of Weldon Owen Inc.

pp 4–5: Travelers headed to the villages south of Pisa pass through vineyards and fields of olive trees, punctuated by cypress trees. **pp 6–7:** Flag throwers perform the *sbanderiata* in Siena's Piazza del Campo, teeming with spectators awaiting the Corsa del Palio. The furious and fiercely competitive horse race is run in three laps around the Campo. The coveted *palio,* a silk banner, is conferred upon the winner, followed by feasting and more pageantry. **pp 8–9:** The façade of the Duomo in Massa Marittima looks down on the Piazza Garibaldi, the town's main square. Built of travertine in the thirteenth century—with a campanile added over a century later—the cathedral is dedicated to St. Cerbone, the patron saint of Massa, whose life is depicted in stone reliefs and in stained glass. Paintings, frescoes, and sculpture by Sienese artists fill the interior. **pp 12–13:** Immaculately plowed farmland rises to a stand of stately cypress, emblem of the Tuscan landscape. In spring, these undulating furrows will be spiked with the first green shoots of new grain.

First printed 2001
10 9 8 7 6 5 4 3 2 1

Library of Congress
Cataloging-in-Publication Data

De Mori, Lori.
  Savoring Tuscany : recipes and reflections on Tuscan cooking/ recipes and text, Lori De Mori; general editor, Chuck Williams; recipe photography, Noel Barnhurst; travel photography, Jason Lowe; illustrations, Marlene McLoughlin.
    p. cm —(The Savoring series)
  Includes index.
  ISBN 0-7370-2070-9
  1. Cookery, Italian—Tuscan style.   I. Title.   II. Series.
  TX723.2.T86 D43 2001
  641.5945'—dc15   00-048920
                                                            CIP